The Passionate Torah

The Passionate Torah

Sex and Judaism

Edited by Danya Ruttenberg

New York University Press   •   *New York and London*

NEW YORK UNIVERSITY PRESS
New York and London
www.nyupress.org

Library of Congress Cataloging-in-Publication Data
The passionate Torah : sex and Judaism / edited by Danya Ruttenberg.
p.   cm.
Includes index.
ISBN-13: 978-0-8147-7604-9 (cl : alk. paper)
ISBN-10: 0-8147-7604-3 (cl : alk. paper)
ISBN-13: 978-0-8147-7605-6 (pb : alk. paper)
ISBN-10: 0-8147-7605-1 (pb : alk. paper)
1. Sex—Religious aspects—Judaism. 2. Sexual ethics. 3. Modesty—
Religious aspects—Judaism. 4. Homosexuality—Religious aspects—
Judaism. 5. Feminism—Religious aspects—Judaism. I. Ruttenberg, Danya.
BM720.S4P37 2009
296.3'66—dc22   2008054007

New York University Press books are printed on acid-free paper, and their
binding materials are chosen for strength and durability. We strive to use
environmentally responsible suppliers and materials to the greatest extent
possible in publishing our books.

Manufactured in the United States of America

c 10 9 8 7 6 5 4 3 2 1
p 10 9 8 7 6 5 4 3 2 1

For Nir, as always, and for my friend Kirsten (Brokhe) Cowan

Contents

Acknowledgments

First of all, much love and many thanks to my superhero agent Jill Grinberg, and to Kirsten Wolf for her copious time and support. Thanks also to Jennifer Hammer for her hard work in bringing this book to light, and to everyone at NYU Press for so much excellence, time, and attention to detail. For their hard work, patience, and blistering smarts, a great big thank you to all the wonderful contributors to this volume. You've all gone far beyond the letter of the law.

Thank you to the 940 Egged bus line (Jerusalem-Haifa) for providing such an obliging place to edit essays, and to Irit and Itzik for being such a good reason to ride it. Thanks to my father and brother for ongoing wonderfulness. As always, thank you also to all my amazing friends, colleagues, and co-conspirators—too many to name—for your encouragement, support, and hevruta time that was sometimes about learning text, sometimes not. Thanks also to all my teachers at the Ziegler School of Rabbinic Studies and to Moshe Benovitz at Machon Schecter.

And, most of all, thank you to Nir, for being everything I could ever think to ask for, plus a whole lot more. (Nelly was right.)

Introduction

Danya Ruttenberg

THERE'S A FAMOUS story in the Talmud about a curious student who takes his studies past the point of what might generally be considered in good taste. Kahane, the yeshiva boy in question, hides under the bed of his teacher, deliberately listening in on the master's lovemaking with his wife. He's shocked by the way they chat and joke together during the coital act but tries his best to remain unnoticed. To no avail, however; in one dramatic moment, his presence—and chutzpah—are revealed.

"Kahane, are you there?" his teacher thunders. "Leave now, because it is rude!"

It is not, and I will not, Kahane calmly replies.

"For this is Torah, and I must learn."

In Judaism, every aspect of human life is a holy piece of Torah, worthy of thought, study, and consideration—and sex is certainly no exception. The Talmud compares the penis sizes of its most venerated Sages and discusses in euphemistic, but excruciating, detail the positions in which a married couple is permitted to make love. Jewish law devotes pages and pages to the prohibition against sex with a menstruant, down to instructions on how to comport oneself if, mid-coitus, it appears that the female partner has just gotten her period. One law code tells us that a widow should not own a dog, because, it seems, there's some suspicion about what a woman who's already tasted the pleasures of the flesh might do with her pet.

In some ways, the tradition's approach to carnal matters indeed appears to be steeped in the wisdom of the ages—such as the mandate that a couple set aside time for sex as often as is reasonably possible. The definition of "how often," in ancient sources, depended on the restrictions inherent in the male partner's livelihood but attempted to be realistic and fair to both parties. The Talmud, for example, tells us that a man who worked as a donkey driver (and was required to come home once a week) could not decide to become a camel driver (who, by the more travel-intensive nature of his work, was required to come home only once a month) without his wife's consent, because his career change would undoubtedly have implications for her sex life. Camels or not, without question, Judaism's mandate to nurture intimate relationships may certainly resonate for many today.

The Talmud also teaches that a couple should not have sex when angry or drunk, or when one partner is thinking of someone else or has already mentally "checked out" of the relationship. Our being fully present with one another is a primary Jewish value—one often missing from the contemporary conversation about sex.

Yet, despite its very real moments of illumination, at other times Judaism seems quite out of step with our contemporary ethos. Some Rabbinic texts, for example, describe the sexual impulse as the provenance of the *yetzer hara*, the evil inclination, and go to some extremes to discourage sexual thoughts and feelings; pious men are sometimes described as those who never looked at their own wives' bodies or who never glanced—not once—at their own genitals. More devastating, some texts tell us that a woman who refuses to sleep with her husband on the grounds that he is disgusting to her may still be forced to remain married, and permitted a divorce only if he chooses to offer her one—and then, too, she is sent out without the monies set aside by her husband at the time of marriage. Many women, no doubt, have preferred to engage in sex with men they found repugnant rather than to be cast out, penniless, without the means to feed or sustain themselves. And, of course, the Jewish legal tradition has not generally taken a kind and welcoming approach to homosexuality or queerness of various stripes. As much as Judaism has to teach us about sexual relationships, there are also places where, from our contemporary perspective, its teachings may feel uncomfortable or deeply troubling, or both.

So are Jewish attitudes about sex enlightened or problematic? Is Judaism an earthy religion of the body or a patriarchal institution? Both, of course, and neither. As with most things, there are many shades of gray in-between these two extremes. Jewish sexuality is nothing if not complex.

And, perhaps, Jewish sexuality—or, at least, our understanding of it—may be more complex now than ever before. Over the last generation or so, the effects of postmodernism, feminism, and queer liberation have become all too keenly felt, creating something of a sea change in how we address sex and sexuality. More people than ever are talking about how to maximize sexual empowerment between consenting adults, and the belief that sexuality itself is a societal construct worthy of examination is becoming increasingly widespread. As a result of work both in the academy and in peoples' real lives, a whole new set of questions with which to address our time-honored traditions has become apparent. There are new ways to challenge the tradition's underlying assumptions, to think about how an ancient idea might speak to our current, ever evolving understanding of human potential, and perhaps to offer thorny sources a little textual healing.

The Passionate Torah was created to offer such a playground for this kind of thinking. Scholars, rabbis, and smart people of various backgrounds have been asked to weigh in on the ways in which our tradition addresses human sexuality, using all the tools and lenses available in the contemporary world.

The Passionate Torah seeks to deepen the Jewish conversation about sexuality and, at the same time, push it forward a little. It seeks to ask questions like, how might new ways of thinking about queer sexuality impact all our understandings of God? Is there a way to address the injunction against sleeping with a menstruant that both takes into account its troubling textual history and offers a new model of practice for the future? In these pages Jay Michaelson and Haviva Ner-David offer insights on these issues, among others.

Rather than excising the problematic, many of the contributors to *The Passionate Torah* choose to grapple with a difficulty until it yields light from a yet unseen angle. Rebecca Alpert examines masturbation through a deceptively simple yet incisive new lens, offering a fresh take on how we can understand solitary love today; Gail Labovitz looks at stories that seem to show rabbinic desire in an entirely unflattering light, and finds among them a powerful vote in favor of female sexual empowerment; and Laura Levitt uses ancient midrash and the writings of the feminist poet and activist Audre Lorde to make a surprising case about partnership.

The book is organized with some help from one of the most noted thinkers of the twentieth century on the subject of relationships, the philosopher Martin Buber. Buber famously distinguished between what he termed an "I-It" relationship and an "I-Thou" relationship. In the former, he explained, the other person is little more than an object at your disposal —the waitress is the object that brings you your food, the cab driver is the object that brings you from one location to another. An I-Thou relationship, on the other hand, is one in which the other person is regarded as a whole being, full of hopes and dreams and selfhood, as created in the Divine Image. The relationship is not bounded by a utilitarian, you-do-for-me-I-do-for-you attitude. I-Thou relationships have no preset boundaries; I-Thou is the model of the relationship that we have with God.

The first section of the book, "I-It: Challenges," focuses on some of the ways in which Judaism has fallen short in helping to foster relationships based in mutuality and caring. To this end, Sarra Lev offers an incisive take on the pornography of the tractate *Sotah*; Judith Baskin looks at how prostitution has been romanticized and demonized, depending on the identity of the prostitute in question; and Melanie Malka Landau looks at the power and limits of legislating intimacy. Others take on everything from human and Divine divorce to the nature—and problems—of scholarly lust. The chapters in this section turn a critical eye on what is—a necessary first step in helping us imagine what might be.

The second section, "I-Thou: Relationships," focuses on connections, on what happens when we set off on the enterprise of loving—others, or ourselves. Some, like Wendy Love Anderson's rollicking history of interreligious coupling, look at what happens when people come together— and how, in this case, the Jewish, as well as the Christian and Muslim, world reacts. Others, like Naomi Seidman's rumination on the erotics of sexual segregation, explore too-long unarticulated aspects of Jewish lived experience. In this section, too, both Elliot Dorff and Sara Meirowitz address issues of relationships unfolding, and their implications for, respectively, procreation and formal commitment. Being in relationship is a messy business, and these chapters address both its magic and its potential.

The third section, "We-Thou: Visions," transcends Buber's formulation to think about ways in which the community as a whole might imagine a shared future. Elliot Rose Kukla gives us a fresh way to think through sex, love, and Jewish gender diversity, and Arthur Waskow brings sexual connection from a narrowly defined "Garden of Eden" model into something far more expansive and multilayered. Other authors in this section examine monogamy, modesty, and sexual agency with an eye toward how we, as Jews and sexual beings, can engage ourselves, one another, and our tradition with the aim of increasing holiness in the world.

For this, too, is Torah. *The Passionate Torah* seeks to deepen the conversation and to open new avenues for dialogue on what Judaism is, what sex is, and who we are and could be.

Come and learn.

I-It: Challenges

1

Sotah

Rabbinic Pornography?

Sarra Lev

> What the public wants is the image of passion, not passion itself.
> —Roland Barthes, *Mythologies*

> Pornography is often more sexually compelling than the realities it presents, more sexually real than reality . . . For the consumer, the mediation provides the element of remove requisite for deniability.
> —Catharine MacKinnon, "Only Words"

THE TEXT OF Mishnah Sotah is a form of literature that does not fit neatly in any one genre. It is not history, as it does not tell of an actual historical case, nor is it fictional narrative, since it functions as instruction rather than description or story. But although it is instructive, it is not an instruction manual or a law book per se, since it confesses to instruct on how to conduct a ritual that is no longer performed. When teaching this text, which focuses on the ritual to be performed when a husband suspects his wife of infidelity, I treat it as a director's manual. I ask my students to "direct" the scene considered in the literature. I ask them, who is on the set or the stage? Who is the camera pointing at? Who is holding the camera? Who is active, and who is passive? Who is narrating? What actions are being performed, and by whom? And, finally, how is the film rated, and why? In this analysis, I also subject the text of Mishnah Sotah to the scrutiny of film theory, primarily the theory of the gaze. Many of the questions I pose here merely reapply theories articulated by scholars such as Mieke Bal regarding fiction, John Berger on the topic of art, and Laura Mulvey concerning film. My claim is that the question of who is looking at whom in the Mishnah of Sotah is of key importance. The reader of the text "views" the crowd viewing the priest viewing the woman, the ultimate voiceless object. The text is often voyeuristic and at times can even be classified as pornographic.[1]

Again, keep in mind, I am not analyzing the ritual as a ritual that actually happened but instead as a novel or script meant to tantalize its readers with scenes of a public or group rape.[2] Whether this ritual ever happened is irrelevant here; of importance is the pornographic portrayal of the rape of a woman for a group of male readers—not in the "actual" ritual but in the depiction of such a ritual. The very fact of its having been written, whether or not it was ever carried out, is enough cause for deconstructing its problematic depiction of women, and the implicit and explicit sexual violence against them.

This chapter thus proceeds as if the ritual itself is fiction. At the same time it is treated as religious fiction, that is, a fiction that is given religious sanction and is imbued with religious sanctity. Whether in fact the violence ever occurred, the two millennia of male readers who have engaged in its study have done so with the understanding that this is an unproblematic text, and have engaged in imagining a scenario in which a woman is publicly raped for the preservation of religious "order."

So, who is the Sotah? According to the Torah, the Sotah is a woman suspected by her husband of having sex with another man. The Torah explains that if a man should suspect his wife of infidelity, he should bring her to the Temple where she ingests a combination of water, dirt, ink, and parchment. Presumably, if she is guilty of said adultery, her stomach will swell and her thighs distend. Of course, according to biblical (and rabbinic) norms, no equivalent ordeal exists for an "unfaithful" husband, since a husband is not required to remain monogamous. The sexuality of the wife belongs to the husband and may not become the property of another. The sexuality of the husband, on the other hand, belongs solely to him. He may use it as he wishes, as long as he does not break one of the prohibitions of Leviticus 18 and 20.

But while the Torah seems to intend the ritual to vindicate the accused woman, the Rabbis who later interpret the ritual ultimately turn it into a humiliation and a punishment for the (only possibly guilty) woman.

The Biblical Ritual

The biblical Sotah ritual takes up twenty verses of Numbers chapter 5, just two-thirds of a single chapter. The text begins:

> Any man whose wife goes astray and commits a trespass [*ma'al*] against him, and a man lies with her carnally, and it is hidden from the eyes of her husband, and is hidden, and she is defiled, and there is no witness against her, and/for she was not caught; and the spirit of jealousy comes upon him, and he is jealous of his wife, and she was defiled; or if the spirit of jealousy comes upon him, and he is jealous of his wife, and she was not defiled, the man should bring his wife to the priest, and shall bring her offering for her (on account of her?). . . . It is an offering of jealousy, an offering of memorial, a reminder of iniquity.

The biblical text opens with the possibility that a woman is suspected of the crime of allowing her body to be used sexually by someone other than her husband. The text uses the term *ma'al*, a term usually reserved for the (mis)use of objects reserved strictly for use by God (signified by the Temple). The obvious correlate in the equation positions the husband as equivalent to God and the woman's sexuality as sacred object, to be used only by her husband. That she allows her body to be used by anyone other than her husband constitutes *me'ila*.

Throughout Numbers chapter 5, the description balances between potential guilt and potential innocence, allowing for the possibility that "the spirit of jealousy comes upon him, and he is jealous of his wife, and she was defiled; or if the spirit of jealousy comes upon him, and he is jealous of his wife, and she was not defiled." The equally weighted possibility that she may be innocent is repeated each time the text mentions her possible guilt —in verses 19–21, and again in verses 27–28 and 29–30.[3]

The text also leaves open the question of whose transgression is being discussed, referring constantly to the jealousy of the husband (using the word "jealous" ten times in twenty verses) and calling the offering that he must bring "an offering of jealousy, an offering of memorial, a reminder of iniquity" (Num. 5:15). Just whose iniquity is being referenced is unclear. Is it the iniquity of the (possibly innocent) woman? If so, if she is innocent, what is her iniquity? Or is it, perhaps, the iniquity of the jealous man? The man of the Sotah ritual, after all, is always jealous, as the entire ritual is triggered by his jealousy. In fact, the very last verse states: "then shall the man be guiltless from iniquity, and this woman shall bear her iniquity," assuming the original iniquity of both man and woman.[4]

The biblical text is consistently ambiguous about the guilt or innocence of the woman, and, moreover, about the possible transgression of the husband. The biblical ritual seems to be directed at ending the husband's jealousy and returning the system to its proper balance, wherein "sacred property" is used for its proper purpose.

The Rabbinic Ritual

In contrast with the twenty-verse biblical ritual, the Mishnah of Sotah constitutes an entire book, much of it focused on the performance of the ritual. The book does not, as one might expect, expand on the intent of the biblical ritual but utterly transforms the original ordeal into a demonstration of sexual humiliation and punishment for a sin not yet proven to have occurred.[5] Unlike the biblical ordeal (in which a man's own jealousy is enough to bring the woman to the priest), the rabbinic ritual is put into action only when a man warns his wife, before two witnesses, not to talk to a certain man. If the wife is then seen going into a "secret place" with this man, and staying there for enough time to have intercourse, the games begin. The ritual is only activated by the presence of observers—in the first case, witnesses who are seen by the wife. In the second instance, however, the observers may be anyone at all—in one opinion, a single witness, or even the husband himself, and they may be entirely invisible to the wife.

The theme of watching and being watched throws us into several discussions prevalent for the past two and a half decades: the discourse of the "gaze" (in film theory); scopophilia,[6] and voyeurism in particular (in psychology); pornography (in feminist theory); and the analysis of the panopticon and its role in discipline in Foucault's book, *Discipline and Punish*.[7] All these discourses form themselves around the question, "What does it mean to watch and to be watched?"

This essay, which engages to a certain extent with all these intersecting theories, focuses primarily on the voyeuristic/pornographic nature of the Mishnah's reworking of the Sotah ritual. In focusing on this element of the ritual, I am not claiming that this is the only lens through which this text may be understood; I merely choose this particular focus for the purpose of delving deeper into this specific aspect of a complex and multilayered text.

Finally, I engage briefly in a discussion of Foucault's panopticism, for while these voyeuristic elements of the ritual are startlingly explicit, they are not the only locus of the subjugation of "woman" as a class in Mishnah Sotah. The other, more insidious, locus of subjugation is visible only through the work of Foucault's *Discipline and Punish*, where he offers an analysis of various "mechanisms" of discipline. But first, let us return to the first order of business: the Sotah ritual as a piece of early pornography.

We left the text above as our Sotah was observed entering a secret place (literally, "house of hiddenness") with the "other man." At this point, the husband takes her to the local court and is assigned two Sages to accompany him to the Jerusalem Temple, in order to watch over them, lest they have sex on the way to Jerusalem.[8] The accused woman sets off for Jerusalem accompanied by the watchful eyes of two scholars, watching not only her but her use of her own sexuality with her own husband. Before the ritual even begins, the Mishnah has introduced yet another stage in which careful observation must take place. In each of these cases, the reader's gaze (and that of the characters watching) is a male gaze. The gaze is also sexualized, as the (male)[9] reader reads first of the husband's insinuation that her talking to another man is "dangerous," then of the townspeople watching her entering a private place (letting his imagination wander), and, finally, as he imagines the two watchers watching her (and her husband) for signs of sexuality on the way to Jerusalem. Here, in the Sotah ritual, the reader is not only innocently watching a woman but is also watching her sexuality. Not only is the gaze a sexualized gaze, but it is also a creative one. The reader does not actually know anything about the true sexuality of the woman; rather, the reader imposes his own idea about her sexuality upon the body that he imagines. The reader watches, and at the same time imposes an imagined sexuality upon her body as he watches.

The watching of the Sotah has only just begun when this odd group of four arrives in Jerusalem. It is here that the watching becomes ever more expanded, as what is watched becomes ever more sexualized and enticing. Upon arriving in Jerusalem the text of Mishnah Sotah 1:3 describes the beginning of the ordeal in which the power relationship and the woman's position in that relationship are established:

> They would take her up to the high court in Jerusalem and intimidate her as they intimidate witnesses in capital cases. And they say to her: My daughter, wine does much [to lead one astray], joking does much, childishness does much, bad neighbors do much;[10] do it (confess) for

the sake of the great name which is written in holiness, so that it is not erased in the water. And they say before her things which she should not have to hear, she and all her family.

In this Mishnah the accused woman is "persuaded" by the high court of Jerusalem. They begin by calling her "my daughter," setting up the power dynamic of kindly father-figure and straying daughter. They attempt to cajole her into confessing her crime (though they do not know yet whether she committed it) by assuring her that her mistake could have been the result of hanging out with the wrong crowd (bad neighbors) or of an excess of wine or frivolity. But we must make no mistake about it: this "kindly" interaction is not benign. It is, in fact, only a calculated piece of a violent process of which this "good-cop/bad-cop" scenario marks the beginning. This power dynamic is hinted at even in the text itself through the use of the word "intimidate" (otherwise translated as "threaten") at the beginning of the description. And again, at the end of the Mishnah, the reader is left to imagine what words "which she should not have to hear" are whispered into the ears of the suspected adulteress. In describing the necessary components of pornography, Susan Cole writes:

> It is important for feminists to identify a patriarchal sexual ideology that is held together by three strands. . . . The second ideological strand perpetuates the women-as-submissive/men-as-dominant configuration within the heterosexual paradigm. . . . Pornography is just one of the cultural institutions committed to this second strain. There is a great deal else done to make our own demise sexually arousing to men. . . . [M]any men and women really "feel" aroused by domination and surrender.[11]

In the buildup to the explicit pornographic climax, the ritual begins by conveying the woman's powerlessness in contrast with the power of the presiding "fatherly" priest or the "administrators" of the ritual. Clearly, if this tactic does not succeed, the next stage will not be as gentle.

In addition to illustrating this power dynamic, this Mishnah also assumes her guilt. The adjuration to confess fails to account for the fact that perhaps the woman standing before us is innocent, and instead stands here before us guilty and sexualized. In addition, unlike the biblical text, which balances every mention of her possible guilt with a mention of her possible innocence, the Mishnah's text never mentions her possible innocence. This stands in stark contrast to a Baraita[12] found in the Babylonian Talmud (BT) which states:

> Just as they intimidate her not to drink, so they intimidate her to drink.
> They say to her, my daughter, if it is clear to you that you are innocent,
> stand by your certainty and drink.[13]

Had this Baraita appeared in the Mishnah, we would have had an entirely different view of the Mishnah's understanding of the Sotah. As it is, however, the only adjuration written in the Mishnah is that which attempts to elicit a confession of guilt. The Mishnah draws the suspected woman as guilty—as always already a whore.

At the same time, at this point in the ritual, as she stands before us—the (male) readers—we remain unsure whether she is innocent or guilty. The possibility that she is innocent must remain, for that is what allows us to carry through with the (reading of the) ritual: we are there to determine whether (or not) she is guilty! The possibility that she is guilty allows us to punish her along the way. In either case, we know that she is guilty of having brought us to this point—having "forced us" to inflict this upon her.

In a strange twist on contemporary pornography, which often positions the woman as either virgin or whore, this text positions the woman neither as virgin nor whore but as the unknown between. Thus the hypothetical woman is, at all points in time, possibly "virgin" and possibly "whore." The enticement of her possible innocence remains a part of the show. At the same time, unlike the biblical ritual that continues to explicitly introduce the feasibility of her innocence at every turn, this particular ritual in some ways actually creates the whore out of the potential virgin.

In Mishnah 2:1 Rabban Gamaliel explains why the Sotah's sacrifice is composed of simple barley with no added oil or incense by stating: "just as her act was the act of a beast, so too the sacrifice consists of the food of a beast." Foucault writes, "The suspect, as such, always deserved a certain punishment; one could not be the object of suspicion and be completely innocent."[14] In the Mishnah, as in Foucault's analysis, it would seem that the Sotah is punished not for the adultery which may or may not have occurred but for the very fact that she has brought herself under suspicion. The ritual, as it is constructed, lets the male spectator say to himself: "it is her fault that we are here. If she had not gone into the secret place, if she had only listened to her husband, if she had not tried to assert her own independence—none of this would be happening!"

Simon Hardy notes that:

> Women could be seen as unique among oppressed groups in that they seem to exercise a certain power over their oppressors. As Richard Goldstein puts it, women are seen to be "powerful, desirable, implicated in their condition and in need of punishment." Indeed, Goldstein even goes so far as to claim that this is why he was able to sustain an erection throughout a film . . . in which women are sexually tortured by a male captor, when, if the victims had been Jewish, or gay, or black and at the mercy of their respective oppressors, he would have "run out of the [video] shop screaming" at the very thought of it.[15]

The Sotah, too, seems to be treated as if she is implicated in her own condition. When viewed as already guilty, it is easier for the Rabbis to both punish her and overtly and publicly sexualize her even further. This sexualization is most explicit in Mishnah 1:5 and 1:6 where the text refers to her bare breasts. This second reference pictures the Sotah's breasts tied with an Egyptian rope, introducing also the imagery of bondage. But this imagery comes only after the actual sexual climax of the text in Sotah 1:5. Here she makes a choice to go ahead with the ritual despite the warning of the "good cop."

> If she says "I am innocent [pure]," they take her up to the eastern gate which is at the entrance to the gate of Nikanor . . . and a priest grabs her clothing. If they are ripped, they are ripped, and if they are undone, they are undone, so that he reveals her breast and uncovers her hair. Rabbi Yehudah says: If her breast is beautiful, he does not reveal it, and if her hair is beautiful, he does not uncover it.

Just as the Sotah is punished for having brought us to this point by defying the controls that have been put on her body, so, too, is she punished for this moment in which she displays her own power of self-determination by refusing to confess. Her refusal to be baited into a confession immediately changes the picture from a passive aggressive display of power to an aggressive one: very little need be said about this part of the ceremony. The ripping of the woman's clothes so that her breasts are exposed before a crowd of men (and women), speaks for itself. As Hardy writes:

One gesture which is richly invested with connotations of power is the tearing of fabric. . . . [T]he ripping of clothing perfectly expresses the paradigm of rape in synchronic terms, out of time, so that its eroticism is not undermined by prior consent. In short, the violent gesture delivers connotations of power which the reader can enjoy, with the mitigating context edited out in the process of interpretation.[16]

We cannot overestimate the level of humiliation involved in this text. In a society where the parts of a woman that are permitted to be seen is regulated even to the point where one rabbinic opinion believes that a woman's heel is an erotic body part,[17] the act of revealing her breasts and her hair were likely the height of shaming and humiliation.[18] If other moments in this process contain elements of the pornographic, this Mishnah screams it out. She has exerted power that did not belong to her, allowing herself to be visible. In response, the Sotah is set up as a spectacle. In the following Mishnah the spectacle continues with a description of her being redressed in shaming clothing:

> If she was dressed in white clothing, he dresses her in black. If she wore golden ornaments or necklaces, earrings or rings, they remove them from her in order to disgrace/denigrate her. And afterwards, he brings an Egyptian rope and ties it above her breasts.[19]

Leaving aside, for a moment, the problematic color allusions, it is clear that this text again creates out of the woman the whore that the Rabbis are afraid she has become, or perhaps the whore that they believe she is, merely for having caused the ritual itself to happen by stepping into the "secret place" with a man other than her husband.

If there is any question of whether my reading of this act as sexual is an imposition of contemporary values upon an ancient and wholly unsexualized text, one need only turn to Rabbi Yehudah's dissenting opinion in this very Mishnah to reveal the ancient understanding of the sexual nature of these proceedings. Here the text itself reads the ritual as pornographic, erotic, or sexually enticing. Rabbi Yehudah's opinion that a woman whose breasts are beautiful does not undergo the ripping of the garments clearly demonstrates his awareness of the obvious potential for sexual arousal in this ritual, which he tries to fend off.[20]

In contrast to the minority opinion of Rabbi Yehudah, who wishes to avoid the arousal of the observers, the majority opinion seems either unconcerned with, or desirous of eliciting, the sexual arousal of either the hypothetical spectators or the actual ones (the readers). One might even say that the text functions to elicit that very arousal, or at least to promote it at every turn. Whereas the Torah text speaks nothing of grabbing the woman's clothes, exposing her breasts, dressing her in denigrating clothing, or inviting spectators, this text is filled with such classically pornographic moves. The reader can simply assume the role of the assaulting priest, and the rest is done for him.

Hardy claims that:

> In textual pornography, instead of assuming the position of the camera, the reader steps into and occupies the position of the Lover in the story. As Robert said, "you picture yourself there, as one of the people." What enabled James to "switch on" sexually was "imagining [him]self in the situation of the bloke."[21]

In addition to identifying with the priest in the scenario, "pictur[ing] yourself there, as one of the people" allows for yet another (male) subject position in the Sotah ritual. One can identify with the actual perpetrator —the priest—who strips the woman and humiliates her or one can identify with the watchers in the crowd, spoken of in Mishnah 1:6:

> And afterwards, he brings an Egyptian rope and ties it above her breasts. And all who wish to come and watch may come and watch, except for her female and male servants, for she is emboldened before them. And all the women are permitted to see her, as it is said "and all the women shall be warned, and shall not imitate your obscenity." (Ezek. 23)[22]

The text here introduces two new roles to the stage—that of the watching man and that of the watching woman. But although these two figures occupy the same field of vision, they are hardly to be understood in the same manner. As already noted, "woman" typically occupies the position of the object of the gaze. Although the audience described within the text is both male and female, the reader of the text is expected to be only male. This sets up a complex matrix of "spectators" and "spectacles," and opens up a question: What are the various dynamics involved in the fact that a group of men are imagining watching (through their reading of the text) another group of men and women watching a priest strip and humiliate a woman?

The male watcher in the text is there for the male reader to identify with, not as an object of the reader's voyeurism. The Mishnah has transformed the biblical ritual from a private affair in which only the high priest takes part to a public humiliation in which each and every step requires the observation and participation of the public. It has moved the ritual out of the private individual world of the husband (and the high priest) and into the public realm of townspeople, local court, high court, priest, and crowd of observers—all watching. At the same time it has reinscribed the power dynamics which allow the ritual to take place in the first place —woman's position as dominated and man's position as dominant. While the watching man is the subject of the gaze, the watching woman is the object of the gaze.

The female watcher is there as object, just like the Sotah herself.[23] The gaze in Mishnah Sotah is clearly a male one. A male voice describes the detailed process by which a hypothetical woman is being watched as she is warned by her more powerful male husband to whom she may and may not talk; watched by surreptitious observers as she enters into a private place with a man not her husband for a period of time which allows the imaginations of the watchers and the readers to flow when thinking about what could have happened there; watched by young scholars as she walks the road to Jerusalem, her sexuality exposed to their imaginings; watched by the men of the high court while she makes her decision about whether to proclaim herself pure or impure; watched by the priest and a crowd of invited onlookers, as she is stripped of her clothes.

Even in the line of Mishnah which invites and perhaps even encourages the women to come and watch the spectacle, the gaze remains a male one. The women are invited by men for the purpose of a warning, and we see no sign of what it means to a woman herself to be watching the abuse. They are there in order to be warned—and thus themselves identified with the wayward woman. They, too, are consequently sexualized—each a Sotah *in potentia*. The male reader watches the women watching the woman.

As we saw from R. Yehudah's response, the stripping of the woman by the priest is interpreted as a sexual act, whether or not it is solely intended to be understood in this manner. In Mishnah 1:6 we add the voyeuristic element of the watchers and the watchers of the watchers, all focused on the woman as a sexual being. Her sexuality is examined both in the form of the story that is told of her (the truth of which will be revealed through the ritual) and in the form of the unclothing of her actual body, innocent or guilty. In both cases, all eyes are upon her as her sexuality is observed and revealed.

I return here to my original contention that whether or not the ritual ever really occurred, the text itself is meant to do the work of the ritual —sexualizing "woman" through the use of an anonymous woman, and tantalizing the reader through its sexual imagery of the woman as object of rape and scopophilia. This becomes particularly evident in an aside found in Mishnah 1:7:

> A person is measured by the same means by which they acted. She adorned herself for a transgression, God disgraced her. She revealed herself for a transgression, God revealed [the transgression] upon her [body]. She began the transgression through her thigh, and then her belly, thus shall she be afflicted first on her thigh and then on her belly, but the rest of her body shall not escape.

This Mishnah brings to the fore each sexual move that the woman (ostensibly) made, and matches it with an equivalent punishment. Since she sinned with her thigh and her belly (probably euphemisms for her genitals and her womb), she is repaid by being afflicted both on her thigh and her belly. The sign of her guilt at the end of the ritual, once she drinks the water, is that her thigh swells and her belly distends.[24]

The contention that the woman deserved her punishment measure for measure is the least problematic element of this text, which mixes "investigation and punishment,"[25] and claims that her (still undetermined) actions led her to this humiliation. But there is another aspect to this particular Mishnah that deserves comment, namely, that it is meant for the reader alone. In other words, nowhere during the course of the ritual are the details of Mishnah 1:7—her alleged actions and her punishment as it relates to them—stated aloud. Unlike other parts of the Mishnah where the text tells us that "he [the husband] says to her" (1:2) or that "they say to her" (1:4), nowhere is the information contained in this Mishnah said out loud. The reader alone has the pleasure of reading this account of the sexual act itself—"she adorned herself . . . she revealed herself . . . she began the transgression through her thigh, and then her belly." Here he is permitted to peek through the keyhole into the "hidden place" where she was seen entering with the other man. Here the reader is given a free ticket to be a voyeur. Here the pornography of the text itself, and not only of the ritual within that text, becomes explicit.

When Adulterers Abounded: The Demise of the Ritual

We have seen that it is possible to see the Sotah ritual of the Mishnah through a series of lenses, all meant to address certain questions: "Who is being watched?" "Who is watching?" and "What is the purpose or function of the watching?" Clearly this ritual includes a much more complex partnership of the mechanisms of watching and being watched than those we have had space to describe here. Throughout we have understood that this ritual never took place. But what might account for the fact that this text stands out as so different from the other ways in which the Rabbis of the period of the Mishnah treat others accused of serious crimes?[26] One cannot say that it is owing to the way women are treated, because other texts do not treat women in this manner. Perhaps the answer may be found in Foucault's mechanism of panopticism:[27]

> Disciplinary power . . . is exercised through its invisibility; at the same time it imposes on those whom it subjects a principle of compulsory visibility. In discipline, it is the subjects who have to be seen. Their visibility assures the hold of the power that is exercised over them. It is the fact of being constantly seen, of being able always to be seen, that maintains the disciplined individual in his [sic] subjection.[28]

> He who is subjected to a field of visibility, and who knows it, assumes responsibility for the constraints of power; he makes them play spontaneously upon himself; he inscribes in himself the power relation in which he simultaneously plays both roles; he becomes the principle of his own subjection. By this very fact, the external power may throw off its physical weight; it tends to the non-corporal; and, the more it approaches this limit, the more constant, profound and permanent are its effects: it is a perpetual victory that avoids any physical confrontation and which is always decided in advance.[29]

It would seem at first glance that the Rabbis disagree. Even while the average woman may understand herself to be watched, particularly by the anonymous masses who may relate her seclusion with the other man to her husband, this watching alone is not enough for the Rabbis to ensure her proper conduct and normative behavior. The Rabbis, in their vision of the entire project, introduce corporal punishment into the picture as well —stripping her and making her drink, thereby inscribing the crime on her (not yet guilty) body. One marvels at the rabbinic mind in this particular tractate, which seems so extreme in its treatment of the woman who may or may not have strayed. But perhaps these Rabbis are perfectly aware of the power of being watched, and fully understand that the ritual will not take place. Perhaps it is this very matter—the fact that they already exert complete control on her watched body—that explains just how far they allow themselves to wander in writing this ritual. The last chapter of the Mishnah tells us:

> When adulterers abounded, the bitter waters were stopped, and [it was] Rabbi Yochanan Ben Zakkai [who] stopped them, as it says [in the Bible] I will not punish your daughters when they go astray or your brides when they commit adultery, for they [too] [stray with whores, and sacrifice with cult prostitutes . . .]

This Mishnah from the final chapter of the tractate makes it clear that the ritual itself, if it ever took place at all, ceased to exist somewhere around the year 70 C.E. When adulterers abound, the mechanism of observation has failed. No longer can we count on the watchers to watch and control. No longer can we count on the watched to feel the gaze of the watchers, even when they are invisible. At this point, the Rabbis can no longer subscribe to the corporal piece of the ritual: there is a danger that it may actually take place.

But make no mistake: that the ritual might not have happened does not exempt or excuse the Rabbis for their brutal portrayal of the public rape of the Sotah. Foucault's panopticism is itself oppressive. It is itself an exertion of power upon the body of the observed. Furthermore, the pornographic novel itself, which the Rabbis create, allows for its male readers to fantasize about the humiliation and degradation of women. And in this model, in which the woman watchers themselves are present at the ritual because of the danger that they, too, will stray, it is not one guilty woman who is at stake but womanhood itself that is condemned as wayward, and forced into objectification and a position of to-be-looked-at-ness.

NOTES

1. Before proceeding to discuss Sotah through the lens of pornography, it is essential to note the often vicious and raging debate regarding the subject of pornography. The debate, which took place primarily in the 1980s and early 1990s, usually centers around the question of whether pornographic literature is "bad for women" and whether it should be legal. In much of the literature, the actual definition of pornography is entirely absent (particularly in the pro-porn literature). In addition, it often seems that the two "sides" are discussing a different object. In this chapter I choose to understand pornography as defined by Dworkin and MacKinnon as that which contains "subordination of women graphically depicted"; see Drucilla Cornell, *Feminism and Pornography,* Oxford Readings in Feminism series (Oxford: Oxford University Press, 2000). That this literature is degrading is a given in this chapter and not a subject of debate. However, in choosing to understand pornography in this way, I take no stand on the debate regarding freedom of speech. My interest is in the genre itself, not in whether it should or should not be permitted.

2. I use the word "rape" here as defined in the Merriam Webster legal dictionary: "Unlawful sexual activity and usually sexual intercourse carried out forcibly or under threat of injury against the will usually of a female . . . NOTE: The common-law crime of rape involved a man having carnal knowledge of a woman not his wife through force and against her will, and required at least slight penetration of the penis into the vagina. While some states maintain essentially this definition of rape, most have broadened its scope esp. in terms of the sex of the persons and the nature of the acts involved. Marital status is usually irrelevant. Moreover, the crime is codified under various names, including first degree sexual assault, sexual battery, unlawful sexual intercourse, and first degree sexual abuse."

3. It is also possible to read verses 31a–b as two scenarios: the first (in which he is cleansed of sin) occurs if she is proven innocent, in which case his "sin" of jealousy is nevertheless cleansed by the ritual; and the second (in which she must carry her sin) occurs if she is proven guilty, in which case, despite the ritual and sacrifice, her sin is not expiated.

4. Although it is possible to read "the man" as referring to the adulterer, it seems more likely that it refers to the husband for two reasons. First, it is unlikely that the adulterous man would be cleansed of sin by means of the ritual if the adulterous woman were to bear her sin. He is equally guilty of "misuse of sacred property" under the laws of sexual conduct in Leviticus. Second, the sacrifice is continually referred to as "a *mincha* [sacrifice] of jealousy."

5. Interspersed between these descriptions are laws about who may eat *t'rumah,* what happens to the materials of the sacrifice if the ordeal is disrupted, under what circumstances the ordeal is disrupted, and various other concerns. Primarily, however, the text deals with the description of the ordeal itself.

6. This is the common English translation of Freud's *Schaulust*, meaning "pleasure in looking," and refers to the sexual pleasure derived from looking, as well as from exhibitionism.

7. Michel Foucault, *Discipline and Punish* (New York: Vintage Books, 1979).

8. It is unclear whether their job is to prevent the two from having sex or merely to monitor and report on the fact that it happened, which would circumvent the ritual.

9. I consciously use the pronoun "he" and assume the reader to be male throughout this chapter for two reasons. First, until the past century, men were almost entirely the only readers of this text. But, more important—and also the reason I use "I" and "we" although some of us are not male—the theory of the gaze positions us as male, regardless of our actual gender. Thus the assumption is that the reader is male, and so we, too, are transformed into male while we read.

10. In other words, "we know that it wasn't really your fault, just tell us that you did it."

11. Susan G. Cole, *Power Surge* (Toronto, Ont.: Second Story, 1995), 40.

12. A Baraita is a source from the same time period as the Mishnah.

13. BT *Sotah* 7b.

14. Foucault, *Discipline and Punish*, 42.

15. Simon Hardy, *The Reader, The Author, His Woman and Her Lover: Soft-Core Pornography and Heterosexual Men* (London: Cassell, 1998), 64–65.

16. Ibid., 90–91.

17. Bavli *Nedarim* 20a

18. See Lisa Grushcow, *Writing the Wayward Wife: Rabbinic Interpretations of Sotah* (Leiden: Brill, 2006), 108.

19. Mishnah Sotah 1:6.

20. This is taken even further in the Talmud's later discussion of this text in which the claim is explicitly made that R. Yehudah's opinion here is the result of his fear of the effects of the lust of the "blossoming priests" who will come to look at her during the proceedings.

21. Hardy, *The Reader*, 130. Robert and James are two of Hardy's interviewees.

22. This verse from Ezekiel is written in the context of God's story of the harlotry of Jerusalem who followed in the path of her adulterous sister. The chapter explicitly recounts in some detail the sexual exploits of the two sisters and the subsequent violent revenge that God takes on each of them.

23. See Lisa Mulvey, "Visual Pleasure and Narrative Cinema," *Screen: The Journal of the Society for Education in Film and Television* 16, no. 3 (fall 1975): 11.

24. This Mishnah refers to the original biblical text which states that if she is guilty her thigh will swell and her belly will distend (Num. 5:27). For a fuller description of the nature of her indiscretion and of the punishments for each of the actions she took, see *Tosefta Sotah* 3:2–5.

25. See Foucault, *Discipline and Punish*, 41.

26. Mishnah *Sanhedrin* 4:1 explains that one of the differences between judging capital cases and civil cases is that in capital cases we hear the evidence in favor of the accused first, treating him as innocent until proven guilty. Ironically, a source from the same time period attributes this decision to the verse in Num. 5:19 which says of the Sotah: "'If no man has lain with you and you have not strayed to impurity [with a man] in place of your husband . . .' from here [the fact that the priest opens his words to the Sotah with the possibility of her innocence, we learn] that one opens in capital cases first to the side of innocence" (BT *San.* 32b–33a). This implies that the understanding of this text is that the Sotah case is equivalent to a capital case, and yet the assumption of innocence given to any other accused on the basis of this verse in Sotah is not given to the Sotah herself.

27. Panopticism is a disciplinary mechanism outlined by Foucault based on a prison (the panopticon) designed by Jeremy Bentham in the late eighteenth century. The prison is designed with a central tower that allows for the prisoners to be watched at all times without knowing whether they are being watched at any specific time. Foucault understands the philosophy behind the panopticon to extend beyond its walls into a great many institutions in society in general.

28. Foucault, *Discipline and Punish*, 187.

29. Ibid., 202–203.

2

Prostitution

Not a Job for a Nice Jewish Girl

Judith R. Baskin

PROSTITUTION AND TRAFFICKING in human beings for the purpose of prostitution have been and continue to be ugly realities of human life. In this chapter, I focus on some portrayals of prostitution in biblical and aggadic (non-legal) rabbinic writings. These traditions often display a romanticized view of prostitutes—as long as they are not Jews. This double standard is evident in attitudes expressed about the "world's oldest profession" and its practitioners in the Hebrew Bible and in the midrashic traditions of the rabbinic era.[1]

Prostitution in the Hebrew Bible

The Hebrew term for prostitution is *zenut* or *zenunim*; a prostitute is a *zonah*. The Hebrew Bible also mentions the *qedesh* and *qedeshah*, apparently male and female "cult" or "temple" prostitutes connected with non-Israelite rituals.[2] Biblical narratives present prostitutes as part of daily life in both the countryside and the city; we catch glimpses of their lives as they ply their trade at twilight (Prov. 7:6–11); attract customers by playing musical instruments (Isaiah 23:16); and sit by crossroads near public events such as sheep shearings (Gen. 38:13–19). One of the unnamed prostitutes who comes to Solomon for justice puts her child's life above her claims as its mother (I Kings 3:16–27).

Women who became prostitutes were orphans, widows, or divorcées on the margins of Israelite society; some may have been released captive women or manumitted female servants or slaves. Certainly, they were outside the mainstream patriarchal system that relegated women to domestic roles under the authority and care of specific men. Some prostitutes, such as the women who quarreled over the infant in I Kings 3, banded together and shared lodgings. Others may have functioned quite successfully as independent entrepreneurs. The biblical authors portray Rahab, the harlot of Joshua 2, as a respected citizen who lived in a private residence where she dried flax on the roof. The wanton woman of Proverbs 7 is said to have coverlets of Egyptian linen and to sprinkle her bed with "myrrh, aloes, and cinnamon" (Prov. 7:16–17).

Prostitutes were a reality in Israelite society, but biblical legislation took a negative view of their occupation. Deuteronomy 23:18–19 forbids male and female Israelites from serving as "cult" prostitutes, and Leviticus 19:29 adjures Israelite men not to degrade their daughters into *zenut*, lest "the land be filled with depravity." Members of the high priestly caste (*kohanim*) are specifically prohibited from marrying harlots (Lev. 21:7, 14), because priests are required to marry virgins, which also rules out widows and divorcées (Lev. 21:14). The daughter of a priest who engaged in *zenut* was to be burned (Lev. 21:9), but no legal penalties are specified for other prostitutes. No Israelite man would have wished his daughter to descend to prostitution, although men facing bankruptcy may have been helpless to prevent it. Jacob's sons, Simeon and Levi, justified slaughtering their putative brother-in-law, Shechem, and all his male kinsmen on the grounds that their sister, Dinah, should not be treated as a *zonah* (Gen. 34:31). Tamar, of Genesis 38, posed as a prostitute and slept with her father-in-law, Judah, when he failed to fulfill his levirate obligation[3] toward her; she is praised and honored as an ancestor of David (Gen. 38). The text makes clear, however, that Tamar would have faced death had she not presented the pledges her father-in-law had left with her in lieu of payment and had he not acknowledged the justice of her claims.

The religious opprobrium directed toward prostitutes is most intensely expressed in biblical passages that invoke harlotry as a metaphor for Israel's betrayal of God. Thus the Israelites at Shittim are described as "whoring with the Moabite women who invite the people to the sacrifices for their god" (Num. 25:1). Jeremiah condemns "rebellious Israel" for "going to every high mountain and under every leafy tree and whoring there" (Jer. 3:6), and Hosea decries those who forsake God to practice *zenut* by worshiping other deities (Hos. 4:11–12). Hosea is ordered to take "a wife of whoredom" who will bear him "children of whoredom" (Hos. 1:2) as living allegories of Israel's lack of faithfulness.

Gentile Prostitutes in the Bible and Midrash

The biblical narrative of the Canaanite Rahab, the harlot heroine of Joshua 2, presents a Gentile prostitute in an extremely positive light. Rahab is portrayed as a strong-minded, independent woman who cleverly saved two Israelite spies from capture in Jericho. Moreover, she had the spiritual capacity to recognize the unique powers of Israel's God, confessing that "the Lord your God is the only God in heaven above and on earth below" (Joshua 2:11). In return for her generosity, the spies she had hidden promised that Rahab and her kin would be saved when Joshua and the Israelites destroyed Jericho. On the fateful day, Rahab hung a red thread from her window and gathered all her family within her house; remembering Rahab's goodness to his spies, Joshua ordered that she and her family be escorted to a safe place outside the Israelite camp. Joshua 6:25 confirms the happy ending: "Only Rahab the harlot and her father's family were spared by Joshua, along with all that belonged to her, and she dwelt among the Israelites—as is still the case." It is instructive that the biblical author depicts Rahab as a woman of substance, living in her home, respected by her neighbors, and in friendly contact with her relatives. This probably reflects the lives of some urban prostitutes in biblical times.

The biblical story of Rahab is exciting and hortatory, and Rahab herself is portrayed as a stalwart, praiseworthy woman. The Rabbis of the midrash and Talmud, moreover, developed Rahab beyond the scriptural parameters of her story. They saw Rahab as a preeminent model of the righteous convert who went beyond all others in her recognition of God's great powers. By imagining Rahab as a repentant fallen woman who found God and joined the community of Israel, the Rabbis also represent Rahab as an exemplar of the efficacy of Judaism and its traditions in taming the disordering powers of female sexuality. Indeed, Rahab's two personae, the good-hearted whore and repentant fallen woman, establish prototypes with far-reaching implications in the Western imagination—from Mary Magdalen of the New Testament to the ubiquitous whore with the heart of gold in the popular cultures of every era.[4]

Why did Rahab become such an important rabbinic model? It appears that both her gender and her profession appealed to rabbinic interpreters looking for engaging female figures of repentance and conversion. In an extended midrash on the Book of Esther in the Babylonian Talmud (BT) *Megillah* 15a, Rahab is also eroticized when she is linked with other

women whom the Rabbis associated with surpassing beauty and irregular sexual behavior. Part of this passage focuses on the unusually seductive
qualities of Rahab, Yael (Judges 4–5), Abigail (1 Samuel 25), and Michal,
the daughter of Saul (1 Samuel 18, 19, 25:44; 2 Samuel 6). Each biblical
character is problematic for rabbinic exegetes because each acted in ways
that included independence, assertion of sexuality, and an apparent willingness to betray the men of her own family and community. The passage,
which is both funny and openly titillating, reads in part:

> Rahab inspired lust by her name; Yael by her voice; Abigail by her mem-
> ory; Michal, daughter of Saul, by her appearance. R. Isaac said, "Who-
> ever says, 'Rahab, Rahab' at once ejaculates." R. Nahman responded,
> "I say 'Rahab, Rahab,' and nothing happens to me." He replied, "I was
> speaking of one who knew her and was intimate with her."

Midrashic traditions about Rahab fall into several groups. First are
those that emphasize her lurid past and then describe her sincerity as a
convert. *Sifre Zuta* on Numbers 10:28 recounts that four names of disgrace
and obscenity pertained to Rahab, and explains that she was called *zonah*
because she was unchaste both with men of her own country and wander-
ers from elsewhere. According to BT *Zebahim* 116a–b, there was no prince
or ruler who had not possessed Rahab the harlot: "She was ten years old
when the Israelites departed from Egypt, and she played the harlot the
whole forty years spent by the Israelites in the wilderness. At the age of fifty
she became a proselyte." This tradition expresses the rabbinic conviction
that women are sexually untrustworthy, particularly non-Jewish women.
However, it stresses, too, the significant lesson that past wickedness is no
bar to present repentance and future salvation. Perhaps the most important lesson is that women, as well as men, are capable of spiritual transformation and are equally welcomed into the Jewish community.

A second category of remarks details Rahab's many distinguished descendants who were said to be priests and prophets in Israel. That a convert and former prostitute could achieve such a name for herself in the an-
nals of Jewish history is proof that those who sincerely return to God will
achieve repentance, no matter how great their previous sins. Rahab's name
can be understood as "breadth" and her past excesses are frequently cited
as evidence of the breadth of the gates of repentance, as in the following
homiletic midrash from *Pesikta Rabbati* 40:3:

"He will judge the world and declare it acquitted / But He will minister judgment to the heathen peoples according to the upright" (Psalm 9:9). What is meant by, "according to the upright"? R. Alexandri said: He will minister judgment to the heathen people by citing as examples the upright ones among them, the example of Rahab, of Jethro, of Ruth. How will he do so? He will say to each individual of the peoples of the earth: "Why did you not bring yourself closer to Me?" And each of them will answer: "I was wicked, so steeped in wickedness that I was ashamed." And God will ask: "Were you more so than Rahab whose house was in the side of the wall so that on the outside she would receive robbers and then whore with them inside? Nevertheless, when she wished to draw near Me, did I not receive her and raise up prophets and priests from her line?"

A third group of traditions revises Rahab's past entirely and transforms her from a harlot to an innocent innkeeper who ultimately married Joshua (BT *Megillah* 114b). Because Rahab is said to have been so intimately connected with prominent figures in Israel, as wife and as ancestor, this revisionist tradition is not surprising.[5] To launder her past in this way, however, seriously undercuts the main message about the warm reception Judaism offers the repentant harlot. Moreover, by transforming Rahab into a pious convert and devoted wife of Joshua, the Rabbis vitiate Rahab's otherness, defuse her dangerous sexuality, and undercut her disturbing independence.

Traditions about Rahab are part of a larger rabbinic repertoire of erotic stories about prostitutes. One midrashic tale in BT *Menahot* 44a (and *Sifre Numbers* 115), for example, appears in a discussion of the importance of observing the precept of *tzitzit* (ritual fringes) and recounts the tale of a student who was very careful in observing this precept. This young man learned about a prostitute "in the cities of the sea" who required four hundred gold pieces as a fee, and he determined to visit her. Sending the money in advance, he set a date for their assignation. When he arrived, the prostitute had prepared seven beds, "six of silver and one of gold; and between each bed there were steps of silver, but the last were of gold." The woman ascended to the top bed and lay down on it naked. When the young man followed her, the four fringes [of his garment] suddenly struck him across the face and he fell to the ground.

The harlot descended from the golden bed and asked what blemish he had found in her to treat her this way. The man replied that she was the most beautiful women he had ever seen, but he explained that his "*tzitzit* had testified against him" and dissuaded him from endangering his life in the world to come by engaging in harlotry. The woman was so impressed that she became a convert to Judaism and married the man who had rejected her when she was a prostitute. The story ends, "Those very bedclothes that had been spread for him for an illicit purpose she now spread out for him lawfully. This is the reward [for observing the precept] in this world; and as for its reward in the future world—I know not how great it is." This appealing and romantic narrative, like the Rahab story, juxtaposes some of the risqué imagined details of its subject's profession with a religious miracle and the spiritually elevating account of her acceptance into the Jewish community.

Rabbinic Ambivalence

Prostitution as a social reality is decried in rabbinic writings. BT *Berakhot* 23a tells the story of a student of the Rabbis who committed suicide when a prostitute revealed their apparent liaison to his teachers. Although contrary examples are given, the Sages advise that men should not practice their vocations in neighborhoods where harlots live (BT *Pesahim* 113a–b). Exodus *Rabbah* 43:7 and BT *Berakhot* 32a explain the Israelites' practice of idolatry in Egypt through the analogy of a man who established his son as a vendor of perfumes in a street where prostitutes lived and then upbraided him for frequenting his customers.[6] *Avot de-Rabbi Nathan* B3 advises:

> Scripture says, "Keep yourself far from her [a forbidden woman]" (Proverbs 5:8). A man is told: "Do not walk down this street or enter this alley, for there is a prostitute here; she is an attractive woman and she seduces all creatures by her beauty. He said, "I am confident that although I walk [there], I won't look at her and I won't desire her beauty." He is told, "Although you are confident, don't go."

However, as is frequently the case in rabbinic *halakhah* (legal rulings), there is a distinction between what is ethically preferred and what is legally permitted. Thus the *halakhah* was decided in accordance with the opinion of R. Judah ha-Nasi (Tosefta *Temurah* 4:8): visiting prostitutes was not forbidden (assuming the prostitute was an unmarried woman so that adultery was not a factor). If a man chose to visit a prostitute, despite moral exhortations to the contrary, there was a definite preference for Gentile women. This is based on rabbinic interpretations of the statements "do not degrade your daughter and make her a harlot" (Lev. 19:29) and "no Israelite woman shall be a cult prostitute [*qedeshah*]; nor shall any Israelite man be a cult prostitute [*qedesh*]" (Deut. 23:18). According to BT *Sanhedrin* 82a, *qedesh* and *qedesha* refer to all prostitutes.

A significant reason for this attempt to deter Jewish men from frequenting Jewish prostitutes was the fear of incest. According to an early midrashic collection on Leviticus, "Whoever hands his unmarried daughter [to a man] not for the purposes of matrimony," as well as the woman who makes herself sexually available not for the purposes of matrimony, could lead to the whole world being filled with *mamzerim* [illegitimate children], since "from his consorting with many women and not knowing with whom, or if she has had intercourse with many men and does not know with whom—he could marry his own daughter, or marry her to his son" (*Sifra Kedoshim* 7, 1–5). Such disastrous misalliances would be far less likely to occur if Jewish men avoided Jewish prostitutes. However, this is not to say that the Rabbis condone sexual contact with Gentiles. It is important to point out R. Hiyya b. Abuiah's saying that "he who is intimate with a heathen woman is as though he had entered into marriage relationship with an idol" (BT *Sanhedrin* 82a).

Jewish Prostitutes in Rabbinic Midrash

A very different tone attends rabbinic narratives about Jewish men and women who were sold into brothels or sexual slavery by Roman conquerors following the failures of the First and Second Jewish Wars (66–70 C.E. and 132–136 C.E., respectively). These grim narratives fall into several categories, but they all portray prostitution as a degradation that, metaphorically, reflects the powerlessness and emasculation that Jews suffered under Roman rule. The prostitutes in these midrashic stories are male and female, but, as Daniel Boyarin has pointed out, all Jews were feminized in their subjugation to Roman rule.[7]

An expression of this is found in a tradition in BT *Gittin* 58a, attributed to the Sage Resh Lakish:

It is related of a certain woman named Tzafnat bat Peniel [the daughter of the high priest][8] . . . that Roman battalion abused her for a whole night. In the morning [one of the captors] put seven veils around her and took her out to sell her. A certain man who was exceptionally ugly came and said: "Show me her beauty." He replied: "Fool, if you want to buy her, buy, for there is no other so beautiful in all the world." He said to him, "All the same [show her to me]. When the woman had been stripped of her seventh veil, she rolled in the dust and cried out, "Sovereign of the universe, if You do not have pity on us why do you not have pity on the sanctity of Your name?" Resh Lakish applied to her situation a verse from Jeremiah, "Daughters of my people, / put on sackcloth and strew dust on yourselves! / Mourn as for an only child; / Wail bitterly / for suddenly the destroyer is coming upon us" (6:26); he explained that since the verse says "upon us," the rape and degradations of the daughters of Israel are also attacks on God.[9]

Other traditions in the same *sugya* (Talmudic discussion) recount the story of four hundred boys and girls who were carried off by the Romans to be placed in brothels (BT *Gittin* 57b). The children knew their probable destination and discussed among themselves the option of suicide, wondering, "If we drown in the sea shall we attain the life of the future world?" When the eldest boy interpreted Psalm 68:23, "The Lord said, 'I will retrieve them from Bashan, I will retrieve them from the depth of the sea,'" in the affirmative, all the girls leaped into the sea. "The boys then drew the moral for themselves, saying, 'If these for whom this is natural [being sexually used by men] act so, shall not we, for whom it is unnatural?' They also leaped into the sea." The anecdote concludes with the citation of Psalm 44:23, "It is for Your sake that we are slaughtered all day long / That we are regarded as sheep to be slaughtered." As this midrash affirms, one of the three permitted reasons for martyrdom in Jewish tradition is to preserve oneself from sexual depredation. The other two reasons to prefer death, whether by suicide or the agency of another, are murder of another human being and participation in idolatry. The strong connection between prostitution and idolatry is constant in rabbinic writings. The tradition that immediately follows the story of the four hundred children is the martyrdom narrative of the woman and her seven sons who choose death over worshiping false gods.[10]

A related group of stories deals with ransoming Jews who were already in Roman brothels. According to the Mishnah, Jews have an obligation to redeem fellow Jews who have been enslaved: "A woman's nakedness must be covered sooner than a man's and she must be brought out of captivity sooner than he. When both stand in danger of defilement, the man must be freed before the woman" (*Horayot* 3:7). One of the most famous of these narratives about redeeming captives is found in BT *Avodah Zarah* 18a, which relates that the Romans martyred the Sage R. Hanina b. Teradion because he persisted in teaching Torah against their orders. As part of his punishment, his wife was also killed and his daughter was placed in a brothel. Her sister, Beruriah, the wife of R. Meir, insisted that her husband attempt to rescue her. R. Meir agreed to do so and set out for Rome with funds with which to ransom his unnamed sister-in-law. On the way he determined that he would only be able to save her if, by some miracle, she had not committed any sexual sin (that is, been sexually violated as a prostitute). The story continues,

> Disguised as a Roman officer, he came to her and said, "Prepare yourself for me." She replied, "The manner of women is upon me." He said, "I am prepared to wait." "But," she answered, "there are many here who are far more beautiful than I am." He said to himself, these [responses] prove that she has not committed any wrong, since she must say this to deter every potential customer. He then went to her warder and said, "Hand her over to me."[11]

A similar story appears in different versions in Tosefta *Horayot* 2:5 and BT *Gittin* 58a recounting R. Joshua b. Hananiah's ransoming of a Jewish boy, "a child with beautiful eyes and face, and hair arranged in locks," who "was in danger of shame" in a Roman brothel.[12] When R. Joshua heard about this child, he stood at the doorway of the brothel and called out, "Who was it who gave Jacob over to despoilment and Israel to plunderers?" (Isaiah 42:24). The child answered, "Surely the Lord, against whom they sinned / In whose ways they would not walk / And whose law [*torahto*] they would not obey" (Isaiah 42:24). R. Joshua said, "I feel sure that this one will be a teacher in Israel. I swear that I will not budge from here before I ransom him, whatever price may be demanded." The boy was redeemed at great cost and he grew up to become R. Ishmael b. Elisha.

In both these stories, each of the Jewish prisoners must pass a gender-based test of virtue and intelligence in order to merit being ransomed. R. Hanina b. Terodian's daughter showed that she had preserved her honor by using her wits to trick customers and deter their advances; this convinced her brother-in-law that she was worthy of redemption. Similarly,

R. Ishmael's demonstration of Torah knowledge ensured his rescue. Clearly, these didactic narratives are meant to emphasize the qualities that the Rabbis believed were essential for Jewish survival under Roman captivity.

Still, the Sages understood that resistance in a situation of virtually certain violation was generally not possible. Thus a related tradition immediately follows the narrative of how R. Ishmael was ransomed from captivity in BT *Gittin* 58a. Linking the related themes of prostitution, incest, and martyrdom, the story relates that R. Ishmael's children were taken captive and sold to different masters in Rome. The young people were both beautiful and their masters decided to mate them and share their offspring. They put them in a dark room overnight, but each sat in a separate corner,

> He said [to himself] "I am a priest descended from high priests, and shall I marry a bondwoman?" She said: "I am a priestess descended from high priests, and shall I be married to a slave?" So they passed all the night in tears. When the day dawned they recognized one another and fell on one another's necks and lamented and wept until their souls departed. For them Jeremiah said, "For these things do I weep / My eyes flow with tears / Far from me is any comforter / Who might revive my spirit; / My children are forlorn / For the foe has prevailed" (Lam. 1:16).

In this tragic narrative, which also appears, in another version, in Lamentations *Rabbah* 1,[13] the young people's strong consciousness of their priestly lineage saved them from committing incest, but their overwhelming horror and grief at their situation led to their merciful deaths as martyrs.

Conclusion

Religious systems promote ethical and moral principles and people depend on these teachings as they struggle with the ambiguities and compromises of human existence. As these biblical and rabbinic traditions about prostitutes and the state of being a prostitute reveal, Judaism and Jews are no different. It is easy to tell romantic tales about idealized and beautiful harlots who are convinced to abandon their wicked, if rather exciting, ways. It is not so pleasant to face the realities of prostitution when one's own identity and one's own loved ones are at risk of violation.

NOTES

1. This chapter focuses on biblical and rabbinic texts. For scholarly research on Jews and prostitution in medieval and modern times, see Yomtov Assis, "Sexual Behavior in Medieval Hispano-Jewish Society," in *Jewish History: Essays in Honour of Chimen Abramsky*, ed. Ava Rapoport-Albert and Steven Zipperstein (London: Halben, 1998), 25–59; Avraham Grossman, *Pious and Rebellious: Jewish Women in Medieval Europe* (Waltham, Mass.: Brandeis University Press, 2004), 133–147; Edward Bristow, *Prostitution and Prejudice: The Jewish Fight against White Slavery, 1870–1939* (New York: Schocken, 1983); Rachel Gershuni, "Trafficking in Persons for the Purpose of Prostitution: The Israeli Experience," *Mediterranean Quarterly* (fall 2004): 133–146; and Nora Glickman, *The Jewish White Slave Trade and the Untold Story of Raquel Liberman* (New York: Garland, 2000).

2. Elaine A. Goodfriend, "Prostitution," *Anchor Bible Dictionary*, ed. David Noel Freedman (New York: Doubleday, 1992), 5:505–510.

3. "Levirate marriage," from the Latin *levir* (brother-in-law), refers to the mandated marriage of a widowed woman to her husband's brother. Levirate marriage in the case of a childless widow is a feature of Israelite religion and has a long history in Judaism. According to the Hebrew Bible, if a man dies and leaves no sons, his widow should not be married to a "stranger" (Deut. 25:6–8). Rather, her husband's oldest brother is to perform the duty of the *levir* (in Hebrew, *yibbum*) and marry her. The first son that the woman bears to her new husband will be considered the heir of the deceased brother, "so that his name is not blotted out in Israel."

4. On rabbinic midrash about Rahab, see Judith R. Baskin, *Midrashic Women: Formations of the Feminine in Rabbinic Literature* (Waltham, Mass.: Brandeis University Press, 2002), 154–160; and Leila Leah Bronner, "Hope for the Harlot: The Estate of the Marginalized Woman," in idem, *From Eve to Esther: Rabbinic Reconstructions of Biblical Women* (Louisville, Ky.: Westminster, John Knox Press, 1994), 142–162.

5. For these traditions, see Baskin, *Midrashic Women*, 157–160; on Rahab's Israelite descendants, see *Sifre Numbers* 78 and *Ruth Rabbah* 2:1; on Rahab as an innkeeper, see *Sifre Numbers* 78; and on Rahab as a linen maker, see *Ruth Rabbah* 2:1, *Sifre Numbers* 78, and *Sifre Zuta* on Numbers 10:28.

6. On this narrative and for other stories about involvements of rabbis with prostitutes, see Meir Bar-Ilan, "Prostitutes," in idem, *Some Jewish Women in Antiquity*, Brown Judaic Studies 317 (Atlanta: Scholars Press, 1998), 132–155, 139–141.

7. Daniel Boyarin, "Thinking with Virgins: Engendering Judaeo-Christian Difference," in idem, *Dying for God: Martyrdom and the Making of Christianity and Judaism* (Stanford: Stanford University Press, 1999), 67–92, 73.

8. The allegorical nature of this narrative is evident in the name of the pro-

tagonist. BT *Gittin* 58a explains that she was called Tzafnat because all gazed "*tzofin*" at her beauty; her father was Peniel because he served as high priest at the Temple's inner shrine in the Divine presence (p'nei El).

9. Concerning the possible influence of Greco-Roman erotic romances on this narrative's themes and construction, see David Stern, "The Captive Woman: Hellenization, Greco Roman Erotic Narrative, and Rabbinic Literature," *Poetics Today* 19, no. 1 (1998): 91–127, 94–96.

10. On martyrdom in rabbinic literature, see Boyarin, *Dying for God*; on this story, see 87–88.

11. This narrative about R. Meir continues with numerous complications and complexities. For fuller discussions than are possible here, see Rachel Adler, "The Virgin in the Brothel and Other Anomalies: Character and Context in the Legend of Beruryah," *Tikkun* 3, no. 6 (1988): 28–32, 102, 105; and Daniel Boyarin, "Thinking with Virgins", 71–73.

12. The earlier version of this story in the Tosefta makes it clear that the boy is in a brothel. By the time the narrative is associated with R. Ishmael and appears in the Babylonian Talmud, the brothel has been changed to a "prison," no doubt out of deference to R. Ishmael's scholarly reputation. However, as with the rehabilitation of Rahab to a different occupation discussed above, much of the point of the story is lost. With thanks to Robert Daum, "Rabbi Ishmael in the Roman Brothel: Early Palestinian Narrative and Babylonian Rabbinic Hagiography," unpublished paper delivered at the Annual Meeting of the Medieval Academy of America, Vancouver, B.C., April 4, 2008.

13. On the somewhat different and more extended version of this narrative in *Lamentations Rabbah*, its erotic overtones, and its transgressive reversal of the typical romance plot, see Stern, "The Captive Woman," 96–97; and idem, *Parables in Midrash: Narrative and Exegesis in Rabbinic Literature* (Cambridge, Mass.: Harvard Unversity Press, 1991), 244–245.

3

Divorcing Ba'al

The Sex of Ownership in Jewish Marriage

Bonna Devora Haberman

THE JEWISH WEDDING is conceived both as a sacred act, *kiddushin*, and in terms of *kinyan*, widely understood to be "acquisition." These two aspects of marriage represent often incompatible realms of human experience. Many contemporary Jewish marriage practices compromise human dignity and well-being. Both in the invocation of wedding commitments and particularly in their dissolution, marriage practices range from the desire for sublime union of body, mind, and soul to behaviors that are utterly profane—such as rape.

The rabbinic Sages have long understood the biblical sources to determine that a man contracts Jewish marriage with a woman's consent and dissolves marriage according to his desire. Deposited with the woman spouse, the traditional *ketuba* documents the wedding ceremony and the man's obligations to support his spouse, particularly in the case of divorce. If and when he wishes, the man dispatches a bill of divorce, a *get*, to his spouse which fulfills the obligations set out in the *ketuba*, the marriage contract. If he chooses, against his spouse's will, not to release her from the marriage, Jewish law forbids her to remarry until she procures a *get*. Without a *get*, any child she might bear with another man is considered a bastard and is prohibited from marrying within the community of Israel. These are the prevalent practices of Orthodox Judaism and the status quo in Israel since the coalition agreement between Prime Minister Ben Gurion and the religious parties at the declaration of the State of Israel in 1948.

The discourse of Jewish wedding and divorce negotiates not only intimate relationships between women and men; wedding is also a symbolic framework for the unfolding relationships among the Jewish people, the Creator, and the homeland. Jewish texts speak of marriage in terms of the connection and estrangement of partners in both personal and national terms. In this symbolic structure, the interactions of alternating male and female identities and archetypes are complex. Biblical and rabbinic texts both affirm and revile unilateral male power over women spouses. Some conceive the Jewish people as a disempowered female spouse abandoned and often punished by her divine partner. A close reading of two narrative passages from the tractate of divorce *Gittin* reveals the structure of *ba'alut-* ownership, which has long possessed Jewish conceptions of sexuality and intimacy, and allows us to question the context of the destiny of the Jewish people and their ethical evolution regarding Jewish sexuality in marriage.

The first instance of biblical exile occurs when God drives humanity from the Garden of Eden, from home.

> So the Lord God *sent* him from the Garden of Eden, to till the soil from which he was taken. He *divorced* the human, and stationed east of the garden of Eden the cherubs and the fiery shifty sword, to guard the way to the tree of life. (Gen. 3:23–24)

The language of the divine decree of banishment is *divorce*. Based on this model, a brief passage in Deuteronomy establishes the root legal concepts of Jewish divorce.

> A man takes a spouse and masters/possesses her [by sex]. She does not find favor in his eyes because he finds something obnoxious about her, and he writes her a bill of divorce, puts it in her hand, and sends her away from his house; she leaves his household and becomes the spouse of another man; then this latter man hates her, writes her a bill of divorce, puts it in her hand, and sends her away from his house. (Deut. 24:1–3)

The Torah authorizes a man to send his spouse away according to his whim, whenever he finds her distasteful, as his passion dictates. In these verses, men are established figures, propertied home owners, the decision makers and actors; women are resource-less, unstable, displaced. Men occupy material and cultural space; women are virtually vaporous, objects more than subjects, concepts more than persons. A woman is sent from one man to another, disdained by both, hated. Her views are not mentioned, her will is undisclosed, presumed irrelevant. To where does the second man send her? Off one page and onto the next.

Consider two stories from the tractate of divorce, *Gittin*.

There was a man who set his eyes on divorcing his spouse, but she had
a large *ketuba*-marriage settlement. What did he do? He invited his
friends—ushers from his wedding—feasted them, made them drunk,
and laid them all in one bed. He then brought the white of an egg and
scattered it among them, brought witnesses and appealed to the *bet
din*. There was a certain elder there from among the students of Shammai the Elder named Baba ben Buta, who said: This is what I have
been taught by Shammai the Elder, the white of an egg contracts when
brought near fire, but semen becomes faint from fire. They tested it
and found that it was so, and they brought the man to the *bet din*-court
and flogged him and made him pay her *ketuba* [marriage contract].
Said Abaye to Rav Yosef: Since they were so virtuous, why were they
punished?—He replied: Because they did not mourn for Jerusalem, as
it is written, "Rejoice with Jerusalem and be glad for her, all you who
love her, rejoice for joy with her all you that mourn over her" (Isaiah
66:10). (*Gittin* 57a)

A certain man once set his eyes on the spouse of his teacher, he being a carpenter's apprentice. Once his teacher wanted to borrow some
money from him. He [the student] said to him [the teacher], Send
your spouse to me and I will lend her the money. So he [the teacher]
sent his spouse to him [the student], and she stayed three days with
him. He [the student] then went to him [the master] before her.
Where is my spouse whom I sent to you? he asked. He replied, I sent
her away at once, but I heard that the youngsters abused her on the
road. What shall I do? he said. If you listen to my advice, he replied
[the student], divorce her. But, he said [the teacher], she has a large
marriage settlement [*ketuba*]. Said the other [the student]: I will lend
you money to give her for her *ketuba*. So he [the teacher] got up and
divorced her and the other [the student] went and married her. When
the time for payment arrived and he [the teacher] was not able to pay
him, he said: Come and work off your debt with me. So they used to
sit and eat and drink while he [the teacher] waited on them, and tears
used to fall from his eyes and drop into their cups. From that hour the
judgement of doom was sealed; some say on two wicks in one candle.
(*Gittin* 58a)

Both stories depict marital abuses by men stemming from their unilateral power to divorce, faithfully implementing the rules in Deuteronomy and their source in Genesis. Commensurate with control over the relationship resting squarely with the man, these texts exacerbate women's powerlessness. In spite of dramatic upheavals in the women's lives, the texts attribute no agency to the women—no response, attitude, personality, motives, or desires. Scripted by the interplay of male puppeteers who control their strings, these women are silent, lifeless, empty forms, marionettes. The first story particularly emphasizes this marionette aspect, where the man literally arrays limp, unconscious bodies. Although the text does not even specify the physical location of the woman spouse during the drama, it seems to imply that her spouse lays her out on the bed among the men and splatters her with egg-white. Does her spouse demonstrate the alleged deed in some way? Does he maneuver her like a manikin into a suggestive or lewd position? Is she clothed? These details are mercifully absent, concealed in the allusive testimony of the witnesses who substantiate the male spouse's charge to the judges in court.

In the second story, the woman executes the directives of the men with august indifference. She travels as a messenger to collect money; she remains with the student; she is divorced; she is sent out of the house of one man into the house of another. At the conclusion, she sits, eats, and drinks with the student, her new spouse, while her former spouse serves them. The text depicts an automaton, a being dispassionate about the central features of her own personal life, her wedded relationship, her sexuality. Although in the text she does not flinch, is it possible that she has no reaction to having been traded between men? Her utter passivity contrasts starkly with the emotional force of the tears shed by her first spouse, tears loaded with the significance of the destiny of the Jewish people. The text declares that the divine decree of the destruction of the Jerusalem Temple coincides with the man's tears: "From that hour the judgment of doom was sealed."

The difficulties in these stories exceed the issues of women's passivity and silence. Postpone for the moment the closing editorial elements in the texts that incriminate men for their manipulations of the legal system, as neither explicitly relates to the sexual violation of women envisioned by the protagonists. In both Talmudic stories, a man fabricates a fiction in which he depicts his current or prospective spouse as a victim of sexual assault, gang rape, in order to extort the divorce he desires on his conditions.

Conceiving the suffering of a woman becomes a man's reward. The men's motive is to render marriage invalid on the grounds of illicit intercourse —adultery. The men imagine the violence in relation to their own spouses, people with whom they are meant to be supremely intimate, human; the women are possibly the mothers of their own progeny. In each story, a man who is meant to be her respectful, trustworthy, and faithful companion schemes against a woman and betrays her, one man from within the marriage, the other from outside it. Men fantasize their *beloved* women as the victim of gang rape for the purpose of promoting their personal interest.

Whereas the biblical divorce text describes the fate of an unwanted woman in a detached, legalistic manner, these stories set women in specific human contexts. Speaking of the woman as a rejected object of hatred, the passage in Deuteronomy opens possibilities that these Talmudic stories aggravate. Such violent sexualized marital episodes are not restricted to human affairs; difficult biblical passages establish grounds for divorce in eroticized divine male vengeance against Israel, God's bride. Ezekiel's sixteenth chapter is a poignant example.

> Therefore, I will gather all your lovers, to whom you have given your favors, all those whom you have loved, with all those whom you have hated; I will gather them against you from every side, and will expose your nakedness to them, that they shall see all your nakedness. (Ezek. 16:37)

The ensuing rape and battery envisioned by the prophet are perpetrated by the woman's *lovers*, the very ones who had earlier participated in transgressive sex with her. The biblical analyst Mary Shields demonstrates how the text maneuvers the reader into identifying with the divine male perspective which sees sexual abuse of the promiscuous woman, Israel, as deserved and just. In Ezekiel, the male lovers are God's accomplices to the violations that the text construes as appropriate punishment for marital infidelity by the woman, Israel.

These texts discipline women to acquiesce to male domination. A form of pornography, the fantasy in both the prophetic biblical and the Talmudic passages encodes the imminent threat and actuality of sexual assault. The violence enforces women's conformity to their role as passive objects of male legislative, economic, spiritual, and physical manipulations. In her formidable research and efforts to legislate against sexual harassment, pornography, and rape-as-genocide, the scholar and legal activist Catharine

MacKinnon points out that such aggressive, misogynist behaviors terrorize women into submitting to patriarchal rule. MacKinnon's recent call to action indicts humanity for waging a war against women that eclipses terrorism in terms of the pervasiveness of its ideology, the annual numbers of homicides and assaults, including rape and concerted tactics of intimidation, degradation, exclusion, and disempowerment. Unwillingly, and often unwittingly, women are coerced to uphold the very system that undermines their humanity by adopting demeaning behaviors, accepting diminished status, and internalizing the values of oppression.

MacKinnon's analysis of the structure of coercion helps to explain the depiction of women in these narratives as totally indifferent. The absence or vacancy of these characters from the acts and scenes that are performed on them is analogous to the behavior of victims of chronic abuse who are similarly denied human agency. In social science and psychiatric literature, and in the courts that apply the testimony of expert witnesses, this acquiescent or cooperative behavior is classified as "Abuse Accommodation Syndrome." The psychiatric researcher Rolland Summit, who heads the Los Angeles County Child Sexual Abuse Treatment Center, lists five reactions to abuse: secrecy; helplessness; entrapment and accommodation; delayed, conflicted, and unconvincing disclosure; and retraction. Women abused by battering or homelessness, or in prostitution, exhibit a similar detachment from their lives and bodies to what is described in these Talmudic stories, a phenomenon alternately called "emotional numbness." Under these circumstances, women suffer higher rates of post-traumatic stress disorder than former combat soldiers.[1] Such afflictions become evident only when there is interest to reveal them; there would be no diagnosis unless caring people directed their attention toward those whose voices are silenced, whose will is erased, and whose character is flattened. In these cases, sensitive reading takes the place of the empathic therapist, social worker, and social critic whose focus shifts from the tacit androcentric interests to the silenced women. For thousands of years students have faithfully transmitted the written and oral Torah in which women are embedded in impenetrable passivity, neither listening for their pain nor probing the anguish of their lives.

Clinical work on "patriarchal terrorism" in marriage is even more applicable to these divorce cases, because it diagnoses the abuse as structural. Patriarchal terrorism apprehends not only physical violence but also "economic subordination, threats, isolation, and other control tactics," and "is rooted deeply in the patriarchal traditions of the Western family."[2] The pattern of abusive behaviors in this model includes physical, emotional or psychological (e.g., ignoring), verbal (e.g., ridiculing), or sexual (e.g., coerced intercourse) by the partner with the intention of controlling or demeaning the woman. While the Talmudic narratives under scrutiny do not *explicitly* indicate the repeated violations that occasion these traumas, the depiction of the women characters in their contexts invokes the diagnoses of "abuse accommodation syndrome" and "emotional numbness" as a result of patriarchal terrorism. Whether biographically authentic or not, these life stories of unknown historicity invoke a social framework that registers selective details and omits others. Rendering women's intimate sexual lives in the manner that they do, the male redactors (re)inscribe their male dominion, a perspective presumed to be shared by the intended male audience. These passages perform acts of patriarchal terrorism on women who are their objects. It is difficult to estimate the extent to which such canonical texts reflect, affect, authorize, or even induce the behavior they portray.

The Talmudic narratives posit that an indictment of adultery against the woman is admissible grounds for divorce even though the alleged *tuma*-impurity is caused by an act of sexual violence against her. The text accedes to a justification of divorce regardless of the woman's experience, suffering, or will. In both stories the accusation is false. In the second case, the story prompts the suspicion that the student does have illicit relations with his teacher's spouse. The text is discreet, however, and alludes to a possible rape by the concluding image of two wicks in a single lamp. The first case states only the man's desire to divorce and his reluctance to pay the required settlement; the man supplies no justification for divorce. In both cases, the men are trying to avoid the price of the *ketuba*-marriage settlement.

Rabbinic Initiative

Where there are no formal obligations between spouses, and the gendered power differential is extreme, the potential for abuse approaches infinity. The horrifying gang rape and murder committed by Benjaminites against the concubine of a Levite when they were traveling through Gibea culminates with her master dismembering her into twelve pieces. This narrative in the Book of Judges indicates how "each man did according to his desire." The *ketuba* and the *get*, marriage and divorce contracts,

signal rabbinic initiative to improve women's status; both attempt to secure women against the whims of their spouses and to instill the gravity
of divorce. Judith Hauptman proposes that the goal of the tractate *Gittin*
"is to ensure that the *get*, the instrument of divorce, is above reproach, and
therefore fully protects women and children from unscrupulous men who
would challenge its validity."[3] But in contrast to the legal material that in-
stitutes *get* procedures, narrative material in the tractate—the two stories
under discussion here, for example—demonstrates how the *ketuba* fails to
remedy women's fate in the dissolution of marriage.

Gendered Economy

The need for the *ketuba* and the *get* as economic and legal remedies arises
from gender-role divisions in society. The *ketuba* functions on the basis of
presumptions about social conventions; it is a one-way male sustenance
obligation to a dependent, resourceless woman that stipulates his financial obligation to her in the event of divorce or his death. These conventions often restrict women to so-called reproductive and unremunerated
labor—home and family management, childbearing, nurturing, rearing,
and educating. Though these functions are the necessary condition for all
forms of productive earnings by a couple and the viability of society, they
do not accrue financial equity. Even when labor is remunerated, Maimonides, for example, establishes that the woman's earnings transfer to the
male spouse.

> All that a woman produces by her means goes to her spouse. And what
> she does for him is according to the practice of the state: if it is a place
> where women weave, she weaves, if embroidery, she embroiders, if it
> is spinning wool or flax, she spins. If it is the way of the women of the
> town to do all of these crafts, he does not force her except to spin the
> wool—because flax is harmful to the hands and lips, and spinning is
> women's special craft, as it says, "all women of wise heart spun with
> their hands." (Ex. 35:25)

Gendered exploitation of human labor withholds from women their
share of the economic resources to which they contribute fully during marriage. Reduced by society to nearly total economic dependence, women
are vulnerable to sexual and other abuses. The *ketuba* is a rabbinic stopgap

measure that intends to address not only the unilateral divorce prerogative, but its devastating consequences where social and economic restrictions disable women from attaining financial solvency. Whereas the Torah and subsequent codes provide for the widow and orphan, they offer no sustenance for the divorcée. Because of her divorced status, even with the *ketuba* money the stigmatized woman is subject to economic hardship and diminished potential for future desirable unions. The two stories from the *Gittin* tractate reflect the Talmud's awareness of the inadequacy of its own remedies.

Release and Detention

Despite women's gains in financial independence during recent decades that have rendered the *ketuba* a virtually symbolic document, abuse persists because the *ketuba* provides no protection against it. Financial solvency definitely fortifies women against the threat and devastation of summary divorce, but the patriarchal halakhic system compensated for the diminished male divorce prerogative by inverting its method of control. Whereas men previously were seeking methods to *terminate* their marriages (while sustaining minimal obligations to their dependent women), the improvement in women's economic condition has led men to *resist terminating* their marriages (in order to procure maximal benefits from their independent women). These spouses are prisoners, denied divorce and unable to remarry. The modern predicament reverses the old one; whereas the women in the Talmudic narratives suffer from imperious divorce, contemporary women suffer from protracted divorce. Women continue to be held captive to men in the Jewish marriage. In communities that observe Orthodox *halakhah*, and throughout the State of Israel where the Chief Rabbinate wields authority over laws of personal status, male rabbinic courts exercise final authority over women's freedom to act independently and to choose when and with whom to have sex. Recent indictments of rabbinic accomplices to male spouses who extort money, sex, wreak vengeance, and afflict women spouses locked in marriages against their will reveal another facet of the vulnerability of women in Jewish marriage.[4]

Current activism to redress the problem of *agunot*-chained women, and women denied a divorce by recalcitrant male spouses, still leaves the fundamental oppressive nature of Jewish marriage intact. Even current halakhic proposals, such as those advanced by Rabbis Monique Susskind-

Goldberg and Diana Villa to alleviate the anguish, both through prevention and retroactive annulment, neglect the structural roots of the problem. Most acrimonious among these approaches, including Zvi Zohar's
view published in *Akdamot*, is the revival of the *pilegesh*-concubine option
—a long-term relationship without marital commitments and obligations.
In the current climate of increasing domestic violence against women, how
can we contemplate a remedy that is intended for polygamy, preserves patriarchal descent and inheritance, and is steeped in the blood of the appall-
ing rape and dismemberment of a person's being? The *ketuba* was intended
to protect women where men's power in society renders women vulnerable
to abuse in intimate and childbearing relations. Insofar as narratives for-
mulate the content and messages of legal concepts, the *pilegesh*-concubine
status (re)invokes the desecration of sexuality and intimacy.

National Divorce

Sexual narratives encode the spiritual and political constitution of the Jewish people. The *Concubine of Gibea* incident portrays strife-ridden tribes
during a decadent period of the biblical "Judges." Similarly alluding to the
social and political malaise of the nation of Israel, the two stories from Gittin are culled from the account of events that led to the decay of Jewish
autonomy in the Land of Israel—one of the most complex and lengthy literary passages in the Talmud. Scrutinizing the closing editorial comments
recorded by the redactor, the stories explicitly identify a causal connection
between abuse of the male prerogative to institute divorce and the destruction of Jerusalem. The redactor, subliminally, reviles the men's loathsome
behavior—the teacher's tears both signal the edict of destruction and
mourn it. At the end of the first story Abaye asks, "Why were they punished" with the destruction and exile of the Jewish people from the land
of Israel, we impute. Rav Yosef answers, quoting a verse from Isaiah, "They
did not mourn for Jerusalem." Yet surely mourning is insufficient to pre-
empt the second destruction. Perhaps the text indicates another cause cor-
responding with the adage, "the personal is political."

Throughout Jewish literature, the intimate partnership of spouses is
overlaid with the metaphoric, often tortured spousal relationship of the
Jewish people with God. These divorce stories are an identifiable genre
in the tractates dealing with marriage and beyond. The cycle of marriage,
faithlessness, adultery, divorce, and reunion is a meta-narrative of Jewish

peoplehood. Broken by the decimation of Jewish power and dignity, estranged from love and home, the pen of history renders the Talmudic Sages, according to their own conceptions, passive and female, the dejected bride of the divine. The Sages take refuge in the textual academies where they renegotiate the terms of their relationship with the Creator. The elaborate tales and detailed rules governing marriage and divorce are among the sublimated and subtle expressions of the experience of exile and the longing for redemption.

These layered metaphors affiliate human sexuality with the human-divine relationship. The literature of Kabbalah and Hasidut expressly envision sexual encounter within the God-head and conceive human mystical union with the divine in sexual terms. The *Iggeret Ha-Kodesh*, a thirteenth-century kabbalistic treatise, directly discusses the optimal qualities of sexual intercourse and its timing on Shabbat. This tract elaborates the cycle of semen and its potency to produce male offspring worthy of fulfilling divine service. The kabbalistic rubric proposes that human sex acts both correspond with union in the divine realms and affect them. The author of the *Iggeret* advocates to men that they seek a union of mind and intention with their spouses, that they arouse the woman to delight, love, desire, and passion. Sex is a vehicle for cleaving to the higher realms, to attaining ultimate knowledge. According to the Zohar, a foundational Jewish mystical treatise, the union of the cherubs on the ark within the Temple invokes and enables divine emanation, efflux, into the lower realms. Interpreting the gender relations portrayed in the *Iggeret*, Karen Guberman, a contemporary student of Kabbalah, summarizes: "In each case, the feminine aspect is not *totally* passive. However, her sphere of positive activity is carefully circumscribed by the masculine force which both initiates and terminates the union."[5] This scholar's remark points to how closely the Jewish mystical conception articulated in the *Iggeret Ha-Kodesh* corresponds with and reinforces the human normative social structure. The male force initiates and terminates the union in both realms; each reinforces the other.

Mary Daly, one of the earliest critics of male-centered theology, pioneered analysis of the similarity between conceptions of human and divine gender.

If God in "his" heaven is a father ruling "his" people, then it is in the "nature" of things and according to divine plan and the order of the universe that society be male-dominated. Theologian Karl Barth found it appropriate to write that Woman is "ontologically" subordinate to man. Within this context a mystification of roles takes place: the husband dominating his wife represents God himself. What is happening, of course, is the familiar mechanism by which the images and values of a given society are projected into a realm of beliefs, which in turn justify the social infrastructure. The belief system becomes hardened and objectified, seeming to have an unchangeable independent existence and validity of its own. It resists social change which would rob it of its plausibility.[6]

In the rabbinic case, the relationships of domination are more complex in gender terms than Mary Daly's linear model: a male God presides over man as man presides over woman; helplessness in marriage, and the gendered female, instantiates the metaphor of the historic and mythic divorce, destruction, and displacement of the Jewish people from the divine partner and homeland of Israel. The Sages feel themselves a woman sent from the house of her beloved, just as the text in legal Deuteronomy 24:1 describes. Isaiah and Jeremiah are explicit about the divorce of the Jewish people from their divine spouse.

> Thus said the Lord, Where is the bill of divorce of your mother whom I sent away? And which of My creditors was it to whom I sold you off? You were only sold off for your sins, and your mother dismissed for your crimes. (Isaiah 50:1)

The divine male partner demeans the woman, mocking her status and her treachery; she is a discarded possession. Jeremiah articulates the marriage narrative of exile and the promise of reunion with clarity.

> 1 ... saying: If a man divorces his wife, and she leaves him, and marries another man, may he ever go back to her? Will not such a land be defiled? Now you have whored with many lovers; can you return to Me?—says the Lord....
>
> 8 And I noted, because rebel Israel had committed adultery, I cast her off and handed her a bill of divorce, yet her sister, faithless Judah was not afraid—she also went and whored.
>
> 9 Indeed the land was defiled by her casual harlotry, and she committed adultery with stones and with wood....

14 Return, rebellious children—declares the Lord; for I have espoused you, and I will take you one from a town, and two from a
clan, and I will bring you to Zion. (Jeremiah 3)

As in the Talmudic stories, alleged sexual infidelity is the pretext for divorce. Jeremiah's verses equate adultery with idolatry—Israel literally uses
the idols of stone and wood for prohibited sexual acts. Indicting Israel for
pursuing her vices, the prophet aspires to reconciliation. Jeremiah tack-
les the biblical prohibition against a man remarrying his former spouse;
according to the divorce law in Deuteronomy, she is defiled because she
has been with another partner. The case of Israel is unique, suggests the
prophet; God promises to gather the exiles to Him in the land because the
betrothal commitment is still binding. Paradoxically, the mythic wedding
of the Jewish people with the Creator weathers infidelity, and at the cost of
incurring male divine wrath and suffering exiles, the Jewish people persist
in desiring reunion.

After the destruction of the second Temple, however, the prospect
of returning to the intimacy of the land is remote. The Sages project their
own fears and displace their pain and helplessness onto the human bride.
Destabilized by the banishment from love and home, they strive to renegotiate the terms of their vulnerability. Even when the judges render righteous judgments in the first story, the court is impotent, according to Rav
Yosef, "because they did not mourn for Jerusalem." Rav Yosef's emphasis
on mourning dismantles the momentum of the justice of the court; the in-
tricately logical and ethical rabbinic construction is irrevocably inadequate
—until redemption. Even moments of justice in the rabbinic court are insufficient against the backdrop of the disempowerment of exile. Caught in
a web of domination, the Sages succumb to and internalize the surrounding abuse. They invent cautious and insufficient protections for the bride,
and for themselves, ignoring or resisting the possibilities of social change
or reform. The resulting legal and narrative framework affirms the forms of
Jewish marriage as a terrifying script of men's power and abuse written on
the parchment of women's dignity.

Why terrifying, and what is at stake? Today recalcitrant spouses bar
thousands of Jewish women from pursuing healthy relationships and a joy-
ous life, exploiting the complicity of the rabbinic courts in the systematic
oppression of women by the religious establishment in Israel and abroad.
Each and every Jewish woman is potentially an *aguna*-chained woman, and
therefore we are all *agunot*. Marriage is a core institution by which society

constructs, replicates, and enforces identity and gender, authorizes sexual intimacy and childbearing, and configures power and belief; every woman and man is subject to its sanctifications and its desecrations.

Ba'alut-Mastery

האישה נקנית—a woman is acquired. According to the Mishnah, one of the three methods by which a man attains his mastery is sexual intercourse: "a woman is acquired by three methods and acquires herself by two; she is acquired by money, and by contract, and by sexual intercourse. . . . She acquires herself by get-divorce contract or by the death of her ba'al-master." For coitus, the text does not use the obvious word for sex that shares the same root as ba'al-master, be'ilah; rather it chooses biah-coming, a rabbinic euphemism. One of the technical descriptors for a married woman is be'ulat ba'al, translated, with difficulty, as "woman-intercoursed-by-a-master." The initial occurrence of the term is in a biblical verse that prohibits a man from having sex with a married woman—the penalty is death. By means of the common concept ba'alut-mastery, these texts conjoin marriage, sex, and ownership.

In the first chapter of *Kiddushin*, the *gemara* queries the mishnaic emphasis on acquiring a woman by means of money. "Why does the Mishnah not articulate the marriage act as *sanctifying* her?" the text asks. The answer is that the Mishnah seeks to demonstrate that marriage *kinyan*-acquisition is enacted by means of money. The Sages derive this meaning from an analogy between קניין-kinyan of a woman and the purchase of a field. Avraham purchases a field to bury his deceased spouse; he is a bereft human aspiring to permanence in the face of transience, mortality, and mourning. Perhaps Avraham also experiences guilt in the wake of betrayal, not only the betrayal that Avraham had unilaterally intended to sacrifice their child, an act to which midrash attributes Sara's death. Perhaps he is also guilty for having twice traded her for riches, once to Abimelekh in exchange for sheep and oxen, male and female slaves, and a thousand pieces of silver, and once to Pharaoh for sheep, oxen, asses, male and female slaves, she-asses, and camels. At the outset of the ordeal, Avraham explicitly states his motive for asking Sara to conceal her identity as his wedded spouse, למען ייטב לי בעבורך —"in order that I benefit on your account" (Gen. 12:13). According to the medieval Bible commentator Nachmanides, the Jewish people suffer four hundred years of exile and servitude at the hands of Pharaoh because of Avraham's violation. Avraham's behavior jeopardizes the safety and undermines the dignity of his female spouse. According to Nachmanides, the patriarch's action is a sign to his descendants. This incident in Genesis—Avraham's descent to Egypt because of famine in Canaan, Pharaoh's agents capturing Sara, the subsequent plague, and finally Sara's release—is a microcosm of the Exodus narrative. Avraham's inappropriate treatment of his female spouse, Nachmanides suggests, brings on the national servitude of the Israelites to Pharaoh for generations later. This interpretation strengthens the meaning of the phrase "the personal is political." Not only is every individual experience of gender-based oppression significant to the public and political discourse, but even the smallest gendered dyad within society is the building block for the larger societal, international, and global relationships of oppression. This theme further intensifies the overlapping human-divine marriage metaphor. Just as Avraham oppresses his spouse by means of Pharaoh's agency, so, too, does the male divine spouse oppress His spouse, Israel, through the agency of Pharaoh. The male prerogative to oppress is inextricable from the idolatry of *ba'alut*-possession.

Mastery of *Ba'al* and control over his servants are marks of the oppression of idolatry. Indeed, the biblical Exodus conceives leaving Egypt as an escape from the servitude of a *Ba'al*, Pharaoh, in order to *willingly* serve the God of Israel, who proclaims: "Let my people go that they may *celebrate* me in the desert." The ensuing narrative of the desert wanderings emphasizes the difficult Israelite struggle to transform its former slave-like attitudes and behaviors toward responsible freedom. Free will is meant to drive sacred divine service, not *ba'alut*-mastery. Although the depiction of the Jewish God and His commandments is often domineering in difficult biblical chapters, its most basic form affirms human choice. The conclusion of the infamous passage in Deuteronomy elaborating the curses that will befall the children of Israel if they do not uphold the terms of the covenant is even more devastating than a return to slavery in Egypt, as it is a severance of all connection.

> The Lord will send you back to Egypt in galleys, by a route which I told you you should not see again. There you shall offer yourselves for sale to your enemies as male and female slaves, but none will buy.

Given this terrible alternative, the Sages compromise their hopes for redemption and cling to the *ba'alut* of marriage, as it is at least one strand of connection during the trials of exile.

When Rashi explains the remorse and fear Israelites felt at the brink of the promised land, he distinguishes between the existential states of Egypt and Israel. Egypt is a land irrigated reliably by the overflow of the Nile, whereas Israel is watered by rain, at divine discretion. Rashi terms this dependency on rain *ba'al,* for the inhabitants are not in control but are dependent. Yet dependence on rain is the divine strategy for holding the inhabitants responsible for their lives and behavior. The Torah suggests that the land is responsive, yielding bounty as a reward for good deeds, and drought and famine as punishment for bad ones. This simple rubric of reward and punishment expresses a structure for the Jewish divine-human connection, whether life experience fulfills or defies it. Whereas abiding in Egypt is conceived as a symbol of exile, estrangement, and divorce, inhabiting the land of Israel is conceived as a medium for the people and a divine partner that coexists in intimate relations.

> For the land that you are about to enter and possess is not like the land of Egypt from which you have come. There the grain you sowed had to be watered by your own labors, like a vegetable garden; but the land you are about to cross into and possess, a land of hills and valleys, soaks up its water from the rains of heaven. It is a land which the Lord your God looks after, on which the Lord your God always keeps His eye, from year's beginning to year's end.

Sowing the grain, and the daily and seasonal fertile processes of life and sustenance, engage the Jewish people with divine abundance, the life force of the Creator. Dwelling away from the land for two thousand years, along with extraordinary creative survival techniques, the Jewish people internalized fear, caution, and conservatism. These traits, particularly fear, forged in the crucible of exile, remain ensconced in rabbinic approaches even after the modern-day return to the land.

Divorcing *Ba'alut*

The contemporary Talmudist Judith Hauptman diagnoses incremental proto-feminist developments in Jewish approaches to the topics of the Talmudic Order *Nashim*/Women; the Sages certainly progress from the biblical virginity purchase and sale legislation. Introducing קדושה-sacredness, the Talmudic Sages reconfigure the wedding as a separation of the woman for the exclusive possession of her spouse; she is מְקוּדֶשֶׁת-sanctified. Like הקדש-*hekdesh,* a consecrated article, the man sets a woman aside for sacred purposes. According to this analogy, the man is likened to God for whom humans set aside *hekdesh*—material, agricultural, and animal property used for the service of the Temple, its offerings and sacrifices. Moshe Ehrenreich, a contemporary halakhic scholar who implicitly recoils at the *kinyan*-acquisition aspect of kiddushin, emphasizes the *hekdesh* concept as being less offensive and more progressive. That a woman is forbidden to all men except her spouse seems more palatable in the current era than the outright purchase and sale of a person. However, identifying the woman as *hekdesh*—an offering or sacrifice dedicated to the service of her male master—produces more gender trouble.

The Talmud and subsequent interpreters conceive both acquisition and sanctification as male acts performed on a female object; the male is *ba'al*-master. The Talmudist Judith Romney Wegner claims that marriage in the Mishnah is equivalent to trading a woman's sexual potency as chattel among fathers and spouses. The less-than-subtle commodification of woman is more than symbolic. Commodification instrumentalizes, dehumanizes, and desecrates the relationship between women and men.

An extreme expression of the abuses of commodification is trafficking in girls and women for sex and profit. Jews have been and continue to be excessively involved in global trafficking. Since the mid-nineteenth century, with a brief interruption during the Holocaust, Jews have been selling their own and other peoples' daughters into prostitution. The Yale professor Edward Bristow documents extensive Jewish involvement in the so-called white slave trade, marketing young women from their destitute *shtetlach* villages in Eastern Europe. Arthur Moro, an officer in an anti-white slavery group, writes in London in 1903:

> We have positive evidence that to almost all parts of North and South Africa, to India, China, Japan, the Philippine Islands, North and South America and also to many of the countries in Europe, Yiddish-speaking Jews are maintaining a regular flow of Jewesses, trafficked solely for the purposes of prostitution.

In Shalom Aleichem's story, "The Man from Buenos Aires," Motek, a Jewish salesman from Argentina, explains obliquely,

> "I supply the world with merchandise, something that everybody knows and nobody speaks of."

"What do I deal in?

Not in prayer books, my friend, not in prayer books."

Commodification fuels the global economy of patriarchy. In 2006 the American State Department put Israel on a special "watch list," citing its "failure to provide evidence of increasing efforts to address trafficking" in human beings. Currently the annual business in the trafficking of women between the former Soviet Union and Israel nets approximately one billion dollars.

Reading these primary Jewish texts with sensitivity to their gendered power structures begins to reveal the processes by which we manufacture the culture of male ownership and mastery. בעלות-ownership and קניין-acquisition participate in and undergird gender-based oppression. The male prerogative to dispose of his bride according to his pleasure is a corollary of the traditional acquisition ritual of the חופה-wedding canopy. The halakhic process has itself become more than a recalcitrant partner. Riveted to a tormented state of exile, each traditional Jewish wedding not only reinscribes the fundaments of male power and enforces the submission of woman; the formulae of *kiddushin* and the *ketuba* encode the commodity transaction. Trafficking in women is a grotesquely exaggerated form of the *ba'alut*-ownership and *kinyan*-acquisition that transpires at most Jewish weddings.

We cannot address these endemic problems at the surface of legal finesse; we must work at the deep layers of meaning where they adulterate intentions to sanctify. Current theories about men's and women's identities and roles expose how they are socially constructed to perpetuate domination and oppression. Tamar Ross, in her Orthodox theology, proposes that *feminism* is part of the ongoing revelation of the Torah. These approaches promise new potential for resanctifying the Jewish wedding.

Reformulating *Kinyan*

Chava-Eve accomplishes the first biblical קניין-acquisition with the birth of Cain, קניתי איש את ה׳ "I have acquired a man with God." In this verse the double transitive objects refer to God, the child, and her spouse as her collaborators in the act of קניין-acquisition. Here, קניין-acquisition connects creators with their partners; there is no exchange of valuables or commodification. *Chava*-Eve attributes shared agency, perhaps responsibility,

certainly divine participation, in her action. Setting aside the psychoana-
lytic nuances of the woman's overlapping allusions to her son and her male
spouse, the next biblical occurrence, Malkitzdek's blessing to Avraham,
shares these alternative valences of קניין-acquisition. Having been van-
quished by Avraham, the King of Sodom comes forth to greet the new
conqueror and exclaims, "Blessed is Avram to God *Elyon*—most high, the
konei-acquirer of heaven and earth" (Gen. 14:19).

Avraham responds with a monotheistic formulation of Malkitzedek's
blessing. This formula is redacted into the daily liturgy of *gevura,* קונה הכל-
acquirer of all, and in its entirety on Shabbat eve, קונה שמים וארץ–acquirer
of heaven and earth. To draw the analogy explicitly, God is *konei*-acquirer
in relation to creation as Chava is *kona*-acquirer in relation to her child and
spouse, in collaboration with God. Dignified partners participate in the
unfolding process of Creation, enabling and sustaining life; each is a responsible agent.

Jewish DNA

The attainment of Jewish statehood in the land proposes a revolution of
Jewish consciousness. Beyond Israel's necessary preoccupation with secur-
ing the safety and material well-being of the Jewish people, Zionism is also
conceived as an experiment, an opportunity to reevaluate, to reinvent Jewish peoplehood. A wedded couple, a gendered dyad of sexual intimacy, is
the DNA of society. Until the 1950s, DNA was thought to participate in,
mastermind, and direct the metabolic and synthetic activities of cells and
organisms. Recent scholarship demonstrates how DNA and its role is a
matter of gender and values.

> Only by ignoring the participation of the rest of the cell and organ-
> ism have molecular geneticists enshrined the magic of DNA—the
> autonomous, all-powerful gene that does not just specify traits but
> produces and controls them. The fact that biologists, who are not usu-
> ally known for their religious commitments, have selected "the Holy
> Grail" and "the book of life" as their metaphors for DNA—not to
> speak of President Clinton's referring to DNA as "the language in
> which God created life"—underlines the ideological content of mo-
> lecular genetics.[7]

The Nobel Prize laureate Barbara McClintock, eschewed for her alternate approach to genetic research from the 1920s to the 1950s, looked at the context of the whole organism:

> She concluded that genes can change their positions on the chromosomes, along with their functions, in response to changes within the plant and around it; this was so contrary to what geneticists believed possible at mid-century that many of them simply wrote her off. Not until the 1970s and 1980s, when comparable observations were made with bacteria, was what McClintock had been saying accepted into the canon of the field.[8]

Similar to DNA, the institution of marriage both produces and responds to the Jewish organism. Many contend that the DNA core, based on oppressive gendered functions, is immutable, and that it determines the stability and continuity of the Jewish people. Divorced from the *kedusha*-holiness of joint responsible creativity by the obsession with *ba'alut*-ownership, the wedding continues to be in captive exile from the hearts and souls of contemporary Jewry. As geneticists have demonstrated the dynamic capacity of the living organism and its DNA, this analysis proposes a dynamic approach to Jewish marriage. One of the most potent conceivable interventions in society would be to adjust the concepts and functions of Jewish marriage to form a nucleus that affirms the dignity of every member of the Jewish people to participate fully in his or her destiny.

Homecoming

The wedding is more than just a window into gender roles and relations. The *gemara* confirms a core tenet of social theory: marriage is a microcosm of relations of power and resources; it constructs standards of social ethics. The well-being of all, including the most vulnerable of humanity, depends on de-commodifying the gendered economy and reformulating the *kiddushin*-wedding. The capacity to invoke and dissolve mortal commitments to each other is one of the profound responsibilities of human society. An investigation into the assumptions, metaphors, meanings, and deficiencies of this evolving institution in Jewish tradition reveals profound ethical exigencies.

Under the חופה-wedding canopy, the shattering of the glass formally invokes the destruction of Jerusalem at a moment of joy; it also portends male incursion into the female sanctum. The purpose is not to persist in the brokenness but to affirm yearning for more wholeness. The Zionist return to the land is a revolution no less momentous than the destruction; it is a radical reformulation of the trajectory of the Jewish people. The prolonged exile and unmitigated longing amplify the significance of the attainment of Jewish statehood. In the grand narrative of the Jewish people, the contemporary Zionist period is an unfathomable reunion with the divine presence in the land of Israel. Although Jews continue to smash a glass under the wedding canopy as the Talmud advocates, the imminent challenge is to create expressions of homecoming for Jewish wedding and marriage.

Throughout its long history, Judaism has usually been held to contribute toward refining the ethical standards of humanity. The recent awareness of the vulnerability of intimacy to gendered violations underlines the urgency to construct Jewish marriage as a more respectful partnership, worthy today of sanctification.

In a divine revelation, the prophet Hosea reconceives betrothal. Speaking to his spouse, whose life has been mired in prostitution and adultery, the prophet proposes to free marriage of ownership and dominion, and also suggests how to accomplish it.

> "And it shall be on that day," said God, "you shall call me, 'my [male] spouse,' and you shall no longer call me, 'my *ba'al*-master,'" for I shall remove the names of the *ba'alim*-masters from her mouth; and they shall never more be mentioned by name. (Hosea 2:18–19)

Overlaying his connection with his human spouse with the metaphoric marriage of God and the Jewish people, Hosea re-institutes marriage on the foundations of righteousness and justice, goodness, mercy, and faithfulness. Just as a condition for sacred intimacy between the people and the divine Creator is the removal of the *ba'alim*-idols-masters-possessors, so, too, is the removal of the expressions of idolatry and desecration—*ba'alut* between spouses, possession and mastery—a condition for the sacred intimacy of Jewish marriage and sex. Divorcing *ba'al* and his abuses invokes the consciousness and will of homecoming in the intimate and monumental narratives of the Jewish people.

NOTES

1. See Nora Macready's study, "Stress Disorder Is Common among Prostitutes," *British Medical Journal* (August 29, 1998); reported by Abigail Zuger, "Many Prostitutes Suffer Combat Disorder, Study Finds," *New York Times*, August 18, 1998, F8.

2. M. P. Johnson, "Patriarchal Terrorism and Common Couple Violence: Two Forms of Violence against Women," *Journal of Marriage and the Family* 57 (1995):283–294; quotes at 284 and 286.

3. Judith Hauptman, *Rereading the Rabbis* (Boulder, Colo.: Westview, 1998), 102.

4. For the indictments of Rabbi Mordecai Tendler (grandson of the great halakhic decisor Rabbi Moshe Feinstein), who was considered an *aguna* activist at the same time as extorting sex from women in his synagogue study, see Rukhl Schaechter, "Rabbinical Council Is Probing Claims of Sexual Harassment," *New York Forward*, August 27, 2004, http://www.forward.com/main/article.php?ref =schaechter200408251025; and Rabbinical Council of America statement about its probe and dismissal: http://www.rabbis.org/news/article.cfm?id=100587. See also *Mekudeshet: Sentenced to Marriage*, videorecording, Amythos Films; producer, Amit Breuer; director, Anat Zuria (New York: Women Make Movies, 1004); Bryna Bogoch and Ruth Halperin-Kaddari, "Divorce Israeli Style: Professional Perceptions of Gender and Power in Mediated and Lawyer-Negotiated Divorces," *Law & Policy* 28, no. 2 (April 2006): 137–163; Ilene R. Prusher, "Divorce in Israel: Men Get the Final Word," *Christian Science Monitor* 98, no. 241 (November 8, 2006); and "Discrimination by Israeli Religious Courts Stops Divorce for Women," *Women's International Network News* 19, no. 3 (summer 1993).

5. Karen Guberman, "'To Walk in All His Ways': Towards a Kabbalistic Sexual Ethic," *Journal of Religious Ethics* 14, no. 1 (spring 1986): 61–81; my emphasis.

6. Mary Daly, "After the Death of God the Father," *Commonweal*, March 12, 1971. For a full version, see idem, *Beyond God the Father: Towards a Philosophy of Women's Liberation* (Boston: Beacon, 1985 [1973]).

7. Ruth Hubbard, "Science, Power, Gender: How DNA Became the Book of Life," *Signs: Journal of Women* 28, no. 3 (spring 2003): 791–800.

8. Ibid., 795.

4

The Sage and the Other Woman

A Rabbinic Tragedy

Aryeh Cohen

WHAT DOES SEX stand in for in rabbinic literature, or in the more specific literature of the Talmud? Torah study is sex in BT *Eruvin* 54b. Indeed, Torah study is like having sex every night as if it is the first time.[1] Torah is the object of sexual desire. Ben Azai refuses procreative sex because of Torah-lust.[2] Rabbi Akiva procreates without sex—twenty-four thousand students in twenty-four years and his wife still at home.[3] Torah study, then, stands in for sex, or, perhaps, it is sex. What, however, does sex stand in for? To ask another question, one posed by Ruhama Weiss in a recent essay: Can a Sage who has sex with Torah have sex with an actual flesh and blood woman?[4] To put a slightly different spin on this, what happens when a scholar, a member of the guild of students of the Sages, one who spends nights as well as days in the study of Torah, actually has sex with a flesh-and-blood woman? The answer, to jump to the end, is that Elijah has to come in to clean up the mess.

The (Other) Woman

The din of the study hall abruptly stops as the disheveled and distraught looking woman comes to the front of the room and demands the attention of the small groups of men clustered around arguments and texts. In her hand she has a cloth bag which she holds aloft as she begins to speak, loudly, at the edge of control, tears streaming down her face:

"These are my husband's *tefillin*/phylacteries that he wore every day and about which you have said that one who lays *tefillin* lives a long life.[5] You well know that my husband studied Scripture and Mishnah abundantly, and that he engaged and served the Sages—and it is written in the Torah, which he read daily: 'For thereby you shall have life and live long.' Why, then, learned masters, has my husband died in his youth?!!"

The silence was thick and uncomfortable, the minutes passed slowly. Finally, the woman lowered the bag that she had held aloft all this time and shuffled out of the room, her question still hanging. Slowly the room returned to its previous state of intellectual ferment, her challenge a nagging annoyance at the edges of the urgent conversations.[6]

This is almost surely not how this story (which, after all, is a story), a version of which appears in Bavli *Shabbat* 13a–b, unfolded.[7] Many aspects of the story are contested in the three versions that survive (BT *Shabbat* 13a–b, Avot de-Rabbi Nathan A [ADRNa] chapter 2, Seder Eliyahu Rabba 16). The Bavli's version itself is different in its details in the various manuscripts.[8] Yet, at the undisputed core of all the stories, the omniscient narrator describes a person as having "read a great deal of Scripture and learned a great deal of Torah."[9]

All the versions similarly agree that this person died in the flower of youth, literally "at half of his days" (*behatzi yamav*). In both the Bavli and ADRNa versions, the woman voices her plaint in terms of Deuteronomy 30:16.[10] Finally, all the versions agree that no one had an answer for her. There is a disturbing second half to the story that allows me to ask what is at stake in this narrative for the Sages—both the Sages of late antiquity, who wrote, revised, and included this story, and the Sages of the middle ages, especially the various compilations of French and Spanish Tosafists who commented on the story.

Before proceeding to the second half of the story, it is only right to transcribe the earlier part that I have already presented in more narrative form in order to point out and attend to the important differences between the versions.

> *Ma'aseh*/It happened with a certain student who read much Scripture, and repeated many [laws and traditions], and served the students of the Sages abundantly, and he died at an early age. His wife would take his *tefillin*, and go around with them to the synagogues and study halls. She said to them: "It is written in Torah: 'For thereby you shall have life and live long.' Why did my husband, who read much Scripture, and repeatedly studied many [laws and traditions], and served the students of the Sages abundantly, die at an early age?!
>
> There was no person to answer her.

The major differences are between the Bavli text above and the Eliyahu Rabba text. In the Bavli text reproduced above, the scene is institutionally focused. The woman demands answers from the Sages in the academies and the synagogues. In the Eliyahu Rabba tale, the woman, who had almost gone mad, went banging on the doors of the homes of her husband's former colleagues. Moreover, in the Bavli text the woman brandishes her husband's *tefillin*, whether as we suggested above, and as the Tosafot Ha-Rosh (fourteenth century) suggest, because there is a tradition guaranteeing long life to those who lay *tefillin* or, as others suggest, that it is to inflict psychic pain, as if to say "this is all that is left of this man."[11] Or, perhaps, it was just as a token of membership in the rabbinic guild. In any event, *tefillin* in hand, the woman makes a rabbinic claim: the promise of long life for learning Torah is stated in the Torah.

This itself is a midrashic promise; that is, it is made on the basis of the mode of reading Scripture which is the hallmark of the Sages. The contextual meaning of Deuteronomy 30:19–20 is quite different:

> [19] I call heaven and earth to witness against you this day: I have put before you life and death, blessing and curse. Choose life—if you and your offspring would live [20] by loving the Lord your God, heeding His commands, and holding fast to Him. For thereby you shall have life and shall long endure upon the soil that the Lord swore to your ancestors, Abraham, Isaac and Jacob, to give to them.

The object of the phrase "for thereby" (which is probably intended in a more literal translation as "for it")[12] is obviously God and God's commandments. God is life. The midrashic move is to read "for it" as referring to Torah. In all the manuscripts of the Bavli the pronoun is feminine (as opposed to the masculine pronoun in the verses referring to God) which makes the reference to the (grammatically) feminine Torah all the more obvious.

The woman makes the midrashic claim against the Sages that her husband should not have died if their way of reading Torah is right. In perhaps the earliest collection of Tosafot commentaries the observation is made that she speaks as a Sage.[13] As a Sage she demands that the study halls and the synagogues answer to her.

The Eliyahu Rabbah version of the story is personal rather than institutional. The woman goes nearly mad and then wanders from door to door, collaring each of her husband's colleagues and confronting them with what they all knew of his life—and demanding an explanation for his death. She does not cite prooftexts.[14] She is not a member of the guild. She is a forlorn widow seeking after the legacy of her husband. (Do we hear the echo of Song of Songs 3:2, where it is written: "I must rise and roam the town, through the streets and through the squares; I must seek the one I love. I sought but found him not"?)

The wife of the Bavli's tale is threatening the whole rabbinic enterprise: "If your midrashic readings are not in some sense 'real,' if they break on the shoals of lived life, then what is the value of the enterprise?" To this there was no institutional response.

In one sense this is a classic question of theodicy. Why do bad things happen to good people? How could God's promise of long life be so wrong? An answer is demanded. When the Sages have no reply, the answer is borne by Elijah.[15]

The Answer

There is an obvious literary break in the move from the first half of the story to the second. The omniscient narrator gives way to the fallible first-person narration of Elijah. This is perhaps apt, as theodicy[16] is a topic in which only partial answers are possible. Elijah, in his exchange with the distraught woman, moves the focus away from the dead man's fulfillment of his duties as a scholar to a more intimate setting.

> Scene 2:
>
> Once I was her guest, I said to her: "My daughter, how did he behave with you during your menstrual period?" She said to me: "God forbid! He did not even touch my little finger."
>
> "During your white days, how did he behave with you?"
>
> "He ate with me, he drank with me and he slept with me in close proximity. But he never even thought of anything else."
>
> I said to her: "Blessed is God who killed him. For he did not show favor to Torah. For Torah says: 'You shall not come close to a woman during the impurity of her menstruation.'" (Lev. 11:18)

Elijah hits the ground running. Without any introduction or pleasantries he immediately sets out to defend the honor of Torah. His agenda seems clear—righteous Sages do not just die. There must have been something wrong with the dead scholar that caused his untimely end. His conversation with the widow is more reminiscent of a prosecutorial deposition than pastoral counseling. The widow seems to have the right answer to Elijah's first question. The young scholar was meticulous in his behavior during her menstrual period. "He did not even touch my little finger."

Elijah, however, presses on. He asks about the "white days," the seven-day period after the menstrual flow ended. The Sages extended the biblical period[17] of impurity, mandating that before a woman may ritually bathe, and thus be pure and able to have sex again, she must be sure that she does not see any menstrual blood for seven days. The severity of the prohibition during this seven-day period is the subject of some debate.[18] The strictest opinion is held by Rabbi Akiva who says that the menstruant is considered completely impure until she ritually bathes, after the period of the "white" or clean days. Apparently Elijah agrees with Rabbi Akiva.

Here is where the widow gets into trouble. By describing the nonsexual though erotic intimacy obtained during the seven clean days, she invites Elijah's wrath. There is one telling line, the second half of the woman's statement: "But he never even thought of anything else." The *vav* that connects this statement with the previous half could also be translated as *and*. The woman admits, in her perhaps bereaved reverie, that when her husband was with her, during those days, he only thought of her and of nothing else; he did not think of Torah. During that time of intimacy she occupied the place of the lover—the place which "rightly" belonged to Torah.[19] Elijah's anger blares forth. "Blessed is God who killed him." The Sage deserved to die, since he did not favor Torah above his wife.[20]

Elijah in this telling is, in a way, the disembodied voice of justice. There is no personal connection on either side. The widow shows no emotion, and Elijah shows no caring. The character of this interaction is especially stark when compared to the Eliyahu Rabba version:

In the ER version the meeting between Elijah and the woman, though intentional ("I entered her courtyard") is in a context of lived life ("I was walking in the market"). Elijah may not even have been planning on pastoral counseling when he set out on his way, since he waits for her to make the first move. The woman is still in the throes of deep grieving verging on madness. She sees Elijah, approaches him, and repeats her tale of woe. Her words are exactly the same as when she was going door to door. The reader senses that she has no idea who the stranger is, but it doesn't matter since

Table 4.1
Elijah and the Widow: Two Versions

Seder Eliyahu Rabba	BT *Shabbat 13b*
Once I was walking in the market I entered her courtyard.	Once I was her guest,
She came and sat next to me and she was crying.	
I said to her: My daughter, why are you crying?	
She said to me: My husband read much Scripture, and repeatedly studied many [laws and traditions]. Why did he die in the flower of youth?	
I said to her: My daughter, how did he behave toward you during your menstrual flow?	I said to her: "My daughter, how did he behave with you during your menstrual period?"
She said to me: Rabbi, he would say to me, "Set aside all those days on which you see blood, and sit an additional seven clean days so that you will have no doubt."	She said to me: "God forbid! He did not even touch my little finger."
I said to her: My daughter, he spoke properly.	
For thus have the Sages taught in regards to men and women with emissions, menstruants and those who have given birth, that after seven days they are pure toward their spouses.	
For it says: And if she is pure from her flow, she shall count, etc. (Lev. 15:28)	
"And during those white days, how did he behave toward you? Perhaps you poured oil for him in your hand and he touched you on your little finger?"	"During your white days, how did he behave with you?"
She said to me: "By your life, I bathed his feet and I anointed him with oil, and I slept with him in one bed. But he never thought of other things."	"He ate with me, he drank with me and he slept with me in close proximity.But he never even thought of anything else."
I said to her: "Blessed is God for there is no showing of favor before Him. For so it is written in Torah: 'You shall not come close to a woman during the impurity of her menstruation.'" (Lev. 11:18)	I said to her: "Blessed is God who killed him. For he did not show favor to Torah. For Torah says: 'You shall not come close to a woman during the impurity of her menstruation.'" (Lev. 11:18)

she is demanding an answer from the universe. She has given up on finding an answer. She is mourning.

Elijah's exchanges with her are gentle and supportive. He always refers to her as "my daughter" (and she responds once by calling him "Rabbi"), as he asks for her story. Although Elijah's second question ("How did he behave toward you during your menstrual flow?") is the same as the first question in the Bavli's version, the context is different. In this context of caring, the woman gives an elaborate answer, as if sharing a memory. Elijah follows her answer with words of praise for her husband, as if saying: "He was truly a Sage, for what he told you was true."

In this environment he pushes on, asking about their behavior during the "clean days," the days of waiting after the menstrual flow stopped. Here the woman opens a window into her intimate life with her husband. One can almost feel the longing accompanying the memory of those days of waiting, when she would anoint him with oil and wash his feet and sleep in one bed with him, close but not touching. She doesn't use the formulaic language of the Bavli: eating and drinking and sleeping.[21] Hers is an intimate description, not a legal formula. In the ER telling she is also the actor. She relates her actions in the first person "I bathed ... I anointed ... I slept." In the Bavli's telling, the focus of the action is the husband, even though the woman is doing the telling.

Elijah's final response is also different. Although Elijah is trying to justify God, he doesn't bless God for killing the scholar. Perhaps he is moved by the woman's passion of her spontaneous "by your life," as she recalled the contact with her lover which would not recur. Elijah only says: "Blessed is God for there is no showing of favor before Him." This formula resonates closely with the blessing prescribed for the mourner's house: "Blessed is the Judge of Truth."[22] Elijah's final word is sad acceptance of the decree of God (even Sages die) rather than a victorious outburst of justification as in the Bavli.

What, then, is going on in the Bavli? When compared to the ER story, the Bavli's tale strikes one as almost vicious. Elijah deflects a critique of the rabbinic guild by way of character assasination—triumphing in the defamation of one whom everyone agrees was a true and good student of the Sages.[23]

Further, the critique itself is contradicted by a midrashic statement that appears in Bavli *Sanhedrin*. The statement comments on Song of Songs 7.

"Hedged about with lilies" (Song of Songs 7:3) for even if only a hedge of lilies was the barrier, they would not breach it. This is what the *min*[24] said to Rav Kahane: You say that it is okay for a menstruant to be alone with her man. Is it possible that there is fire in the chaff and it does not burn? He said to him: The Torah testified concerning us "hedged about with lilies." For even if only a hedge of lilies was the barrier, they would not breach it.

Rashi, the twelfth-century Talmudic commentator in northern France, explains Rav Kahane's allusion to the hedge of lilies:

> Hedged about with lilies, in other words, with a gentle warning and a slight differentiation they are distanced from the sin and there is no need for a stone wall to separate them. Even if they were only as far as a hedge of lilies from the transgression, they would not breach it.

In other words, the presumption is that one of the characteristics of a scholar is his ability to set his own boundaries. A scholar has no need of physical separation ("a stone wall") from the possibility of transgression. Were this true, what might have been the scholar's transgression? Why not believe his widow that he never even thought of anything else? We are caught in a dilemma. If we believe the widow, then her challenges to the rabbinic project stand. If we do not believe her, then Rav Kahane's claims about the spiritual and moral self-control of Jews (or at least Sages) ring hollow. Is this not the barrier the Sage had set between himself and his wife? Why is this not a perfect example of Rav Kahane's point rather than a point for the prosecution, a justification of God's ineffable judgment?

Nachmanides, in Christian Spain in the thirteenth century, writes: "Rather we will explain that she would ritually bathe [in the *mikveh*] at the end of her menstrual period as defined by Torah law. However, since he belittled and breached the fence of the Sages he was bitten by a snake, for all their words are as burning coals." This dense statement sums up Nachmanides' attempt to make sense of a detail in the story that disturbs many of the medievals. Why does Elijah distinguish between the days of the "menstrual period" itself and the "clean days"? Nachmanides points to Bavli *Shabbat* 64b where Rabbi Akiva is reported as having said: "She will be in her *nidah* [impurity] until she immerses in the waters [of the *mikveh*]." According to this reasoning there is no distinction between the days of actual blood flow and the clean days following. The only line of separation is the immersion in the ritual bath which signals purity.

Nachmanides, among others, speculates that there was a custom of immersion to separate the Torah-mandated impurity of the days of menstrual flow and the rabbinic-mandated clean days afterward. A woman would have immersed herself twice every month, once at the end of her flow and again after the seven so-called clean days. Nachmanides again speculates that this first immersion was abandoned because it was a "stringency which brought a leniency in its wake." In other words, the stringency of the *extra* immersion immediately after the period (and before the clean days), marking the end of the Torah-mandated period of impurity, caused people to act improperly leniently regarding the clean days in which the woman was still *nidah* (impure) by rabbinic ordinance.

Elijah, according to this reading of Nachmanides, was asking the widow about the way that her husband had treated this rabbinic prohibition. When Elijah found out that the husband had not held it as strictly as the first separation, then he had his justification of the death of the young Sage. In a number of sources the following verse, from Ecclesiastes 10:8, is cited as proof that death will come to one who disregards an ordinance [*gader*] of the Sages: "He who breaches a stone fence [*gader*] will be bitten by a snake."[25] Similarly, in various sources the words of the Sages are compared to coals or embers of which one must be wary lest one is burnt by them.[26] Nachmanides places this conceptual frame around Elijah's triumphant "blessed is God who killed him."

The Tosafists Speak Up

Another point of the story that bothers some commentators is that no one had an answer for the woman. How could this be? Does this not point to a real flaw in the system if this type of tragedy cannot be accounted for theologically? This quandary may have rested especially heavily on the Tosafist academies for whom the memory of the Crusades was alive—a time of widespread martyrdom in these very circles.[27]

A comment in the earliest collection of Tosafot (twelfth century), which seems to have been written in the academy of Rabbi Yitzhak ha-Zaken of Dampierre,[28] one of the two central personalities in the Tosafist academies, points to a text in BT *Hagigah*.[29] The discussion in *Hagigah* relates a tradition from Rabbi Yohanan that whenever he would come to a certain verse—Job 15:15—he would cry; the verse reads: "He puts no trust in His holy ones." The Talmud explains that the intent is that God causes the holy ones to die before they are able to sin.

Perhaps the young Sage was one of those whom God took up before he would sin? Whatever we might think of this answer, it is a response to the widow's question. Why did no one offer this as an answer? Rabbi Yitzhak ha-Zaken suggests the following:

> However, one can say that this is what was meant [by "there was no one to answer her"]: according to her understanding there was no one to answer her since it was settled for her, that even though she was a haverah [a member of the guild of Sages], and she would say "it is written in Torah, etc.," in any event it was not settled for her that because of "He puts no trust in His holy ones"—he should have died before his time—since it is [also] written in Torah "for it is your life, etc."[30]

She was, then, a Sage but had not completely bought the party line. She dismissed the idea that God might gather up one of His holy ones out of fear that they might sin. Thus there was no person in the study halls or synagogues who could answer her questions.

A later collection of Tosafot from Spain, edited by Rabbenu Asher of Toledo, suggests that the Sages might have given the widow a different answer. The author wonders why she was not told that "the lengthening of your days" refers to "the world which is eternal," that is, the world to come.[31] The Tosafot of Rabbenu Asher suggest that the colleagues of the young Sage were themselves not convinced of the verity of this answer, "since it is written, 'for it is your life and the length of your days,' which implies 'your life' in this world and 'the length of your days' in the world to come."[32]

The world to come is not intended as a substitute for long years in this world, but rather as an additional reward. The young Sage should have had them both, according to this understanding, and so the study hall was silent.

While Elijah delivered the party line, it bothered the Tosafists that none of the Sages had spoken up. Two different schools or collections of Tosafists supplied two different answers. Are these the answers they told themselves as they heard the stories coming from Mainz and Worms and Spires, of the destruction of the great centers of Torah, the murder of Sages and their families during the Crusades? Did some find comfort in the tradition that sometimes God took God's beloved scholars away before they were able to sin? Did others find comfort in the teaching that reward awaits in the next world and here, in this vale of tears, we cannot presume to understand the Divine accounting? Perhaps they took comfort in being able to dismiss these answers as specious. Perhaps they were the widow —she was, after all, a *haverah*, a member of the guild—and they found comfort in being able to voice her disdain for any of the proffered answers; that is, until Elijah will turn up and put things back together again.

Sex and the (Not So) Single Scholar

The gender of Rabbis is complicated. They seem to be gendered male— and heterosexual—in relation to the Torah with which they want to have sex each day as if it were the first day. They want to penetrate Torah.[33] They lust after Torah.[34] They are still gendered male—yet, at the least, homo-erotic, if not homosexual—when they lust after each other (as, for exam-ple, Resh Laqish and Rabbi Yohanan did) and die of heartache when their lovers (*hevrutot*) die.[35] Then when, like Israel, they are abandoned at the *huppah* (bridal canopy) by God,[36] they are gendered female.

Yet it seems that the Tosafists' problem with the story is the crux that points to its meaning. The story in BT *Shabbat* comes at the end of a legal discussion generated by the question: What is the law regarding a woman, who is in her state of menstrual impurity, who would sleep in the same bed as her husband, when both of them are clothed?

The *stam*, the anonymous editorial voice of the Talmud, leads the dis-cussion through differentiations and distinctions between sexual boundar-ies and other sensual boundaries, specifically eating that which is permitted though in context might be forbidden.[37] The discussion is brought toward what would seem like its conclusion with the introduction of a statement attributed to Rabbi Pedat, a Palestinian Sage of the third generation (ca. third to fourth century CE): "The Torah only forbade explicitly sexual closeness." This would mean that sleeping clothed in the same bed, with no thought of other activity, would be permitted.

Rabbi Pedat's statement is followed by an anecdote about 'Ulla, a Babylonian contemporary of Rabbi Pedat. 'Ulla, it is recounted, upon re-turning from the academy would kiss his sister on the breast. If non-sexual closeness would be forbidden, 'Ulla would not have done this, since sexual relations with one's sister are, of course, forbidden.

The *stam*, however, upsets this well-constructed conclusion, claiming that 'Ulla disagrees with himself. This anecdotal evidence of sisterly breast kissing is apparently contradicted by a statement attributed to 'Ulla:

Any closeness is forbidden, just as the Nazirite is told "Go away!" "Go away!" do not come near the orchard.

The story of the ill-fated Sage and his widow follows immediately upon this statement. The story, which is generated by a terminally ambiguous discussion, lives in that space of ambiguity. 'Ulla's reported acts were of the affectionate kind, whereas he forbade acts that might approach real desire. Perhaps.

It is the Tosafists' question that again serves as a hermeneutic index. The problem is not abstract desire, but rather the passion that leads to sex with a woman. The woman is always the "Other" woman. Torah is, of course, the only object of desire for the Sages. When there is a conflict between the Sage's desire for Torah and the Sage's desire for his woman, death can result. Loving desire in the rabbinic eco-system, it seems, is not a renewable resource.

When R. Yosef, the son of Rava, who was in the middle of a six-year stay at the academy of Rabbi Yosef, decided to visit his wife, he found that it is not so easy to return home.

> R. Yosef the son of Rava [was] sent [by] his father to the House of Study to study with Rabbi Joseph. They set for him six years of study [i.e., he had been married and it was decided that he would be away from home for six years]. After three years, on the Eve of Yom Kippur, he said: I will go and visit my wife. His father heard, and went out to him with a weapon. He said to him: "You remembered your whore [zonah]?" (Another version: You remembered your dove [yonah].) They fought, and neither of them stopped.[38]

Rava saw his son's wife explicitly as the other woman, as his whore. There are two versions of what Rava said. The second version, which is inserted by the editor, is one letter away from the first version. I would like to read the two versions as part of the fight between father and son. The son's yonah, or "dove," is to Rava a zonah, a "whore." It is passion for the "other" woman that leaves Rava—one of the giants of the Babylonian rabbinic tradition—enraged and violent.

I suggest that this very possibility of desire for the other woman, a passion delicately traced in the version of the story found in Eliyahu Rabba, left the Sages in the study hall silent. Death was not foreign to them. Theodicy was part of their vocabulary. They were, however, strictly monogamous.

When the young widow raised the possibility that one could love Torah and also love a woman, that one could penetrate Torah and also have sex with a woman of flesh and blood, they were all speechless. Elijah had to come and restore the balance. Elijah had to show that the Sage was not as pure as they thought, and therefore his transgressive relation with his wife was *actually, legally* transgressive. The study hall would then still be the site of the only real desire.

NOTES

1. "Why are the words of Torah compared to a loving doe? To teach you that just as a loving doe whose womb (i.e., vagina) is narrow and is as beloved each time to her lover as the first time, so, too, are the words of Torah." Cf. Ari Elon, *From Jerusalem to the Edge of Heaven: Meditations on the Soul of Israel* (trans. Tikva Frymer-Kensky) (Philadelphia: Jewish Publication Society, 1995).

2. BT *Yebamot* 63b.

3. BT *Ketubot* 62b–63a. This story has received much critical attention. For a review of the literature and a suggestion for a different reading, see my *Rereading Talmud: Gender, Law, and the Poetics of* Sugyot (Atlanta, Ga.: Scholars Press, 1998), 97–120, and note 69.

4. Ruhama Weiss, "Of Holiness and the Trampled Infant," *Sh'ma* 38 (September 2007), 4.

5. BT *Menahot* 44a–b; Tosafot HaRosh *Shabbat* 13a *s.v. vehayta* p. 46.

6. It should be clear by the style and context that this is my own creative reconstruction of the story that appears in various versions in the texts cited in the next paragraph.

7. In addition to the other issues mentioned further on, there were almost surely no brick-and-mortar study halls until very late in the history of rabbinic Judaism. On this point, see Jeffrey Rubenstein, *The Culture of the Babylonian Talmud* (Baltimore, Md.: Johns Hopkins University Press, 2003).

8. I consulted the available manuscripts on the CD of the Lieberman Project: Vatican 127, Oxford (Oppenheim 336), and Munich 95. Vatican 127 is available as a facsimile on the אוצר כתבי יד תלמודיים Web site of the Jewish National and University Library at http://jnul.huji.ac.il/dl/talmud/. The importance of the facsimile is that Vatican 127 also has Rashi's commentary. I also compared the versions with the version in Alfasi's *Halachot*, and that cited by Rabbenu Asher.

9. The Bavli and the ADRNa version also state that he "abundantly served the Sages" (*shimesh talmidei hachamim harbeh*).

10. "For thereby you shall have life and live long." It is noteworthy that all the manuscripts read *ki hi* ["for it," feminine] rather than the masoretic *lo hu* ["for it," masculine].

11. E.g., *Maharsh'a*, Rabbi Shlomo Eidels *ad locum*.

12. *Lo hu*. And see note 10, above.

13. Cf. *Tosafot RI HaZaken Ve-Talmido*, 10. The index of her being a Sage, according to this commentary, is that she says "it is written in Torah."

14. See note 13, above.

15. All the commentators assume that the first-person voice in the second half of the narrative is Elijah. In the Bavli, this is probably because of the attribution of the story to the school of Elijah. There is mention of a book written by Eliyahu, called *Seder Eliyahu* in Bavli *Ketubot* 106a. This is almost certainly not the *Seder Eliyahu* we have today (where we find the alternative version of the story) which is dated to the Geonic period (ninth century). However, Elijah's name is only mentioned once, and then in only one of the manuscripts of the Bavli. The Oxford manuscript (Oppenheim . . .) introduces the second half of the story with the phrase: "Father Elijah said." (Nachmanides also has this reading. See his novellae *ad locum*.) Elijah's name is not mentioned in ADRNa nor in the version in Seder Eliyahu Rabba, although it is assumed that the narrator of the pseudepigraphic Seder Eliyahu Rabba is the prophet Elijah.

16. On the complicated rabbinic practice of (anti-)theodicy, see Zachary Braiterman, (*God*) *After Auschwitz: Tradition and Change in Post-Holocaust Jewish Thought* (Princeton, N.J.: Princeton University Press, 1998).

17. Leviticus 15:19

18. See BT *Shabbat* 64b and Tosafot BT *Shabbat* 13b *s.v. biymey lybunech*.

19. My thanks to Jennifer Hammer, who pointed me toward this reading.

20. This is starkly different from the version of the story in Eliyahu Rabba, where it is obvious that God does not show favor for other reasons.

21. See this formula in a completely unrelated context in BT *Eruvin* 44a.

22. ברוך דין האמת. See BT *Berachot* 46b; cf. M *Berachot* 9:2.

23. My concern here is not to determine the chronological relationships between the stories, that is, whether ER was drawing on the BT version or the ADRNa version or some other independent version which we know nothing about. My interest, instead, is in the contrasts between the stories as I have pointed them out and what that might say about the *sugya* in the Bavli. The ADRN story seems to share some characteristics with the BT and some with ER.

24. Scholars disagree over whether a *min* was a sectarian, a Christian, or a non-rabbinic Jew. See, e.g., Richard Kalmin, "Christians and Heretics in Rabbinic Literature of Late Antiquity," *Harvard Theological Review* 87, no. 2 (April 1994): 155–169; Christine Hayes, "The 'Other' in Rabbinic Literature," in *The Cambridge Companion to the Talmud and Rabbinic Literature*, ed. Charlotte Elisheva Fonrobert and Martin S. Jaffee, 243–269 (Cambridge: Cambridge University Press, 2007).

25. *Sifri Eqev* 12; BT *Avodah Zarah* 27b.

26. E.g., ADRNa 15:4; *Genesis Rabba* 52:4.

27. See Haym Soloveitchik, "Catastrophe and Halakhic Creativity: Ashkenaz—1096, 1242, 1306, and 1298," *Jewish Quarterly Review* 94, no. 1 (2004): 77–108; no. 2 (2004): 278–299.

28. See Avraham Shoshana's discussion in Avraham Shoshana and Yehuda Amitai Shoshana, eds., *Tosafot R. Isaac b. Samuel of Dampierre (Ri the Elder) and Early Tosafists on Tractate Shabbat: edited for the first time from MS Guenzberg, Mos 636 Russian State Library, Moscow*, Vol. 1 (Jerusalem: Ofeq Institute, 2007), 21–27 (hereafter, Tosafot Ri haZaken).

29. BT *Hagigah* 5a.

30. Tosafot Ri haZaken, 9–10.

31. This answer is found in other theodic contexts; cf. BT *Kiddushin* 39b, and *Hullin* 142a, inter alia.

32. Yitzhak Shimshon Lange, ed., *Tosafot HaRosh al Masechet Shabbat*, 2nd ed. (Jerusalem: n.p., 1977), 46. It is noteworthy that MS Vatican 127 has this explanation in its text. If we were to read that version as an "authentic" version and not a scribal error, her argument would be that the world to come is an addition to this world and not a compensation or substitution for this world. The version of Vatican 127 is: כי היא חייך ואורך ימיך בעו׳ הזה ואורך ימיך לעו׳ הבא. Though this version is clunky, it could still be an alternative reading.

33. Cf. BT *Yevamot* 92a.

34. See note 2, above.

35. BT *Baba Metzia* 84a.

36. *Lamentations Rabba* 46.

37. For example, two people are sitting at a table, and one is eating meat and the other cheese.

38. Rashi's interpretation of the last line is that neither of them ate the "separation meal" before the fast of Yom Kippur. This is a plausible interpretation, although the literal meaning is as I have translated it, and its literary payoff is greater.

5

Intermarriage, Gender, and Nation in the Hebrew Bible

Esther Fuchs

THE BIBLICAL REPRESENTATION of "foreign" women has been the object of intense inquiry in recent years.[1] Initially feminist criticism highlighted the condemnation and stigmatization of national outsiders, such as Potiphar's wife, Delilah, and Jezebel, and linked it directly or indirectly to biblical patriarchal and ethnocentric ideology.[2] Cheryl Exum, for example, notes: "The negative image of the foreign woman is a given in the Bible; it is simply assumed, and exceptions like Ruth only prove the rule. Proverbs warns the young male repeatedly against her." [3] Danna Nolan Fewell criticizes Ezra-Nehemiah's objection to marriage with foreign women, linking it to sexism and xenophobia: "What was Israel's sin? Not following YHWH. How did they not follow YHWH? They worshiped other gods. Why did they do that? They were influenced by foreigners. Specifically foreign women. If only they had not associated with foreign women."[4] Claudia Camp elaborates on the association of foreign women and sexual strangeness:

> I suggest, however, that female ethnic foreignness is intimately linked, via several different modes, to other significant conceptual fields: it is linked, by ideological framing, to worship of foreign gods; by metaphor to sexual strangeness (adultery, prostitution and, in general, women's control of their own sexuality); by extension of the sexual metaphor to deceitful language; by metonymy to incorrect ritual practice; by moral logic to evil; by onto-logic to death; and by patri-logic, to loss of inheritance and lineage.[5]

If these readings reject the exclusivist rejection of foreign women, more recent postcolonial readings reject the colonizing acceptance of foreign women like Ruth. Laura Donaldson argues: "For 'Ruth the Moabite,' the translation from savagery to civilization or from Asherah to Yahweh similarly involves the relinquishing of her ethnic and cultural identity."[6] Musa Dube argues that the foreign sexualized woman, specifically Rahab the Canaanite prostitute in the Book of Joshua, is both a symbol of the conquered land and a colonized woman who is made to identify with her enemies against her own national interests. As such, the foreign woman is a pawn or cipher of colonial ideology: "It is, therefore, proposed that this flexible, yet recognizable and reoccurring, pattern of the use of gender in imperializing rhetoric should be recognized as a literary-type scene of land possession in the rhetoric of God, gold, glory, and gender."[7] Challenging Dube's representation of Rahab as a stereotypic "loose woman" and a "sell-out," Kwok Pui-lan defends Rahab's sexual and political choices as heroic strategies of survival: "Like the story of the colonized, hers is a fragmented, incoherent, and half-erased tale."[8]

By reframing the object of inquiry, by adding to gender as an analytic lens those lenses of nation, sexuality, and, to some extent, class, feminist critics have effectively demonstrated the double marginalization of the foreign woman as sexual and national other. In this chapter, however, I focus on the Israelite woman as a national identity construct, arguing that the feminist analysis has, so far, only managed to invert rather than subvert the traditional dichotomization of Israelite man versus foreign woman. This inversion obfuscates and erases the Israelite woman as insider/outsider in the body politic and as the body on which national boundaries are inscribed. Whereas earlier discussions of the foreign woman tend to configure the Israelite woman as a subcategory or variation of the foreign woman, later postcolonial discussions tend to assimilate her into the male Israelite subject.[9] Earlier discussions tended to emphasize the victimization of Israelite women as a manifestation of an "otherness," and later postcolonial treatments posit Israelite women as oppressors. The polarization of the Israelite woman as victim or oppressor sheds no light on her role in the construction of the nation as imagined community.[10] Nor does it acknowledge her status as both insider in the nation's body politic and outsider whose relationship to the nation is mediated through men (father, husband, or son).[11] The Israelite woman is the subject that is neither foreign nor normative—she is different from the dichotomized terms of reference in the above feminist interpretive binary. She exceeds and disrupts both categories and, as such, has the potential to deconstruct rather than reproduce them. Does the recent interest in the foreign woman have to displace or erase the Israelite woman? By focusing on the Israelite woman, we can illuminate the collusion between sexual and national politics that has been obscured by the critical focus on the binary opposition between Israelite masculinity and foreign femininity.

Sexuality and the Nation

The binary of the male Israelite and female foreigner reifies and naturalizes national identity as pre-given and evident. But just as the term "woman" has been recognized as an essentialist abstraction that cannot contain the plurality and complexity of that which it signifies, the nation is also culturally contingent, textually mediated, and ideologically contradictory.[12] The much quoted imperative, in Ezra 9:12 and 10:3, against marrying foreign women, based on the explicit warning in Deuteronomy 7:3 against intermarriage, is followed neither by Israel's male progenitors nor by Israel's leaders. Abraham has conjugal relations with Sarai's maid, the Egyptian Hagar who bears him a son (Gen. 16:4), and marries Keturah after Sarai's death (Gen. 25:1–6). Joseph marries Asenath, daughter of the Egyptian priest of On (Gen. 41:45–46), who bears him two sons who become two tribes in Israel (Gen. 41:45; 50–51); Moses marries the Midianite Zipporah who bears him two sons (Exod. 2:21–22), in addition to marrying a Cushite woman (Num. 12:1), and Solomon marries the Pharaoh's daughter and numerous foreign wives (1 Kings 3:1; 11:3). This practice is indicted by the authorial narrator only once, in the case of Solomon. It is therefore arguable that exogamy itself is not indicted here but rather the exaggerated number of foreign women (seven hundred) that he married —in addition to the three hundred concubines he is reported to have had (1 Kings 11:4–5). There is no evidence even in Ezra-Nehemiah that the legal proclamations against exogamy were ever followed or carried out. If postcolonial critics may argue with a measure of justification that these instances of exogamy entail the assimilation of the foreign woman into Israel's body politic, their position is more tenuous regarding the category of the "unattached" yet sexually desirable foreign women. Positioned at key moments in the nation's history are the representations of the Pharaoh's daughter who saves Moses's life and adopts him (Exod. 2:5–10), the Canaanite Rahab who collaborates with the Israelite spies (Joshua 2:1–21), the Midianite Jael who smites Sisera (Judg. 4:18–21), and the admirable queen of Sheba who validates Solomon's wisdom (1 Kings 10:1–13).

Why should the narrator highlight the fact that the nation's male leaders married foreign women, and why would he highlight their contribution to the national weal? Might one argue that at least some of these outsider women are being constructed as border-crossers, or as porous and ambiguous symbolic borders between Israel and its neighbors? Is it possible that on some level they are seen as both foreign and Israelite, as hybrid constructions of bi-national and bi-cultural identity?[13] Rather than framing foreign women as coherent totalizing identities, as postcolonial feminists suggest, I posit a more contingent picture where they are both insiders and outsiders. What may we learn by asking what effect the diverse representations of foreign women have on the Israelite women as consumers of their national narrative? Although the Israelite woman, as we will see, is also both insider and outsider in her own nation, at this point I invoke her simply as a material subject, a reader of the male-produced imagined community. Do these representations of foreign women empower her as a national subject or threaten her as someone who can be replaced or displaced by an "other" woman? If foreign women are just as effective, if not more so, as both national agents and marital partners, to what extent is the Israelite woman's place secured as a partner or helper? To what degree does the approbation of foreign women as marital partners and national agents displace the already tenuous relationship of the Israelite woman to the nation?

A more accurate theory of the foreign woman ought to take into account her dual representations as attractive and fearsome, the same and the other, desirable and forbidden. If her national identity suggests distance, her sexuality is feared and coveted, as she appears to have both sexual appeal and natural reproductive abilities. Her freedom to move between national boundaries also releases her from the strict configurations of Israelite women as wives or mothers. There is a complementary rather than antagonistic relationship between Israelite and foreign female sexualities. Sexual excess may be taken as a marker of alterity, as several postcolonial theories have suggested, but, as a literary trope attributed to women by male writers, it may also reveal repressed heterosexual desire and subliminal rebellion against doctrinal propriety.[14] The contradictory representations of foreign women as threatening and alluring, dangerous and enticing, correspond to a contradiction in the national self-representation of Israel as on the one hand endogamous–rejecting marital associations with foreigners–and on the other exogamous–open to marriage with outsiders.[15]

On one hand, Israel is separate and sacred, and, on the other, it is interdependent and interrelated with foreign cultures. The ideology of endogamy may explain the sexualized and threatening representations of foreign women, the likes of Potiphar's wife, Delilah, and Jezebel. Yet the approving representations of foreign wives such as Hagar, Zipporah, and Ruth suggest a contestation of this injunction, an exogamous ideology that accepted and approved of marriage with foreign women. The tension between these narrative discourses may correspond to what Homi K. Bhabha identifies as the tension between the idealized, prescriptive, or "pedagogic" script and the actual, experiential or "performative" narratives of the nation.[16] Although pedagogic texts, such as laws, prescribe endogamous marriage exclusively within the community for both men and women, the biblical narrative suggests that endogamy was meant for women alone. Thus strictures against adultery (outside marriage) and menstrual purity (inside marriage) were national identity markers meant exclusively for women. Whereas narratives of male intermarriage indict neither the practice nor the practitioner, narratives of female intermarriage are deeply aware of the problem of national boundaries, and they seek to deny that the marriage took place or describe the disastrous outcome of such potential liaisons. The most celebrated biblical woman who escapes criticism, Esther, becomes the queen of the Persian king Ahasuerus (Esther 17:18) under exceptional circumstances that involve the possible extinction of the entire nation.

A comparison of "foreign" and "Israelite" women suggests that, although the boundaries of the nation are inscribed on the body of Israelite woman, this body is often constructed as defective or damaged sexually and reproductively. Israelite women are presented as sexually violated daughters (Dinah, Tamar, and Pilegesh of Gibeah), sexually repressed wives, and barren mothers, whereas foreign wives and lovers are presented as sexually irresistible and assertive (Potiphar's wife, Delilah, Jezebel, and Vashti). Foreign mothers are also naturally fertile (e.g., Hagar, Bilhah, Zilpah, and Ruth). As a sexual and maternal subject, the Israelite woman is depicted as requiring supplementary assistance. The discursive construction of Israelite women is mediated through strategies of domestication, by which I mean a system of intersecting familial and conjugal dependencies. The production of collective national identity depends on the suppression of female sexuality, and thus it proscribes sexual desire for women and promotes instead asexual motherhood, propriety, purity, and virtue.[17]

The reproductive imperative—key to all nationalisms—often denies

Israelite women the ability to give birth and attributes to them a barren-
ness that is reversed only through divine intervention.[18] The repression
of sexuality in the Israelite insider group finds compensatory expression
in the foreign group. The endogamous narrative, which seeks to present
insider women as virtuous, is oppressive in its strategies of domestication
in ways that are different from, but arguably equivalent to, the exogamous
strategies of colonization applied to sexually "loose" foreign women. Foreign women are shown to move about and cross geographic, social, and
national boundaries at will (e.g., Rahab, Queen of Sheba, Jezebel, and
Ruth), but Israelite women who cross domestic boundaries (e.g., Dinah,
Jephthah's daughter, Tamar, and Pilegesh of Gibeah) are brutally violated
and textually silenced.[19] Is the material and discursive repression of Israelite women less onerous than the stigmatic descriptions of foreign women?
More important, whose interest is served by constructing their reciprocal
functions as antagonistic, as a contest? The sexual suppression of Israelite
women marks the inner limits of the nation in much the same way that
the sexuality of foreign woman marks its outer bounds. The multiple restrictions on women's sexual access to outsiders, to men other than their
husbands, and to their own husbands during regular periods inscribe the
sexual ethos of the nation on the women's bodies.

The frequent narrations of these interlocking representations attest to
the need of the national narrative to constantly check its fabricated boundaries, at times stressing oppositional relations of exclusions, at times seeking in the others opprobrium and validation of its imagined coherence.
As Andrew Parker, Mary Russo, and Doris Sommer note in their book
Nationalisms and Sexualities:

> Like gender, nationality is a relational term whose identity derives
> from its inherence in a system of differences. In the same way that
> "man" and "woman" define themselves reciprocally (though never
> symmetrically), national identity is determined not on the basis of its
> own intrinsic properties but as a function of what it (presumably) is
> not. Implying "some element of alterity for its definition, a nation is
> ineluctably shaped by what it opposes."[20]

Patriarchy and nationalism are systems that produce gendered hierarchical
relationships, because they always already originate in masculine humiliation, aspiration, and hope. In this sense Norma Alarcon, Caren Kaplan, and
Minoo Moallem are right: "Women are both of and not of the nation."[21]

The Gender of Intermarriage

In *Sexual Politics in the Biblical Narrative*, I suggest that two types of scenes are constitutive in the representation of marriage in the Hebrew Bible: the adultery type and the contest type, each of which are described below.[22] In that work I dealt with the patriarchal implications of these type scenes, pointing up the gendering of adultery as the validation of male control of women's sexuality and the gendering of reproduction as the validation of male control of female procreation.[23] For our purposes, I focus on the narrative inscription of national identity on women's bodies through sexual and exogamous proscriptions and restrictions. Israelite "nationness" is defined by the performance of coerced feminine propriety defined in conjugal and procreative terms within the sanctioned family unit, the inner sanctum of the national body politic.[24]

The adultery-type scene presents a wife, a husband, and a covetous powerful king. The high status of the sexual rival suggests that not even a king is exempt from the prohibition of extramarital relations with a betrothed or married woman. This scene begins with a point of irresolution and then moves through descriptions of the violent punishment of the covetous interloper and on to the happy resolution of patriarchal monogamy. As I put it elsewhere, "The wife is ultimately united with only one lawful husband: she is either restored to her original husband or transferred to her new husband."[25] Sarah, in the Book of Genesis, is restored to Abram after the Egyptian Pharaoh is duly penalized (Gen. 12:10–20). In a variant of this, after the transformation of their names, Sarah is again restored to Abraham (Gen. 20:1–18) as is Rebekah to Isaac (Gen. 26:1–12) after the Canaanite king of Gerar is duly penalized for his transgression. In 2 Samuel 11–12 Bathsheba is transferred from Uriah the Hittite to King David but only after the latter is punished and castigated for his inappropriate behavior. The repetition of these adultery scenes offers a dramatization of the actual performance of the legal proscription against adultery: "Thou shalt not covet they neighbor's wife" (Exod. 20:13; Deut. 5:17). Though the proscription of adultery appears as a sexual restriction addressed to men, it is an asymmetrical restriction that is ultimately imposed on betrothed and married women (Deut. 22:22–27).

As the contest-type scenes make clear, biblical adultery laws ultimately restrict married women to an exclusive monogamous relationship, while permitting their husbands to have sexual relationships with additional co-wives, concubines, and prostitutes.[26] (The contest-type scene presents us with two co-wives competing with each other for the husband's attention and the reward of male offspring.) It is the Israelite wife who is made to undergo the terrifying ordeal of the *Sotah* at the temple on her husband's least suspicion of infidelity (Num. 5:11–31).[27] Biblical adultery is thus gendered because the asymmetrical prohibitions imposed on the wife validate a hierarchical conjugal relationship that grants the husband exclusive control of his wife's sexuality. But the biblical adultery-type scene is not only gendered, it is also racialized in that it attributes adulterous behavior to foreigners alone. This is not the case in the scene involving King David and Bathsheba, the only biblical scene in which a married woman is eventually lawfully transferred to a covetous king and the only one in which the covetous king is an Israelite.

This suggests that an additional stricture is embedded in the Genesis adultery-type scene—the foreign nationality of the covetous kings. What makes the transference of the wife from husband to powerful king impossible in this context is the foreign nationality of the powerful king. The severe penalties suffered by the Egyptian and Canaanite kings for their involvements with Sarah and Rebekah are meted out not only in response to the violation of conjugal boundaries but also for the violation of national boundaries, as the Israelite woman's body is not to be claimed by a non-Israelite. The adultery type-scene is a dramatic proscription of adultery as well as of female intermarriage. The disastrous results of the violation of female adultery and intermarriage are presented in great detail, and usually it is the interloper who is severely punished whereas the husband is compensated for the temporary loss of control over his wife's sexuality. In Pharaoh's case, in Genesis 12, the punishment is especially severe and involves the death of offspring. The text uses the word "plagues" (*ng*), which appears again in the context of the collective punishment of Egypt's male infants shortly before the deliverance of the Israelites in the time of Moses (Exod. 11:1). The association between the punishment for adultery and exogamy and the punishment for oppressing the people of Israel suggests that the private violations of sexual law have national implications. In the case of David and Bathsheba, both the wife and the interloper are punished. Much has been written about the discursive "rape" of Bathsheba, but is it possible that her discursive suppression and the death of her child are penalties for her violation of the law of exogamy? David is explicitly penalized for violating the law of adultery, but Bathsheba also lost a son.[28] Is it possible that Uriah the Hittite, despite his devotion to David, simply had to die? In other words, could it be that his elimination was required because he violated the unspoken rule of gendered exogamy when he intermarried with Bathsheba? Perhaps David and Bathsheba are eventually rewarded with the birth of Solomon, the heir to the throne, because their marriage does not violate the proscription of gendered intermarriage. I suggest that this interpretation is indeed possible despite the explicit protestations of the narrator and the prophet Nathan. Innocent or not, the foreign man who is a potential exogamous husband is severely punished or violently eliminated. The Israelite wife in question, meanwhile, is textually silenced; her desires or preferences are all but repressed, as if to camouflage, deny, and erase, even in the process of telling the story, the very possibility of her interest in and potential marriage to a foreign contender.[29]

This is indeed the case as well in the rape story of Dinah. Although Shechem, the eponymous leader of a major Canaanite city, is stigmatized, he is presented as innocent and even well intentioned, much like the kings of Egypt and Gerar. The point is not to excoriate an individual foreign ruler but to present a range of sexual behaviors as foreign, non-Israelite, and in some sense antinational. Indulging in such sexual behaviors is precisely the definition of foreignness. The sexual appropriation of an Israelite female body requires strict adherence to distinct patriarchal procedures, the violation of which is unpardonable. If adultery is condemned as foreign in the preceding scenes, in Genesis 34 it is rape that is racialized.[30] What is satirized and severely punished is the failure to follow proper procedure and realize the gravity of the violation of sexual laws and the law of exogamy (Deut. 22:28). The story implicitly pokes fun at the sexual foreignness of the Shechemites, who nowhere show concern about the rape itself or apologize for it. Instead of approaching the girl's father, as the law requires, Shechem approaches his own father, Hamor (literally, "donkey"). This clearly violates the appropriate decorum implied by the betrothal-type scene.[31] Shechem begins to fancy Dinah *after*—not before—he has sexual relations with her (Gen. 34:3). To first claim a woman sexually and only later negotiate for her is how one deals with a prostitute, not with an honorable daughter of Israel. This may well be what Dinah's brothers mean when they ask: "Should our sister be treated like a whore?"[32] Hamor offers financial compensation to Dinah's brothers and then seems to add fuel to the fire by proposing collective intermarriage: "Intermarry with us: give your daughters to us, and take our daughters for yourselves (Gen. 34:9).

Exogamy is associated here with rape, and both transgressions are severely punished, this time by the victim's brothers. Again, the lesson driven home is that under no circumstances, not even in the extreme case of the rape of an unmarried woman, is marriage to a foreign man to be considered. The proscription of exogamy seems to overrides the law on rape, because Shechem's belated proposal is eventually rejected. The verb "defiled" (*tm'*), which the brothers use to explain their subsequent vindictive punishment, suggests that a crime of this order can only be set right through violence and bloodshed (Gen. 34:25–29).[33] The desecration of Dinah's body is presented as tantamount to the subversion of the integrity of Israel's first family and, by implication, its national identity.[34] Although Dinah is not held responsible for her rape or its bloody aftermath, the story begins with her departure from her proper place. We are told that she "went out to visit the daughters of the land" (Gen. 34:1). Venturing out, departing from domestic space, are actions that have serious consequences for Israelite daughters (e.g., Jephthah's daughter, Pilegesh of Gibeah, and Tamar).[35] The spatial enclosure of female Israelite bodies offers a vivid contrast to foreign women's bodies (e.g. Hagar, Zipporah, Ruth, and the Queen of Sheba) whose bodies are discursively captured in motion.

The violence often unleashed against Israelite women represents them as vulnerable bodies in need of (male) protection. This differs greatly from the frequent representation of foreign women as projecting force up against male bodies (e.g. Jael, Delilah, and Jezebel). The story of Dinah and Shechem inscribes on the body of the raped virgin the national boundaries that must under no circumstances be violated. Exogamy is forbidden even for a virgin in straits, a virgin who has been assaulted and "defiled," even if the rapist is willing to marry her and is of high royal status.

The Book of Esther seems at first to counter the national narrative of exogamy, because here an Israelite, or actually a Jewish woman, is shown to marry a foreign emperor. The Jewess seems to cross familial, national, and sexual boundaries, and is imagined as a foreigner. As the foreign woman, Esther must hide her national identity from Ahasuerus, her king and husband, as her people have been marked for destruction by the vindictive and bloodthirsty Haman (Esther 3:7–15). Esther reveals her identity only on the verge of genocidal catastrophe, shortly before Haman's edict to annihilate the Jews of the empire is to go into effect (Esther 4:1–2). She does so reluctantly, not because she herself desires to overturn Haman's edict but because she is urged, even threatened by Mordecai, her cousin and adoptive father, to do so (Esther 4:12–17). Esther's reluctance to go out on a limb and save her own people is underscored by the text. Her initial refusal to approach the king suggests that she has been colonized or assimilated in a way that Mordecai was not. Her response refers to the emperor's law as supreme, all but oblivious to the laws that govern her hidden identity: "All the king's courtiers and the people of the king's provinces know that if any person, man or woman, enters the king's presence in the inner court without having been summoned, there is but one law for him—that he be put to death" (Esther 4:11).

Esther's initial response, then, reflects a kind of fearfulness and lack of national solidarity that are implicitly juxtaposed with Mordecai's refusal to accept any laws that challenge those governing his national identity. He refuses the gift of clothing Esther sends him and insists on wearing sackcloth and ashes, in solidarity with his people who are "mourning, fasting, weeping, and wailing" because of the imminent genocidal decree (Esther 4:1–4). Though agitated and upset, Esther still does not seem to understand "why and wherefore" he refused her gift (Esther 4:5). The emperor's law that forbids mourning clothes in front of the palace (Esther 4:2) seems to override for her the genocidal law that triggers Mordecai's decision to wear mourning clothes. She is reluctant to speak out on behalf of her people, even after Mordecai produces the "written text of the law" (*patshegen haktav*) revealing the plot to dispossess and destroy the Jews (Esther 4:8).

This is not to deny Esther's contribution to her people's weal. Yet her strategy is remarkably different from Mordecai's. Esther's performance of submission seems excessive, and although some praise her strategy as effective diplomacy, I argue that this approach is both gendered and ethnicized.[36] Esther's hyper-femininity constructs the exiled Jewess as an object of beauty and the subject, in the sense of subjection to male power. If her body is converted into a desirable object through successive treatments of cosmetic oils and perfumes (Esther 2:9–14), her subjectivity is trained through successive encounters with masculine authority, until she finally emerges as a true queen, capable of signing off on edicts that complement those composed by Mordecai (Esther 9:29). As an object of beauty, Esther's identity converges with the foreign queen Vashti, whom she replaces, and the two hold up contrasting models of femininity: Vashti stands up to the emperor and refuses his invitation to parade her beauty in front of his officers (Esther 1:10–12). In this regard, Vashti's femininity continues the biblical construction of foreign women who challenge male authority (e.g. Delilah and Jezebel). As Timothy Beal points out, Queen Vashti has more in common with Mordecai than with Esther.[37] If Vashti's determination is unacceptable as a model of Jewish femininity, it seems to return as a repressed model in the construction of Mordecai.

The Book of Esther implies that only a collective national crisis justifies the exceptional violation of the law against intermarriage. Although the narrative admits that exogamy has taken place, it virtually eliminates explicit references to Esther's legal, economic, sexual, or matrimonial bond with Ahasuerus. Toward the end of the story, the king is said to have granted Esther Haman's estate (Esther 8:1). Significantly, she is said to have transferred the estate to Mordecai (Esther 8:2). To the extent that Mordecai plays the role of father, this transference is in keeping with matrimonial rules of *mohar*, or bride gift (Exod. 22:16). To the extent that Mordecai plays the role of Esther's true, though secret husband (he, too, is officially unmarried and childless), the transference is in keeping with the customs of patriarchal marriage. Either way, matrimonial law is being upheld despite the foreign context and the power of empire.

The suppression of explicit indicators regarding marriage suggests that the original prohibition of exogamy is also upheld, albeit imperfectly, given the political constraints. It is especially peculiar that in a book obsessed with descriptions of royal procedure and etiquette, there is virtually no reference to a marriage ceremony. Nor is there any reference to a written contract between Ahasuerus and Esther. As Mieke Bal has pointed out, although the Book of Esther reflects "lots of writing" there is not even one reference to the writing or signing of a marriage contract.[38] The most explicit reference to marriage is rather general and surprisingly vague: "The king loved Esther more than all the virgins. So he set a royal crown on her head and made her queen instead of Vashti (Esther 2:17–18). The "royal crown" (*keter malkut*) is mentioned in chapter 1 in reference to Queen Vashti, who refuses to display it as the emperor requests (Esther 1:11). This lone reference to marriage suggests that it amounted to a coronation rather than to nuptials. Apparently the king is more interested in finding an appropriate substitute for Vashti than in building a new family. This marriage does not produce offspring. As a national heroine, Esther, like Deborah and Miriam, is deprived of descendants. In Esther's case, this is in keeping with the implicit irony that erases even as it inscribes the violation of female intermarriage. The king's preference for Esther is skin-deep; her looks please him, although he may not know the difference between sexual attraction and "love" (*/hb*). Despite his "love," we hear later on that the king has not called for Esther for thirty days (Esther 4:11). That the king reads the Book of Records during his sleepless nights (Esther 6:1–4) suggests that the couple may not sleep together. The alleged marriage between Ahasuerus and Esther does not seem to grant her automatic permission to see him whenever she pleases. Esther has to wait for her husband to extend his scepter to her, and she must touch it first before addressing him (Esther 5:2; 8:5). The highly stylized and formal discursive relationship between the royal couple continues even during the party Esther throws for the king and Haman. The king's offer to share as much as half his kingdom with Esther is an obvious courtly speech performance: "At the wine feast, the king asked Esther, 'What is your wish? It shall be granted you. And what is your request? Even to half the kingdom, it shall be fulfilled" (Esther 5:6; 7:2).

Sublimated as reading and writing in classic Freudian fashion, sexuality is also displaced by feasting and drinking at banquets.[39] The first half of the story emphasizes that eunuchs supervised the elaborate cosmetic processing of the virginal candidate, and the second half implies that the lavish banquets that framing social life in the imperial palace follow the same rigorous regime of royal decorum as daytime diplomacy. Obsessed with propriety and etiquette—or simply drunk—the king mistakes Haman's desperate pleading for his life at the feet of Queen Esther during the second party as a sexual advance or, worse yet, an attempt to literally "conquer" (*kbs*) or claim the queen's sexuality. This misperception costs Haman his life (Esther 7:7–10). Thus, amid the opulence and excessive indulgence of the Persian colonial court, Esther, despite her status as sexual object, is desexualized, in keeping with the national ideals of feminine virtue. And in the context of the most publicized and apparently condoned exogamous violation in the Bible, the narrator weaves his tale in such a way as to deny it.

Esther, like Sarah, Rebekah, Bathsheba, and Dinah, is both an insider and outsider in the nation. Although Mordecai shapes her character as subjective and interior, her body is inscribed by the national ethos of sexuality: she is both an object of beauty and a virgin. She is desirable, but her own desire is repressed. Unlike Vashti, who is driven by her desires—her desire to object to the king's command, for example—Esther's desires are not known. Like most other sexually attractive Israelite women, it is not clear whether she wants to be "taken" (*lkh*) into the king's palace. The repression of the Israelite woman's desire in stories about potential or actual exogamy highlights her status as a body inscribed with national meaning. In the case of Sarai/Sarah and Rebekah, the body is taken into the foreign palace but is not violated.

In Esther's case, however, the fate of the entire nation seems to hinge on the violation of both the law and the woman's body. Does the Book of

Esther attempt to represent both? Does it mean to display the sexual desirability of the female body as the means by which the nation is rescued and at the same time deny its matrimonial and sexual appropriation by the national other? Though eventually Esther does request that she and her people be spared from destruction, it is her sexual desirability and the king's jealous possessiveness that win the day. Unlike Sarah and Rebekah, Esther is "taken" (*lkh*) into the foreign king's palace and not returned to her lawful guardian and custodian; unlike Dinah, Esther is not "taken back" by her relatives.

Even in the extreme circumstances of exile and genocide, intermarriage is, nevertheless, both admitted and erased. Whereas the female body may and often does symbolically represent the entire nation, its sexuality marks it as "strange" and therefore its identity converges with the foreign king. The concept of *issa zara*, or "strange woman," remains contentious, because it infers both sexual strangeness and foreignness. Marked sexually and nationally, foreign women may indeed be seen as doubly other, but the Israelite woman—if such an abstraction is possible—is both of the nation and not of the nation.

Conclusion

Musa Dube argues that Israelite women ought to be studied as colonizers and oppressors of the foreign nations that, according to the Book of Joshua, occupied the land of Canaan before the conquest of the land: "Narratively speaking, the position of Israelite women changes from the colonized in Egypt to the colonizer as the journey to the promised land begins."[40] Dube implies that key moments in the trajectory of Israel toward national sovereignty empowered Israelite women, whereas I argue that the national narrative tends to eclipse and diminish the power of Israelite women.

The transition from imperial subjugation in Egypt to national symbolic liberation in the desert and to territorial conquest in Canaan progressively suppresses the presence and agency of Israelite women. Shortly before the constitutive event of Sinai, which interpellates the former subjugated crowds as a holy nation, Moses defines women as outsiders and sexual relations with women as somehow polluting: "Moses came down from the mountain to the people and warned the people to stay pure, and they washed their clothes. And he said to the people: 'Be ready for the third day: do not go near a woman'" (Exod. 19:14). The repetition of the word "people" ('m) is not accidental. The exclusion of women is not merely the result of religious legislation and communal arrangements— as was already argued—it is the event, par excellence, that constitutes the Israelites as a nation.[41] Women signify a sexual category within the nation that is potentially polluting, a pollution that cannot be eliminated through the simple washing of clothes (Exod. 19:14). Women signify the other within, much as the foreign nations that are to be eliminated during the conquest of Canaan are the external others that construct the nation from without (Exod. 23:23–33).

The discursive suppression of Israelite women in the story of wanderings and Joshua corresponds to their sexual repression. The ambiguous representation of the foreign woman, Rahab, in the Book of Joshua has been explained as a result of her status as a colonial subject. The story of Rahab, who offers a safe haven to the Israelite spies, racializes prostitution and attributes to the colonized woman a ringing endorsement of the appropriation of Canaan. Although the rigid proscription of relations with foreign women is challenged by the ambiguous presentation of Rahab as both prostitute and shrewd diplomat, as Canaanite enemy and Israelite ally, Israelite women are not mentioned as distinct groups or individuals. The Book of Judges seems to sustain the ambiguous presentation of foreign women by assigning them the roles of national rescuers (e.g., Jael) and dangerous enemies (e.g., Delilah). The lone figure of Deborah as a military leader hardly substantiates the claim that the struggle for national sovereignty grants women a greater share of power. For the most part, Israelite women in the Book of Judges are presented as victims of male violence (e.g., Jephthah's daughter and Pilegesh of Gibeah).[42] The Kingdom of David, the height of monarchic sovereignty, also offers little evidence for a positive correlation between national consolidation and the ascendance of women. David's own daughter, Tamar, emerges as a victim of incestuous rape in a story that attributes to David's son, Amnon, a sexual crime originally attributed to Lot's daughters, the matriarchs of the Ammonites. The narration of King Solomon's reign attributes prostitution to Israelite women and is much less generous toward the Israelite prostitutes than Joshua 1 is toward Rahab, the Canaanite prostitute. The scene that dramatizes the sordid contest of the prostitutes presents the male king as the wise protector of lowly Israelite women, whereas the story of Rahab represents her as the wise protector of Israelite men (1 Kings 3:16–28). The only woman who claims power and wisdom equal to the king is the foreign Queen of Sheba. Solomon is not indicted for marrying an Egyptian princess (1 Kings 3:1), but for allying himself with a large number of foreign consorts—"seven hundred royal wives and three hundred concubines," to be precise (1 Kings 11:3). National sovereignty, as represented in the Bible, is rarely correlated with the ascent of Israelite women.

It is therefore misleading to construct Israelite women as mere extensions of their male counterparts. Though the oppressed can indeed be oppressors, and the biblical narrative should be read from both gendered and postcolonial perspectives, a mere inversion of the terms of reference is not sufficient. An interrelational consideration of both inside and outside women is necessary in order to fully appreciate the narrative strategies of national ideology.

As I tried to show throughout this chapter, feminist postcolonial analyses of the Hebrew Bible must consider the Israelite woman as well as the foreign woman as mutually constructing national representations. Israelite women are often depicted as sexually repressed and barren, in ways that often justify intermarriage, but the stigmatizing and titillating depiction of foreign women reveals a contested ideology that both condemns and condones intermarriage for Israelite men. This contested ideology corresponds to the double narration, both "pedagogic" and "performative" of the nation, but it largely applies only to the nation's men. Narratives of female intermarriage lead to disastrous consequences for the foreign men involved. The examples on which I drew—the adultery-type scene involving Sarai/Sarah and Rebekah and Bathsheba, the story of Dinah and Shechem, and, most notable, the story of Esther leave no doubt about the unacceptability of female intermarriage. In Esther's case, a virtual genocide is needed to justify female intermarriage, and even here the text erases its probability. In this sense, intermarriage in the Hebrew Bible is gendered —and so is the nation. To focus on the exclusions and stigmatization of foreign women at the expense of the Israelite woman risks obscuring the mechanisms and narrative strategies that gender patriarchy and narratives of the nation.

NOTES

1. The qualifier "foreign" is in quotation marks here, because this concept is relational, and therefore incomprehensible without its necessary complement the "Israelite," who is just as much a relational construct. Yet recent feminist criticism has largely treated the "foreign" woman as a historical entity and a distinct essential identity. My reference in what follows to "foreign" and "Israelite" women is

decidedly heuristic, and the absence of quotation marks should not be mistaken for an attempt to naturalize or legitimate these highly unstable constructions.

2. J. Cheryl Exum, *Fragmented Women: Feminist (Sub)versions of Biblical Narratives* (Valley Forge, Pa.: Trinity Press International, 1993), 61–93; Danna Nolan Fewell, "Imagination, Method, and Murder: Un/Framing the Face of Post-Exilic Israel," in *Reading Bibles, Writing Bodies: Identity and the Book,* ed. Timothy K. Beal and David M. Gunn, 132–152 (London and New York: Routledge, 1996); Alice Bach, *Women, Seduction, and Betrayal in Biblical Narrative* (Cambridge: Cambridge University Press, 1997); Laura E. Donaldson, "The Sign of Orpah: Reading Ruth Through Native Eyes," in *Ruth and Esther: A Feminist Companion to the Bible,* ed. Athalya Brenner, 130–144 (Sheffield, U.K.: Sheffield Academic Press, 1999); Claudia V. Camp, *Wise, Strange, and Holy: The Strange Woman and the Making of the Bible* (Sheffield, U.K.: Sheffield Academic Press, 2000); Musa Dube, *Postcolonial Feminist Interpretation of the Bible* (St. Louis: Chalice Press, 2000); Gale A. Yee, *Poor Banished Children of Eve: Woman as Evil in the Hebrew Bible* (Minneapolis: Fortress Press, 2003); Harold C. Washington, "Israel's Holy Seed and the Foreign Women of Ezra-Nehemiah: A Kristevan Reading," *Biblical Interpretation* 11, no. 3/4 (2003): 427–437; Judith E. McKinlay, *Reframing Her: Biblical Women in Postcolonial Focus* (Sheffield, U.K.: Sheffield Phoenix Press, 2004); Kwok Pui-lan, "Sexual Morality and National Politics: Reading Biblical 'Loose Women,'" in *Engaging the Bible: Critical Readings from Contemporary Women,* ed. Choi Hee An and Katheryn Pfisterer Darr, 21–46 (Minneapolis: Fortress Press, 2006).

3. Exum, *Fragmented Women,* 68.

4. Fewell, "Imagination, Method, and Murder" 135. See also idem, "Changing the Subject: Retelling the Story of Hagar the Egyptian," in *A Feminist Companion to Genesis,* 2nd series, ed. Athalya Brenner, 182–194 (Sheffield, U.K.: Sheffield Academic Press, 1998).

5. *Wise, Strange and Holy,* 28.

6. Donaldson, "The Sign of Orpah," 144.

7. Dube, *Postcolonial Feminist Interpretation of the Bible,* 76. Judith E. McKinlay sees Ruth also as a colonized woman to the extent that she had to leave her own country and throw her lot with Judah. See McKinlay, *Reframing Her,* 37–56.

8. Kwok Pui-lan, "Sexual Morality and National Politics," 39.

9. For discussions of the first approach to categorizing the foreign woman, see, for example, Claudia Camp, "Sister, Brother, Other: The Israelite Woman Estranged," in idem, *Wise, Strange, and Holy,* 191–322. Though aware of gender distinctions between Israelite men and women, Musa Dube nevertheless sees Israelite women as colonizers: "As women from the colonizer's side, Israelite women become the measure and keepers of the purity or holiness of their nation. Thus their role emerges clearly when the identity of the Israelites is pitted against the identity of the Canaanites" (Dube, *Postcolonial Feminist Interpretation of the Bible,* 75).

10. My reference to the nation as imagined community does not mean that

the nation is an illusion or phantasm; rather, the nation is a social category of difference which, like gender, is historically reconstructed, reinvented, culturally performed, and continuously contested. See Benedict Anderson, *Imagined Communities: Reflections on the Origin and Spread of Nationalism*, 2nd ed. (London: Verso, 2006 [1983]).

11. Esther Fuchs, *Sexual Politics in the Biblical Narrative: Reading the Hebrew Bible as a Woman* (Sheffield, U.K.: Sheffield Academic Press, 2000).

12. See Judith Butler, *Gender Trouble* (New York and London: Routledge, 1990); Chris Weedon, *Feminism, Theory, and the Politics of Difference* (Malden, Mass., and Oxford, U.K.: Blackwell, 1999).

13. On the attribution of Israelite traits to foreign women, see Susanne Gillmayr-Bucher, "'She Came to Test Him with Hard Questions': Foreign Women and Their View on Israel," *Biblical Interpretation* 15, no. 2 (2007): 135–150. On gender and bi-cultural hybridity, see Gloria Anzaldua, *Borderlands/La Frontera: The New Mestiza* (San Francisco: Aunt Lute Books, 1987); Trinh T. Minh-ha, *Woman, Native Other* (Bloomington and Indianapolis: Indiana University Press, 1989).

14. Ania Loomba, *Colonialism/Postcolonialism* (London: Routledge, 1998), 151–172.

15. On endogamy and exogamy as expressions of contradictory Israelite identity constructs, see Regina Schwartz, *The Curse of Cain: The Violent Legacy of Monotheism* (Chicago: University of Chicago Press, 1997), 83–102.

16. Homi K. Bhabha, *The Location of Culture* (London: Routledge, 1994), 199–244.

17. On the linguistic mediation of the ideology of female asexuality, see Athalya Brenner, *The Intercourse of Knowledge: On Gendering Desire and 'Sexuality' in the Hebrew Bible* (Leiden: Brill, 1997).

18. Fuchs, *Sexual Politics in the Biblical Narrative*, 44–90.

19. Lynda E. Boose, "The Father's House and the Daughter in It: The Structures of Western Culture's Daughter-Father Relationship," in *Daughters and Fathers*, ed. Lynda E. Boose and Betty S. Flowers (Baltimore, Md.: Johns Hopkins University Press, 1989), 1–18.

20. Andrew Parker, Mary Russo, and Doris Sommer, introduction to *Nationalisms and Sexualities, ed. idem*, 1–20 (New York: Routledge, 1992), 5.

21. Norma Alarcón, Caren Kaplan, and Minoo Moallem, "Introduction: Between Woman and Nation," in Caren Kaplan, Norma Alarcón, and Minoo Moallem, eds., *Between Woman and Nation* (Durham, N.C.: Duke University Press, 1999), 12.

22. Fuchs, *Sexual Politics in the Biblical Narrative*, 116–176.

23. By "gendering," I refer to the hierarchical and asymmetrical power relations implied in the legal appropriation of the wife's sexuality and reproductive labor.

24. The family unit is often referred to as *bet av*, literally, the father's house. See Carol Meyer, *The Invention of Eve*.

25. Fuchs, *Sexual Politics in the Biblical Narrative*, 119.

26. Prostitution is tolerated to the extent that it is presented without censorship or condemnation, and it is gendered in that only women are defined as prostitutes. See Phyllis Bird, "The Harlot as Heroine: Narrative Art and Social Presupposition in Three Old Testament Texts," in *Women in the Hebrew Bible: A Reader*, ed. Alice Bach, 99–118 (New York and London: Routledge, 1999).

27. Alice Bach, "Good to the Last Drop: Viewing the Sotah (Numbers 5:11–31) as the Glass Half Empty and Wondering How to View It Half Full," in idem, *Women in the Hebrew Bible*, 503–522.

28. See for example, Cheryl Exum, "Raped by the Pen," in idem, *Fragmented Women*.

29. The word *tm'* (defilement), which appears in the scene referring to Bathsheba's postmenstrual ritual purification, is rarely attributed to a specific woman (2 Sam. 11:4). The only exception is Dinah, who as we shall see is raped and claimed by a foreigner. The purification may be mentioned to signal Bathsheba's partial commitment to laws of purity, ironically highlighting her more radical defilement through exogamy that can only be eradicated through murder, death, and bereavement.

30. According to Lyn M. Bechtel, Genesis 34:2, specifically the succession of verbs "and he took her, and he lay her and he oppressed her [*inah*]" does not refer to rape. See Bechtel, "What If Dinah Is Not Raped? (Gen. 34)," *Journal for the Study of the Old Testament* 62 (1994): 19–36. But see, too, Susanne Scholz, "Through Whose Eyes? A 'Right' Reading of Genesis 34," in Brenner, *A Feminist Companion to Genesis*, 150–171; and Fuchs, *Sexual Politics in the Biblical Narrative*, 200–224.

31. Fuchs, *Sexual Politics in the Biblical Narrative*, 91–115.

32. Literally, "will he make our sister into a whore (*znh*)." Here I am following *The Jewish Study Bible* based on the Jewish Publication Society *Tanakh* Translation (Oxford: Oxford University Press, 2004).

33. This word also appears in the story of Bathsheba and David, although it refers to Bathsheba's menstrual impurity (2 Sam. 11:4). In light of our analysis, her act of purification could be interpreted as referring to her previous marital relationship with her Hittite husband.

34. The root *tm'* in the sense of menstrual impurity also appears in the story of David and Bathsheba.

35. Fuchs, *Sexual Politics in the Biblical Narrative*, 200–226.

36. For positive assessments of the literary representation of Esther, see, for example, Sidnie Ann White, "Esther: A Feminine Model for Jewish Diaspora," in *Gender and Difference in Ancient Israel*, ed. Peggy L. Day, 161–177 (Minneapolis: Fortress Press, 1989); Michael Fox, *Character and Ideology in the Book of Esther*

(Columbia: University of South Carolina Press, 1991); Timothy K. Beal, *The Book of Hiding: Gender, Ethnicity, Annihilation, and Esther* (London and New York: Routledge, 1997).

37. "And thus the Jewish hero Mordecai and the non-Jewish heroine Vashti are once again identified with one another" (Beal, *The Book of Hiding,* 79).

38. Mieke Bal, "Lots of Writing," in *A Feminist Companion to Ruth and Esther,* ed. Athalya Brenner (Sheffield, U.K.: Sheffield Academic Press, 1999), 212–238.

39. Cheryl A. Kirk-Duggan, "Black Mother Women and Daughters: Signifying Female-Divine Relationships in the Hebrew Bible and African American Mother-Daughter Short Stories," in Brenner, *A Feminist Companion to Ruth and Esther,* 192–211.

40. Dube, *Postcolonial Feminist Interpretation of the Bible,* 74.

41. Judith Plaskow, *Standing Again at Sinai: Judaism from a Feminist Perspective* (San Francisco: HarperCollins, 1990), 25–28.

42. Mieke Bal suggests that the daughter figures that are frequently assaulted and victimized are eventually avenged by the repressed mothers who are erased from the text (e.g., Deborah, Jael, and Delilah). See "Dealing/With/Women: Daughters in the Book of Judges," in Bach, *Women in the Hebrew Bible,* 317–334.

6

Good Sex

A Jewish Feminist Perspective

Melanie Malka Landau

WHEN WE THINK of "good sex" we think of sex that feels good and gives pleasure. Some less affected by advertising and popular culture may think of sex as acts between humans that create connection. But we know that sexual relationships are not only between two atomized individuals but are located within a complex set of contexts and relationships. If good sex is about sex within an ethical context, then good sex from a feminist Jewish perspective has its own set of questions to account for. This chapter asks: How can we make sex holy as feminist Jews while grappling with the gender injustices that emerge through the male-centered textual tradition?

At the outset I acknowledge that I am limiting this discussion to heterosexual relationships. I think the heterosexual relationship is the potential site for radical gender transformation on the level of gender roles and the separation between gender and biology. At the same time I believe that this is limiting, because it reinforces the idea that there really are two polarized sexes as opposed to a continuum of sexual beings attested to by the existence of intersex people. A focus on heterosexual relationships also bypasses the gender injustices that abound for Jews in same-sex partnerships.

The question now is this: Can a just and good sex be retrieved and fashioned from the compulsory heterosexuality of a male-centered rabbinic tradition? Judith Plaskow argues that "the question of what constitutes good sex from women's perspectives simply cannot be asked within the framework of the system." [1] In this chapter I ask this question in dialogical relationship with the tradition. This process of retrieving and refashioning, which I aim to achieve here, builds on the exciting scholarship that shows love and passion for both rabbinic texts and radical feminism while creating an evocative dance that weaves together the strands of their commitments.

We enter the discussion on good sex from the House of Learning (*Beit Midrash*) and the experience of women reading about sex from the voice of men in the Talmud. The Talmud places a high value on learning, and yet rabbinic culture excludes women from this most prized practice. David Biale argues that the exclusion of women from the highest cultural value of learning and the dominant male role in sexuality were intimately and inseparably linked. Although women's business was highly important, the textual tradition attributes superior value to men through their focus on learning and because they have more religious obligations than women do. Moreover, compared to non-Jewish men and Jewish men who did not fit the scholarly ideal, the rabbis considered themselves to be a sexual elite which was manifested through their sexual restraint. Women and Torah are used interchangeably as objects of male desire.[2]

When people are reduced to objects, even by being classified in one group or another, their full range of humanity and of possibility is denied. To acknowledge objectification is to recognize that there is no particular correlation between the way that women are represented and the lived reality of those women. When we read texts about women, we may learn more about the dominant discourses from which they come than about the women themselves. Thus, how man and woman are seen to be is actually a construct upon which whole societies, economies, and religious systems are based.

A story in the tractate *Menahot* 44a in the Babylonian Talmud illustrates one way of seeing the move from objectified to subjectified sex. My reading of this story also shows how rabbinic texts can be appropriated for a feminist agenda. Narratives yield a multitude of interpretations that usually reflect the ideological commitments of the interpreter.

In this particular story, a rabbi paid a lot of money to come to a world-renowned prostitute who lived by the sea. He had to travel very far and schedule his appointment with her well in advance. Finally, his turn had come. After waiting for some time he was escorted to a luxurious room with seven levels of elaborate beds—six silver beds crowned by a golden bed on the top. The woman for whom he had been waiting was naked on the top bed, waiting for him to come up. He undressed as he climbed the beds; after he removed his shirt, the *tzitzit* attached to his undergarment smacked him in the face, as if to admonish him for what he was about to do. Castigated and embarrassed, he went back down and sat naked on the ground. When the woman saw this, she came down after him; they faced each other naked on the ground. She had never been rejected. Before she let him leave, she wanted to know what blemish he had found in her that caused him to react in this way. He told her that she was the most beautiful woman he had ever seen in his life, but he explained that there is a commandment called *tzitzit* that called him to account for himself by appearing as four witnesses as he ascended the beds to have sex with her.

The woman was totally transformed by this encounter. She did not let the man leave until he told her his town and the name of his teacher. She then divided her property three ways: one-third for the poor, one-third for the government, and one-third she took with her. When she arrived at the study house of Reb Hiyya, who was this rabbi's teacher, she told him that she wanted to convert to Judaism. The rabbi asked her if she had taken a fancy to one of the students. She handed him the note that the man had written for her with the name of his town and his rabbi. The Sage then told her she could now fully consummate her relationship with that man with whom she had nearly had relations. The tale ends with her spreading the same linen for their marital union that had been previously spread for their anticipated illicit union.[3]

The rabbi in our story undergoes an inner transformation that results in his no longer seeing the woman—the prostitute—as an object. His "sin" is interrupted by the ritual fringes. I contend that this man did not only think prostitution was wrong because it is against the law—rabbis found various justifications for seeing prostitutes—but rather that it was not how he was meant to relate to another human.

Even if it is too speculative to suggest that he saw her as a subject, once he interrupted the process of objectification she then took upon herself autonomy as a subject and could see herself in a new way. It is a near miraculous moment when the horizon of possibility opens up and humans see that there is a range of alternatives in a given situation. A force of no less than Divine proportion—the mythical intervention of the *tzitzit* —was needed to interrupt the objectifying relationship.

This may be a reminder about the intensity of the drive to objectify. In this story the Divine voice—through the vehicle of the *tzitzit*—is used as a way to promote the shift to subject. At other times Divine authority, at least through the force of the law, is used to reinforce unequal power dynamics between men and women in a relationship.

The image of the rabbi and the prostitute sitting on the ground, face to face and naked, evokes a deep sense of human connection. They have experienced a transformation in each other's company.

The story is comforting in that it reports a transformation from de-personalised sex to a grounded meeting between two people. In one sense it actually represents the way in which the social construction of women and men sets them up to relate to each other in a certain way that does not necessarily serve either of them particularly well. In the story it is the fringes of the garment that intervene to effect the transformation to a way of relating, stripped (literally) of the other roles they had been playing. Being stripped of roles, as crucial as it may be, can only ever be a temporary position; we see, in the end, that the two resume other defined roles of husband and wife according to the rabbinic tradition. Despite this, the moment of nakedness does show the contingency of our roles and the possibility that they can be disassembled. This story repeats some of the stereotypes and oppressions of women; it features a prostitute, after all, who is absorbed back into society through the respectable channel of marriage. Yet, at the same time, it also interrupts the objectification of the prostitute and shows the human vulnerability inherent in their relationship.

This story has in it all the kernels of the conundrum of kosher sex. There is a move from impersonal sex to "sex in a relationship." The twentieth-century Jewish legal and philosophical scholar Eliezer Berkovits calls this movement "the humanized transformation of the impersonal quality of the sexual instinct" and claims that this is "the climax in man's striving for sexual liberation."[4] Good sex, according to Jewish tradition, takes place within the marital relationship. This means that it is between a Jewish man and a Jewish woman in a committed relationship at the right time. The ultimate resolution of our story depicts the gentile prostitute becoming the Jewish wife of a scholar. Although intermarriage is frowned upon, as a convert the prostitute is welcomed into the fold. The rabbi suspected that perhaps she only wanted to convert to get married, but when she told him the story he was reassured that she wanted to adopt Jewish life and values for herself and not just to get a Jewish husband. Bad sex, here, becomes good sex. In one way it could be seen that the sex that began as "illicit" becomes "holy" within the appropriate framework; however, it resonates more to say that the relationship became transformed from an I-It relationship to an I-Thou relationship. Although "good sex," traditionally, is any sex within the pre-scribed framework, this essay argues that "good sex" also encompasses a deep recognition of humanity. A committed relationship is not a definite guarantee against an I-It relationship.

Not only is married sex potentially holy, but, in fact, it is part of the husband's marital duties. The obligation of the husband to have sex with his wife or, more specifically, his obligation to give her sexual pleasure, suggests that the dynamics of object and subject are potentially harder to ascertain. This obligation is referred to as *onah*, a Hebrew word meaning "time period." The rabbinic tradition lists, according to occupation, the required amounts of sex that a husband needs to "give" his wife. For example, a Torah scholar is obliged once a week on Shabbat (if he is in town).[5] Where sex is expressly considered the husband's obligation to his wife, the role of consent as well as the woman's right to refuse sex also become further complicated. Carol Pateman argues that, "unless refusal of consent or withdrawal of consent are real possibilities, we can no longer speak of 'consent' in any genuine sense."[6]

The movement from illicit to permitted and sanctified sex in the above story is notable, for whereas a sex worker is financially compensated for her services, a wife in Jewish marriage is not recognized as providing sexuality to her husband—because, at least in part, it is seen as the man's obligation to give his wife sexual pleasure. The expectation of sex in marriage is covered over in the guise of the male duty to sexually please his wife. Although it is not without its problems, there is something refreshing in not viewing sex as something the woman *gives* to the man. If the woman does feel obliged to have sex, however, then the man's obligation to please her obscures her own sense of obligation, which means that one may not even be able to question it.

The marital duties that the man owes the woman as articulated in the Bible but developed by the rabbis include clothing, food, and sex. The male's right to sex was preserved alongside a rabbinic sexual ethic that neither permits a husband to rape his wife nor promulgates the idea that women want to be ravished.[7] Women are constructed as needy for sex, and men constructed as service providers.[8] As Daniel Boyarin writes, "through the construction of sexuality as a form of the husband taking care of the wife's needs and through the construction of her needs as both compelling and in part inexpressible . . . although the wife has the right in principle to refuse sex on any occasion, her consent can be understood through silence and necessarily ambiguous signs." [9] Boyarin continues in a footnote: "By coding male sexuality as a form of service to women, a mystifying protection of male access to female bodies is secured."[10] Male access to ongoing

heterosexual sex from their partners is secured through the guise of a commandment incumbent on the male to pleasure his wife. It is questionable
to what extent the act of Jewish marriage (*kiddushin*, the explicit acquisition of a woman or her sexuality by the male partner) means that the man
has bought a right to sex with his wife.

It is significant that forced sex, per se, was never permitted in a Jewish
marriage.[11] The idea of consensual sex between willing husband and wife
is a value. This is promising, especially given that only in the recent past
has common law acknowledged and made illegal the possibility of rape in
marriage. However, the woman's consent in sex is potentially ambiguous,
perhaps because sex is construed as part of her husband's obligation to her.
A woman's refusal to have sex is also a woman's thwarting of her husband's
attempts to fulfill the commandment of giving her sexual pleasure. There
are a range of scenarios referred to by the rabbis that result in the break-
down of the marriage and that, in effect, form the limits of the rights of the
woman to refuse sex within marriage.

A woman who refuses to be sexual with her husband is called a *moredet*, a rebellious woman.[12] One reason she might refuse her husband is because he has become disgusting to her. There is a debate within the rabbinic tradition about whether the husband, in this case, should be compelled to grant a divorce. The tension is between not wanting a woman to
be trapped in her own marriage and wariness, on the rabbis' part, about allowing her to leave her husband when she is sick of him and find someone
else. The nonreciprocal nature of the Jewish marriage and the husband's
capacity to withhold a divorce from his wife can severely undermine her
freedom and autonomy.

In order to explore the situation in which a woman refuses to have sex
with her husband, we need to investigate the details of Jewish divorce. One
consequence of the one-sided nature of Jewish marriage, where the man is
viewed as acquiring the woman, is that only the man can grant a divorce.
Two exceptions to this, where the religious courts have historically had
jurisdiction to compel the husband to grant a divorce, include the following:[13] first, marriages that contravene the law, for example, someone from
the priestly line married to a divorcee; and, second, marriages that are in-
tolerable for the woman because of something about the husband, whether
it is within or outside his control.

In his Code of Law, Maimonides differentiates between various motives of the rebellious wife. For one type of woman, he advocates forcing

the husband to grant a divorce. In Laws of *Ishut* (Personal Status) 14:8–9, Maimonides says:

> She is asked why she rebelled. If she says, "He is loathsome to me and I cannot willingly have relations with him," then pressure is forthwith exerted upon him to divorce her because she is not like a captive that she has to have relations with a man who is hateful to her. However, when she exits [the marriage] it is without anything whatsoever of the *ketubah* [marriage contract] entitlements. . . . But if when asked she says, "My purpose is to torment him in retaliation for such and such that he did to me or for his having cursed me or quarreled with me and the like," then she is sent away from the Beit Din (legal court) with the following threat: "Be advised that if you persist in your rebellion, then even if your *ketubah* is worth a hundred *maneh* you shall forfeit it all."

When goodwill and benevolence break down between people, then legal obligations become the skeleton of the relationship. They provide the bare minimum, but they alone do not make a healthy body. The *ketubah* was put in place by the rabbis as a protection for women, that is, to deter husbands from leaving their wives because they had to pay a lump sum upon divorce. Obviously, if only that amount is preventing the husband from leaving the wife, the relationship requires a lot of fixing. On the one hand, the *ketubah* does "protect" women but, on the other, the shadow side of protection is that it constructs the woman as someone needing protection and thus reinforces her role as a victim. In fact, the *ketubah* may only protect her as long as she is a victim. As we see from the above law, if the woman initiates the complaint, she also gives up her right to collect the *ketubah*. Therefore, the protection symbolized by the *ketubah* only has valence when she decides to stay in the marriage regardless of what the husband is doing. If the woman wants to stay in the marriage and she withholds sex to retaliate against her husband, then, according to Maimonides, she cannot obtain a divorce. It is unclear whether this category includes only a woman who is retaliating or whether it also includes a woman who takes too long to make up after a fight. Maimonides does indicate that the woman had been cursed and in a quarrel, and so perhaps it is not necessarily a clear-cut act of retaliation.

However, coercing the husband to give his wife a divorce has not been a popular strategy. Even as early as Rabbenu Asher (the Rosh), less than two hundred years after Maimonides, we see the rabbinic turnaround against coercion of the husband, especially regarding the wife having been disgusted with him. The Rosh advocates for the husband's right to remain in the marriage, even against the wife's will. He says:

> Moreover, I say the [earlier decisors] that ruled as they did were acting on what appeared to be the imperative of the hour for the sake of the daughters of Israel. Today the situation is the opposite; the daughters of Israel are immodest . . . therefore it is best to stay far away from coercion. A great wonder at Rambam for saying that she is not like a captive that she has to have relations with a man who is hateful to her. Is that a reason to coerce a man to divorce and to permit a married woman? Let her refrain from relations with him and remain in living widowhood all her days! After all, she is not obligated to be fruitful and multiply (Rosh, Clal. 43:8).

Rabbenu Asher implies that it is more important to stop a woman from getting another, more desirable husband than actually ensuring that the current husband is also in a loving and sexually active partnership. When he condemns the woman to live as a widow, it is uncertain whether he is implying that, despite her need to be celibate, if she is not having sex with her husband , that the husband would have access to other sexual relationships outside the marriage. It is also unclear whether the husband would be prevented from fulfilling his mitzvah of having children because she did not want to have sex. If so, would Rebbeinu Asher say that procreation is less important than actually stopping her from getting out of the marriage?

The halakhic system attempts to legislate for humanized sexual relationships: rabbinic guidelines stipulate that one should not have relations when one is fighting. Sex may bring you together, but it should not take the place of good old talking or even when either party is reluctant. The Babylonian Talmud tractate *Nedarim* 20b recognizes the coercive nature of threats when it comes to rape. It lists nine categories of objectionable intercourse; one includes all forms of coerced sex, whether one "consents" out of fear (*eimah*) or is aggressively forced to have intercourse (*anusah*).[14] When subject to pressure, intimidation, and fear, a person is afraid to say no and loses the ability to express any meaningful consent. Other situations where sex is forbidden is when (1) the husband hates the wife and is thinking of another woman; (2) one of the parties is excommunicated; (3) a husband who has two wives has intercourse thinking that he is with the other wife; (4) one party is angry with the other; (5) one party is drunk; (6) the husband has already decided to divorce the wife; (7) the wife is sleeping with another man; (8) a woman brazenly demands relations.[15]

The laws of *nidah*, the physical separation of husband and wife during menstruation and for one week after, enable relationships to focus substantially on nonphysical aspects of connection. Whereas feminists have described marriage as implying a continuous male sex right, the laws of menstrual separation interrupt any implied female sexual availability. As one contemporary observant woman writes:

> Quite simply, for non-Jews, marriage means that the other is always sexually available to them, subject to an unspecific, largely unenforceable notion of consent. The Jewish laws of Family Purity and those that mandate the explicit consent to sexual relations make it clear to Jewish men from the outset that even marriage does not enable perpetual access to a woman's body and that sexual relations are not an inalienable and constant right purchased through the transaction of marriage.[16]

Yet women may also use this issue of availability as a way to engage in a power play with their husbands and withhold sex *not* because they do not want to be intimate per se but as a weapon to punish their partners. I think this actually objectifies men and their sexual desire, and takes advantage of their vulnerability. At the same time, perhaps, women withhold one of their most significant values in marriage in order to transform their power as objects. This exemplifies how the categories of subject and object may become fluid and indiscrete. In a situation where a woman feels powerless, she may use her capacity to withhold or delay sexual encounters with her husband as a way to reclaim a sense of autonomy and power in the relationship. In fact, the Palestinian Talmud recounts such an episode:

> Shmu'el wanted to sleep with his wife. She said to him: "I am in the status of impurity." But the next day she said: "I am in the status of purity." He said to her: "Yesterday you were in the status of impurity and today you are in the status of purity!?" She said to him: "Yesterday I did not have the same strength as today." He went to ask [the opinion

of] Rav, who said to him: "If she gave you a plausible reason for her words [which she did] she can be believed.[17]

As this story reveals, Shmu'el's wife has a measure of control over the couple's sexual life, which is couched as her control over the way laws of menstruation are practiced. Charlotte Fonrobert also reads this story as a symptom of the rabbi's anxiety about women making halakhic decisions to their advantage as well as undermining the rabbi's authority through questions of believability.[18]

The critical reading of classical rabbinic and medieval texts about sexuality—as well as the reading of contemporary practices—can locate resistance within the texts themselves to some dominant paradigms of heterosexuality. Through an activist interpretation of these sources the feminist project of rebuilding gender relations can be achieved from the ground up, using the foundations of the tradition to seed the support for a constantly developing vision for Jewish practice and community. Similarly certain interpretations of the sources can reinforce gender hierarchies and masquerade gender constructions as natural and biological differences between women and men. The desirable relationship between men and women is not about exchanging male dominance for female dominance; rather, it is about transforming the relationship beyond power dynamics to a dance of giving and receiving, of communication and openness. This can only be achieved by acknowledging the various contexts in which the heterosexual relationship is located. It is within this paradigm that, in the best case, certain strands of tradition will guide us.

NOTES

1. J. Plaskow, "Authority, Resistance, and Transformation: Jewish Feminist Reflections on Good Sex," in *The Coming of Lilith: Essays in Feminism, Judaism, and Sexual Ethics, 1972–2003* (Boston: Beacon, 2005), 193–205, quote at 196.

2. D. Biale, *Eros and the Jews: From Biblical Israel to Contemporary America* (New York: Basic Books, 1992), 36.

3. BT *Menahot* 44a.

4. E. Berkovits, *Essential Essays on Judaism,* ed. D. Hazony (Jerusalem: Shalem, 2002), 114. One might question what Berkovits calls the "sexual instinct" and his assumption that it is naturally and originally impersonal. One may agree that it is impersonal but may not agree that it is naturally so, but rather that it is a

function of many interrelated social processes. Nevertheless, its transformation is still significant even if there are different understandings regarding its origin.

5. For more information about the male marital obligations, see D. Boyarin, *Carnal Israel: Reading Sex in Talmudic Culture* (Berkeley: University of California Press, 1993), 143.

6. C. Pateman, "Women and Consent," *Political Theory* 8, no. 2 (May 1980): 149–168, quote at 150. Pateman continues:

> To examine the unwritten history of women and consent brings the suppressed problems of consent theory to the surface. Women exemplify the individuals who consent theorists have declared uncapable of consenting. Yet, simultaneously, women have been presented as always consenting, and their explicit non-consent has been treated as irrelevant or has been reinterpreted as "consent."

7. D. Boyarin, *Unheroic Conduct: The Rise of Heterosexuality and the Invention of the Jewish Man* (Berkeley: University of California Press, 1997), 170. See also BT *Ketubbot* 61b.

8. Boyarin, *Unheroic Conduct*.

9. Ibid., 171.

10. Ibid., 172.

11. See *Eiruvin* 100b: Rami b. Hama citing R. Assi further ruled: "A man is forbidden to compel his wife to the [marital] obligation, since it is said in Scripture: 'Without consent the soul is not good; and he that hurries with his feet sins'" (Prov. 19:2); *Ba'ailei ha-Nefesh, Sha'ar ha-Kedushah; Hil. De'ot* 5:4; *Even ha-Ezer* 25:2. Available at http://www.jsafe.org/pdfs/pdf_032206_2.pdf (accessed 22 May 2007; p. 10).

12. Incidentally, the husband who refuses to have sex with his wife is called a *mored* (rebel), and for every week that he refuses to have sex he has to add more payment to her *ketubah*. At any point the wife can also choose to divorce, in which case the Beit Din will force the husband to divorce her. See *Shulchan Aruch, Even Haezer* (Laws of *Onah*) 77:1. The wife can also prevent her husband from working in a certain place if it will reduce his capacity to fulfil her sexually. If he chooses to be a Torah scholar, however, then she cannot prevent him from moving. Even without her permission, he may go away for two or three years; with her permission, he can go away for even longer (76:5). These laws, which trump a husband's religious obligations to his wife, demonstrate the extremely high cultural value attributed to learning Torah.

13. I. S. D. Sassoon "*Ra'ah ma'aseh ve-nizkar halakhah*," *Judaism* (winter/spring 2005).

14. Available at http://www.jsafe.org/pdfs/pdf_032206_2.pdf (accessed 22 May 2007; p. 12), in reference to *Nedarim* 20b.

15. Ibid.

16. J. Shmaryahu, "We Will Do and We Will Listen," in *Total Immersion: A Mikvah Anthology*, ed. R. Slonim (New York: Jason Aronson, 1996), 35.

17. PT *Ketubot* 2:5, 26c; and quoted in Tosafot, BT *Ketubot* 22b. Translation from C. E. Fonrobert, *Menstrual Purity: Rabbinic and Christian Reconstructions of Biblical Gender* (Palo Alto, Calif.: Stanford University Press, 2000), 26.

18. Ibid.

I-Thou: Relationships

7

The Erotics of Sexual Segregation

Naomi Seidman

JERUSALEM IN THE late 1980s was full of American Jewish hippies discovering messianism or existentialism or both, vegetarian spiritual seekers who heard personal messages in Bob Dylan's songs, bearded graduate students working for years on dissertations in Kabbalah, yoga students who spent an hour a day on their heads. I lived in a small apartment in Nahlaot, with the only phone among my circle of friends. Parents would call from Pittsburg or London or Flatbush, and I would relay messages to their sons and daughters.

On the Purim of my second year in Jerusalem my friend Menahem took me along to a party in the Old City, full of Shlomo Carlebach Jewish hippie types—the men with extravagant *payes* and oversized *kippot*, the women with beautiful headscarves and a baby on one hip. People passed me joints and little plastic cups of Slivovits and whiskey. Menahem had long disappeared into the crowd when two women approached me to ask if I would like to go to a "women's party." As had been the case for as long as I could remember, I was cross-dressed for Purim, but they must have seen beyond the tsitsis and hat to the fact that my moustache had been applied with eye-liner. When I said that I was in no condition to go anywhere, the two women put my arms around their shoulders and walked me down a few alleys and up a long flight of stairs. The apartment was blessedly quiet. In the flickering candlelight I saw women lounging on couches and on the floor. A woman who seemed to be the leader gave a meandering, earnest, endless talk. She was wearing red from her neck to her stocking feet, and around her neck was hung a sign: "Tell the Israelites to bring you a red heifer without blemish or defect, one which has never borne a yoke" (Numbers 19:2). Behind me, invisible hands rubbed my shoulders through the suit jacket. If I learned anyone's name, I immediately forgot it. At a break in the Red Heifer's Torah talk, I asked, my voice erupting too loudly into the silence, "Is this a cult?" Someone laughed, and I hurried to add, "No, no, I don't mind. If it's a cult I want to join."

It was dawn by the time I lurched my way back to Nahlaot, stopping at Menahem's cave of an apartment to explain where I had vanished to. Even with his face going in and out of focus, I could see his envy: "They were all beautiful? Where was the apartment?" But I had no idea where I had just spent the night. A few months later, when I had begun to wonder whether I had dreamed the whole party, I bumped into the Red Heifer at the shuk, looking like an ordinary housewife with her string bags of tomatoes and eggs. That Friday evening I was back in the apartment, sober enough this time to recognize these women as of this world rather than mythical. Nevertheless, there was something magical in the singing, the teaching, the easy intimacy between the women around the Red Heifer's Shabbat table. The world of women, as I experienced it in Jerusalem, was a world beyond couples and families, a world with fluid boundaries between whom I was permitted to touch and whom I was not, whom I was allowed to love and those whose love I was required to stand outside of and watch.

I had tasted this particular flavor a decade before, in my Orthodox girls' school—also in Jerusalem—and liked it. The teachers at Michlala, the girls seminary I attended for a year after high school, had helpfully arranged for us American students to spend Shabbat with families in the surrounding neighborhood, and for a few months we did, sitting nervously at the far corner of the dining room table as some middle-aged paterfamilias pumped us with the familiar questions—where we came from, were we enjoying our studies, which yeshiva our brothers were learning in, did we know this family or that one.

But as that first wet Jerusalem winter descended on the campus, a few of us somehow managed to slip the knot and evade the Friday exodus, making Shabbat for ourselves on the wonderfully deserted campus. Over the remains of the *chulent* we had cooked for ourselves, we sang every tune we knew for every one of the Shabbat *zemirot,* hands pounding the table. To sing out loud was not something we took for granted: a woman's voice was immodest, not to be displayed before men to whom we were not related. At those strange Shabbat tables, and even at school events—where there were also a few of our male teachers present in the sea of girls and women —we were not supposed to even hum along. Away from all men, we sang our hearts out, praising the Sabbath Queen, the day of rest, the time we had snatched away for ourselves from the regimen of classes and adults.

Afterward, heavy with feeling and *chulent*, we drew the shutters closed and crawled into our beds with a book or a friend.

For American Jewish feminists, traditional synagogue architecture has been viewed as encoding the hierarchies of patriarchal Judaism, with the primary symbols and ritual objects of Jewish prayer and worship firmly situated within the male sphere, while women are relegated to the role of spectators of—at most, marginal participants in—Jewish religious practice. This marginalization of women in the synagogue—and, by extension, in the world of Jewish practice—is traditionally justified as a way to separate the spiritual from the sexual realm. Women, in this justification, represent sexual temptation to men—the sexual temptation men present for women is deemed irrelevant, as witnessed by the fact that men may not look at women but women are encouraged to look at men during synagogue services. In the Orthodox synagogue in Berkeley and, no doubt, many other similarly reconfigured synagogues, feminist awareness has led to a restructuring of this symbolic space, with the *mechitzah* lowered to allow women a roughly equal view of the happenings and the Holy Ark and the *bimah* positioned so that half of it is in each space. In these and other reconfigurations of the traditional synagogue, the *mechitzah* retains its role as controller of sexuality, even if women and men are now viewed more equally as subjects within this system of sexual control.

Control over sexuality has been discussed perhaps most fruitfully, in academic work, by the French philosopher Michel Foucault. In his *History of Sexuality* Foucault argues for a new, post-Freudian reading of the narrative that views modernity as having brought in its wake freedom from the Victorian restraints on sexuality. In Foucault's analysis, the modern period (writ more broadly to include the Victorian era) brought with it a new focus on individual sexuality, with people increasingly expected to submit to the required mechanisms of sexual confession. Our own era, which imagines itself more sexually liberated from the past, in fact has seen a continuation and even an intensification of this cultural imperative to sexually confess. As Foucault puts it, "Western man has been drawn for three centuries to the task of telling everything concerning his sex," and this confession, far from being a sexually repressive mechanism in the Victorian era, as opposed to the liberating function we imagine for it today, has always worked to create as well as control sexual forces: "this carefully analytic discourse [on sex] was meant to yield multiple effects of displacement, intensification, reorientation, and modification of desire itself."[1] Confession, in other words, generates as well as suppresses desire. Sexual confession, in Foucault's view, did not, or did not *only*, control sexuality by bringing it to the light of day. It was also itself sexual, multiplying and intensifying the variety and character of sexually charged human connections, and lending erotic excitation to a range of power relationships from doctor-patient, teacher-student, parent-child, and so on—any situation, in other words, where an authority figure might have an investment in the sexual behavior or thoughts of those under his or her control.

My own interest in Foucault's argument here is primarily in its structure; that is, I suggest that some of the mechanisms in traditional Jewish society—particularly the sexual segregation of Jewish ritual practice—have not been, or have not *only* been, mechanisms of sexual control but have also been mechanisms of "intensification, reorientation, and modification of desire itself." In other words, ostensible modes of sexual control and censorship such as the radical separation of men and women in various spheres are *productive of* rather than (only) suppressive of erotic connections—sexual segregation, like the requirement of telling about sex, incites desire, channels sexual energy, and creates new eroticized power relationships. The Old City apartment of the Red Heifer or the dormitories of Michlala were not devoid of eroticism—although they conformed to an ostensibly conservative ethos that segregated the sexes. On the contrary, they provided new avenues for the productive interplay between the religious and the erotic, precisely through the mechanism of sexual segregation.

Much more than Foucault's, my argument is vulnerable to at least two pitfalls: I worry that I am participating in what has been an apologetic discourse of Orthodox Judaism, which argues that tradition makes full use of such mechanisms as sexual segregation and "family purity" laws in order to increase marital attraction and thus stabilize families and maintain some ideal level of reproduction. That is, sexual segregation is productive of erotic energy not only in the homosocial sphere but also in the heteronormative sphere of family life. This discourse has often justified the continued marginalization of women and female sexuality, and I have no intention of contributing to this justification. An additional danger is that I am romanticizing or exoticizing tradition, as if it were organic, authentic, and free of the alienations and ruptures of modernity (for someone who considers herself to have "escaped" Orthodoxy, this would indeed be a partial view of my own experience of tradition). In fact, the strictest and most ramified forms of sexual segregation—as in the Hasidic court or the Lithuanian yeshiva—did not arise in some purely "traditional" realm, if such a realm could be discovered, but in the nineteenth century, and, one might argue, under the pressures of secularization and modernity.

The nineteenth century was a period in which intensely sexually segregated spaces, at least for men, increased and became more socially complex; it was also a time when various Jewish marriage and gender practices were radically reconceived. Modernity cast itself in the role of liberating Jewish youth from arranged marriages and, in its more advanced forms, freeing women from their second-class status. But the crises of modernization, immigration, and secularization had another effect: they also sharply narrowed the traditional erotic investment in community. Because the heterosexual couple and the nuclear family are, for modernity, both the site of primary erotic investment and the scene for the gender dialectic, they have become the template by which the traditional world is retrospectively judged; when traditional marriage is the sole focus of critique, other models of communal relationships are radically de-prioritized. Sexual orientation and gender roles have similarly determined the narrative we tell of tradition and its aftermath. The modern processes of delaying marriage, removing the marriage brokers and parents from the business of finding a spouse, and raising to an ideal the values of free choice, sexual attraction, and companionate marriage seem so clearly an improvement on the traditional arrangements for marriage and family life that the modernizers had no sense that these transformations also entailed a certain erotic loss. The sexual organization of traditional life, however, had another, complementary dimension: its homosocial structure. The traditional world offered a wide range of same-sex environments, each with its distinctive patterns of interaction, class or religious associations, and so on. Male domains such as yeshivas, study halls, bathhouses, synagogues, and the Hasidic court were all part of a ramified, single-sex socio-religious culture that supplemented, indeed sometimes supplanted, the mixed-sex spaces of home and marketplace. Less ramified but still important were the same-sex spaces for women, including the women's section of the synagogue (which once had a wider variety of functions than it does now) and perhaps also the cemetery and ritual bath. Once the erotic importance of this social configuration is acknowledged, the erotic consequences of modernity become more complicated to calibrate.

What does it mean to call sexual segregation, and the homosocial space, erotic? In Eve Kosofsky Sedgwick's use of the term "homosocial," the sexual component of the relationship is supplied by the rivalry of men for a female object of desire. In the traditional Jewish world, such a hetero-sexual triangulation is specifically ruled out, although it may appear sym-bolically through the introduction into the male sphere of such feminine figures as the Torah or the Sabbath or any number of religiously charged terms with a feminine valence. The eroticism is produced, or permitted, by the absence of members of the opposite sex, allowing for physical, emo-tional, and religious intimacies and connections forbidden in mixed groups —the shared ecstatic song and dance, common meals, and worship that is the peculiar genius of intensely religious or traditional societies. The ho-mosocial scene is erotic in another sense as well, insofar as the connections forged in such spaces are intimately linked with marital and family ties; the practice of arranged marriage (so excoriated by the Jewish modernizers) in fact often represented a heterosexual consummation of a bond contracted in a homosocial space—the yeshiva or Hasidic court, for example. In this traditional system, homosociality is both strictly separate from and richly productive of reproduction and kinship.

The particular erotic phenomena I trace here seem to be possible only in homosocial formations, even if these formations are ideologically jus-tified by sexual abstinence. The erotic power of the homosocial structure may lie less, however, in its single-sex character than in a derivative of this: in its transcendence of the limitations and borders that inevitably govern both the sexually linked couple and the family and kinship ties that grow from this link. It seems evident to me that these homosocial formations are vastly richer and more common in conservative rather than liberal re-ligious communities, traditional rather than modern Western groups, even if all societies continue to maintain sexually segregated spaces. Modernity recognizes the erotic forces it has let loose but not those it has consigned to history. In the literature and culture of post-traditional Jewish experi-ence, homosocial nostalgia—a sense of modernity as erotic loss—often nevertheless rises to the surface.

To restate my argument briefly: in moving to a heterosexual model of free romantic choice as the ultimate form of human erotic engagement, modernity sacrificed another form of Eros and did so largely unwittingly; given the modern understanding of sexuality, this loss is also discursively nearly incoherent. Modern sexual arrangements foreclosed the erotic spaces tradition had provided beyond the couple, and indeed beyond the individual, and weakened the internal attachments of the group whose sol-idarity was guaranteed by both external and internal forces—the Hasidic Rebbe, Torah, God, and tradition itself. Such social configurations were erotic both despite and because of their independence from individual character or "sexual orientation" and the vagaries of erotic attraction.

In the twentieth century the homosocial scene sometimes returned as a memory of some cultural dimension that had been forgotten or repressed. In such wildly popular Yiddish films as *Yidl mitn Fiddle* and others in Molly Picon's cinematic corpus, a young woman cross-dresses as a boy in order to play in an all-male klezmer band or, as in Isaac Bashevis Singer's short story "Yentl the Yeshiva Boy," to study in a yeshiva. There, the cross-dressed young woman meets an attractive young man, and the predictable romantic misunderstandings ensue. The short story and films have been read both as an exploration of Jewish gender roles and as evidence of the "queerness" of the Jewish erotic character. I suggest another reading: Yidl and Yentl each occupy an ambivalent space between the imperatives and conventions of the modern heterosexual romance and the lost and reimagined homosocial scene. The romances described in these cultural productions are made spicy by their religious and sexual transgressions, but they are also enriched by what is available only by sexual segregation: a camaraderie, equality, and authenticity that their writers imagine as native to the homosocial scene, and suspect is impossible in the spaces modernity has constructed for courtship and romance. In Singer's tale, after Yentl (who has taken on the male name Anshel) has confessed to Avigdor that she is a woman in disguise, their friendship becomes awkward: "their intimate talk, their confidences, had been turned into a sham and delusion," Avigdor feels. But soon enough the friends enjoy renewed intimacy:

> Gradually the two went back to their Talmudic conversation. It seemed strange at first to Avigdor to be disputing holy writ with a woman, yet before long the Torah reunited them. Though their bodies were different, their souls were of one kind. Anshel spoke in a singsong, gesticulated with her thumb, clutched her sidelocks, plucked at her beardless chin, made all the customary gestures of a yeshiva student. In the heat of argument she even seized Avigdor by the lapel and called him stupid. A great love for Anshel took hold of Avigdor, mixed with shame, remorse, anxiety. . . . For the first time he saw clearly that this was what he had always wanted: a wife whose mind was not taken up with material things.[2]

In cross-dressing fantasy, if nowhere else in the architecture of modernity, the erotics of the heterosexual and the homosocial can meet and marry.

My hypothesis that traditional sexual segregation had its erotic attractions may be bolstered, as well, by examples drawn not from the realm of literature but rather from sociology. Writers who document the recent trend of a "return" to tradition, and, in particular, the entry of secular, liberal, and feminist women to Orthodoxy and ultra-Orthodoxy (e.g., Lynn Davidman, Sharon Balcove, and Debra Kaufman), speak of this as a puzzling if not paradoxical phenomenon. Writing of feminists who have joined Hasidic groups, Kaufman asks:

> What maintains these women's commitments to a past not of their own making and to a patriarchal present? How can one conclude that these women's lives are anything but oppressive and "alienated"?[3]

Kaufman answers her own questions partly by recourse to the answers provided by the subjects of her research, the newly Hasidic women themselves, who represent themselves as the guardians of community tradition in the face of a materialistic and self-indulgent dominant culture. Comparing these women's words to those of other women in the Religious Right, Kaufman concludes that Orthodox Judaism, along with "evangelical theology and institutions, may be flexible resources for renegotiating gender and family relationships."[4]

The puzzlement Kaufman feels about Hasidic women, though, would only be heightened for the significant numbers of Jewish lesbians who join the traditional world, since Orthodoxy is at least as homophobic as it is patriarchal; nor is it clear what it might mean for lesbians rather than heterosexual women to renegotiate family relationships within an Orthodox context. The power of homosocial desire, perhaps particularly within the post-traditional culture of East European Jews, may provide a key to the attractions of the traditional world for women of a variety of sexual, political, and cultural "orientations." Feminism, from one point of view, can be seen as a political-epistemological cousin to homosocial desire; it is at least possible, then, that conservative Orthodox communities, with their complex homosocial structures, satisfy one particular aspect of feminist desire—what was referred to, in an earlier time, as "sisterhood." The relationship of homosexual and homosocial desire may be more complex, but I would caution against the assumption that homosocial desire is a "cover" for the deeper or more profound dimension of sexual orientation. Our social desires may be as profound as our sexual ones, and certainly as deep as our political stances; they may also be productive of sexual orientation or political affiliation. The paradox sociologists confront in the phenomenon of the turn to conservative religious communities may be no paradox at all: it may be patriarchal traditions, segregating the sexes in the name of sexual control, that still best produce and shelter homosocial communities, and thus satisfy homosocial desire. In Jerusalem I felt the force of that desire, and now, in Berkeley, I feel the force of its loss.

NOTES

1. Michel Foucault, *History of Sexuality*, Vol. 1, *An Introduction*, trans. Robert Hurley (New York: Random House, 1980 [1976]), 23.

2. Isaac Bashevis Singer, "Yentl the Yeshiva Boy," in idem, *The Collected Stories* (New York: Farrar, Straus and Giroux, 1983), 165.

3. Debra Kaufman, "Engendering Orthodoxy: Newly Orthodox Women and Hasidism," in *New World Hasidism: Ethnographic Studies of Hasidic Jews in America*, ed. Janet S. Belcove-Shlain (Albany: State University of New York Press, 1995), 151.

4. Ibid., 152.

8

Reclaiming *Nidah* and *Mikveh* through Ideological and Practical Reinterpretation

Haviva Ner-David

THE TRADITIONAL JEWISH approach to heterosexuality encourages giving and receiving sexual pleasure, but only within certain boundaries. Once one complies with these restrictions, sex is not only allowed but is a *mitzvah*, a Divine commandment. For instance, sex between certain partners, such as sister and brother, father and daughter, or a man and woman not married to each other, is forbidden. Once a heterosexual couple is married, however, sex is obligatory. Nevertheless, even within the marital relationship, sex is not permitted *all* of the time.

In the book of Leviticus, we are introduced to a complex set of laws regarding *tumah*, imperfectly translated as "ritual impurity." *Tumah* is contracted primarily from various physical phenomena, such as eating non-kosher animals, coming in contact with a corpse or a rodent, becoming ill with leprosy, or experiencing certain bodily emissions. One also contracts *tumah* secondarily by coming in contact with another person who became *tameh* from a primary source.

When a woman contracts *tumah* because of a uterine flow of blood, whether her regular menstruation or some other irregular bleeding, sex with her and by her is forbidden. The first place this issue arises, in Leviticus 15:19–33, appears in the context of a discussion of ritual impurity contracted from both male and female bodily emissions. One of the emissions that cause ritual impurity, or *tumah*, is menstrual blood. A woman who has contracted ritual impurity from a flow of menstrual blood is called a *nidah*. *Tumat nidah*, the *tumah* of a *nidah*, can be transferred further through contact between the *nidah* and other people, utensils, clothing, and food; contact with objects the woman sits or lies upon; and by the act of sexual intercourse.

Although sexual intercourse transfers *tumah*, these verses do not indicate that intercourse itself is forbidden. Still, we learn that a man who has sexual intercourse with a woman in *nidah* becomes *tameh*, ritually impure, to the same degree of severity that she was *t'meah*. He, too, becomes *tameh* for seven days.

In two other biblical passages, however, we do find a prohibition on sexual intercourse with a woman in *nidah*. The context of these two verses, Leviticus 18:19 and 20:18, is a list of forbidden acts (many of them sexual) that, if performed, prevent one from becoming *kadosh*, or holy. Although *tumah* may be contracted in various ways, including via seminal emissions and contact with the dead, only the *tumah* of uterine blood carries with it a sexual prohibition. Sexual intercourse with and by a *nidah* is punishable with *karet*, which has been interpreted by the Rabbis to mean either excommunication or death by the hands of God.

Even though it is forbidden to sleep with a menstruant, Leviticus does not stipulate that it is forbidden to contract *tumah*. Moreover, the status of *tumah* is temporary and reversible. A woman who is a *nidah* is *t'meah* only for seven days, after which she automatically exits her ritually impure status.

The Bible states that one who contracts *tumat nidah* secondarily must wash. Proper washing was interpreted by the Rabbis to mean immersion in a collection of water called a *mikveh*, which means either a natural body of water such as a spring, lake, or ocean, or, if that is not possible, in a man-made pit filled with rainwater or a ritual bath. The Rabbis also required the *nidah* herself to immerse, since they assumed that if one who contracts *tumah* from a woman must wash, so, obviously, must she, even though the biblical text makes no such explicit requirement.

In other words, from the time a woman experiences uterine flow (whether it be her regular menstrual or some other irregular flow) until she immerses properly and timely in a *mikveh* (a man-made ritual bath or a natural spring, lake, river or ocean) sex between even a married man and woman is forbidden. This regimen of sexual separation and reunion is commonly referred to in Jewish religious circles as the practice of "family purity."

An approach to sexuality within marriage that limits permissible sex to only certain times during the month can be a positive or a negative influence not only on the couple's sex life but on their relationship in general, depending on the couple's spiritual and emotional attitude toward this sexual regimen. For instance, if they see their time apart as an opportunity to give each other individual space within the marriage, or as a time when they can strengthen their nonsexual connection, this regimen can be a healthy and beneficial one. If, however, they view their time apart as a curse or a challenge that they cannot possibly meet, then they set themselves up for failure and for a sexual relationship wrought with tension and guilt. Similarly, if the man perceives his wife to be repulsive or a potential source of sin when she is ritually impure (*t'meah*), this is also a recipe for emotional and psychological disaster. The same applies to the woman's attitude about herself, her biology, and her body. Experiencing her body when she is *t'meah* as dirty or dangerous or the potential source of sin can cause deeply ingrained negative attitudes about herself, her body, and her sexuality.

Yet consciously constructing a psychologically positive ideological approach toward the practice of family purity is not enough. Even if the couple communicates an approach to these sexual separations that is about strengthening their emotional bond together rather than focusing on the woman's forbidden sexuality, certain specific practices within this larger framework will continue to send messages that contradict their ideology. Therefore, while it is vital to stress to couples who practice this sexual regimen the importance of healthy, balanced, egalitarian interpretations of this way of life, it would be irresponsible to do so without encouraging them to make changes within their actual praxis itself so that the ritual reflects their ideological viewpoint.

Sex and Impurity

As the term "family purity" suggests, this set of laws and ritual impurity are strongly connected. A woman's sexual status is determined by her *tumah* status. As noted, when she is *t'meah*, sex by and with her is forbidden, and when she is *t'horah* (in a state of ritual purity), it is permitted. Thus, as soon as she emerges from the *mikveh*, her *tumah* status is reversed and therefore so is her sexual status. Yet, worth noting is that the connection between *tumah* and the modern practice of these laws is not axiomatic.

According to the Bible, a person who is *tameh* (ritually impure) may not enter the Tabernacle, the portable and temporary sacred space that the Jews carried with them in the desert when they left Egypt. Later, when the Jews entered the Land of Israel, a ritually impure person could not worship in the permanent Holy Temple in Jerusalem.

When the Second Temple was destroyed, most practices relating to ritual purity and impurity fell into disuse; with no Temple, *tumah* in general became irrelevant. With no holy space, *tumah* had no practical ramifications.

Although people may have avoided contracting *tumah* because being *tameh* had ramifications in Temple times, they were never forbidden to become *tameh;* rather, *tumah* was apparently a natural part of life in Temple times. Moreover, although they may have tried to reverse their *tameh* state as quickly as possible, they were not forbidden to remain in this state as long as they did not enter the Temple precinct. Therefore, when the Temple was destroyed, although *kohanim* (priests) were still biblically prohibited from contracting *tumah*, the common Jew had no reason for concern in this regard.

However, the rituals connected to one type of *tumah*—that of impurity contracted from uterine blood flows—were kept alive by all Jews after the Temple's destruction, because, unlike other *tumah* states that contain no sexual prohibition, this particular type of *tumah* remained relevant precisely because of its related sexual prohibition.[1] Though it may be logical, the fact that this *tumah* ritual is still enforced *en masse* today has negatively influenced both men's and women's perception of women and their bodies. Because all *tumah* ideology and associations after the Temple's destruction have focused on the bleeding woman, today only women are perceived to even have the biological capacity to become ritually impure.

Since the destruction of the Temple, the *tumah* state a woman enters as a result of menstruation has been interpreted in misogynistic ways. Jewish scholars and authorities, as well as the mass Jewish culture, have understood it as being a lower spiritual state, connected to filth and danger, and antithetical to the holy. These characteristics have, in turn, been associated with women in general, regardless of their state, because all women are potential bleeders. Defining all women as *t'meot* (with all the connotations that status implies) for a significant part of each month has, conveniently (for the men who have had the power to disseminate these negative interpretations of women's *tumah*), reinforced the patriarchal power structure that gives these men their power.

We cannot escape the integral connection between *tumah* and the laws surrounding menstruation. A woman's sexual status depends on her *tumah* status. Moreover, *tumah* ideology and language is still integral to the way these rituals are understood and expressed. In addition to the common usage of the term "family purity," most current manuals on the practice of these laws use *tumah* terminology, and some *mikveh* attendants even refer to a woman as *t'horah* (ritually pure) after she immerses properly in the *mikveh*. This continual use of *tumah* terminology in itself is not harmful, but without positive feminist reinterpretations of *tumah* dominating the general social consciousness, applying *tumah* terminology in the context of a modern-day woman in this state can be extremely damaging.

However, though it is useless to deny the inherent connection between *tumah* and these laws and practices, we can influence the way this *tumah* status is understood and experienced in our modern reality. On the one hand, men have interpreted its history in misogynist ways that have caused harm to women's perceptions of themselves as both physical and spiritual beings. On the other hand, however, these rituals focus on the woman and her body and therefore have the potential, when interpreted in positive, feminist ways, to be the source of spiritual expression and fulfillment for women.

One way to do this is to promote feminist interpretations of what it means to be *t'meah* from a uterine flow. We must also promote similarly positive interpretations of the rituals connected to these laws, such as *mikveh* immersion, internal vaginal checks to determine the cessation of the blood flow, and a limited curbing of sexual interaction within a long-term intimate relationship. Of course, these interpretations should not be apologetic but rather transparently critical of previous misogynist rabbinic interpretations while presenting new approaches that truly speak to our modern feminist sensibilities.

An interpretation I personally have adopted stems from one meaning of the root of the word "*tumah*." In rabbinic usage, the term *mitamtem* means to block. In tractate *Pesahim* 42a, a fatty dairy food is said to block (*mitamtem*) the heart, and in tractate *Yoma* 39a, sin is said to block (*mitamtem*) the heart. In this latter source, the midrash actually uses as a proof text Leviticus 11:43. The context is forbidden foods, and the author of the midrash does a word play on *timtum* and *tumah*. Rabbinic literature thus draws a connection between *tumah* and blockage.

I have found that this is one way I relate to being *t'meah* from my uterine flow. It is a time when I feel generally more closed within myself, less open to giving to and receiving from others. This is one way of being blocked, of setting clearer boundaries. When I am *t'meah*, the side of me that sets boundaries is stronger. And though this may close me off in certain ways, even spiritually, setting boundaries is a necessary part of being able to function in my relationship with my husband Jacob in particular, but also in all my relationships. In fact, setting boundaries is a necessary part of being able to function in the world.

Something works for me in the together/apart cycle inherent in the *nidah* ritual. It speaks to my need to balance the two sides of myself that are both strong but also seemingly contradictory: my willing side and my willful side, my open side and my closed side, my externally-directed side and my internally-directed side, my giving side and my boundary-building side.

Living a life conscious of *tumah* and *taharah* is about being aware of these two sides of myself and making room for them to exist simultaneously in my life. Sometimes my *tumah* side is dominant, and at other times my *taharah* side is dominant. This is fine, as long as each is given its appropriate time to dominate.

This manifests itself in a literal way in my relationship with my husband. When I am in this *t'meah* state, I am less open to him, at least in a physical way. My physical boundaries influence the general energy I project. And when I am *t'horah*, I must send off signals that are more willing and available in general. We all fluctuate in our degrees of readiness to give and receive. But what this rhythm does is regulate these swings so that they do not go out of control in either direction.

While it may be harder for my husband to deal with the side of me that is boundary-building, and also more difficult for him during these times, he loves me even then. That is important for me to know.

It is not as though when I am in *nidah* (when I have my period) I am always closed and self-absorbed, and when I am not, always open and giving. But perhaps I *am* more in one direction than the other depending on my *nidah* status. Maybe when I am *t'meah*, I have permission to be more closed, and when I am *tehorah*, I am more open. But I think the cycle is less literal for me. I believe it is about recognizing that I have both these elements within me, and that this is okay, as long as they are balanced in a way that is beneficial to my growth. Just as too much willfullness can be bad, so, too, can too much willingness. The two must learn to make room for each other at the proper time.

This is especially compelling for me when I am trying to conceive. When my period comes, I turn inward. I am disappointed, even saddened, by the loss of potential life inside me. I may even become resentful. I need my space to grieve, and that is what I get—days and days of *tumah* space. And then, when the time comes to return to the *tehorah* state, I welcome immersion in water as a way to transition from one state to another. I return to the womb, to that safe fluid space where everything and anything seems possible, and I am filled once again with hope. My spirit is renewed. I am reborn, refreshed, and ready to try again. I am open to receive God's blessings or to be hurt once again.

This is one aspect of what it means for me to be in a state of *tumah* from my uterine flow. I am sure the experience is different for other women. We are all entitled to our own private meanings. But for this ritual to survive in an authentic and sincere way, it is our responsibility as women to reclaim this ritual and reinterpret it, express what it means for us in the twenty-first century to be *t'meot* from our uterine blood. For too long we have let men tell us what this means. Menstruating women have been seen in rabbinic sources as dangerous, filthy, sinful, and profane as a result of their *tumah*. It is time we take matters into our own hands.

However, although these types of reinterpretation make these separations meaningful, even empowering, to the modern, feminist woman, this is clearly not enough. The current practice and application of the traditional "family purity" laws are often unnecessarily degrading to women in a basic way. For this reason I propose an approach that combines changing both ideology and praxis. It is not enough to promote a feminist reinterpretation of "family purity" while continuing to practice rituals that perpetuate the message that a woman who is *t'meah* (ritually impure) from her uterine flow is spiritually inferior, dirty, or dangerous. It is not enough to say that these laws are meant to improve the marital bond if the onus of their application is exclusively on the woman.

In the remainder of this chapter, I share a few changes I have made in my own practice of "family purity" so that my praxis more accurately mirrors my ideology. But first, a few words about these laws, their biblical origins, and their rabbinic development.

Biblical versus Rabbinic Practice

In Leviticus 15 the *nidah* is juxtaposed with the *zavah*, a woman who experiences a discharge longer than seven days or not at the regular time of her menstrual flow. When her blood flow stops, she then counts another seven bloodless "clean" days and brings a sacrificial offering before she can resume worship in the Temple. Considering that the *zavah* is experiencing an abnormal, unexpected flow of blood from her uterus, it is understandable that the Bible requires her to adopt a wait-and-see approach, unlike the approach required of the *nidah*, who is experiencing her regular menstrual period. The *nidah* exits her *t'meah* state as soon as seven days (the period of time that the Bible apparently considers the outermost range of normal for a menstrual flow) have passed since the first day of her flow. (It is important to note that the rabbinic interpretation of the Bible forbids intercourse with a *zavah* as well as a *nidah*.)

The Bible clearly distinguishes between the *nidah*, the woman with a regular menstrual flow, and the *zavah*, the woman with an irregular menstrual flow. The *nidah*, according to biblical law, is automatically in a state of *tumah* for seven days from the time she starts bleeding, as long as her flow lasts for seven days or fewer. If her flow lasts for more than seven days, or if she bleeds for three days or more during a time when she is not expecting her regular period, she is a *zavah* and must wait until her flow stops and then count seven "clean days" before she can resume relations.

In the late mishnaic period, the *nidah* was conflated with the *zavah*. According to rabbinic law, any woman who bleeds from her uterus—whether it is during the time she expects her period or whether it is for one day, three days, or fourteen days—must wait a minimum of four or five days (depending on whether one is Sephardic or Ashkenzic in origin) and then perform an internal check to determine that the bleeding has in fact stopped and then wait seven clean days before she immerses in the *mikveh* and resumes sexual relations. In other words, rabbinic law turned a healthy menstruating woman into a sickly woman experiencing an irregular flow.

What does this say about the way the Rabbis view the bleeding woman? If all women are *zavot*, then our bleeding is not normal; it is infirm, irregular, dangerous, frightening, and even threatening. In short, it is unnatural.

This stricture mostly came, apparently, as a reaction to and categorization of women's menstrual blood as dangerous and abnormal. Men conflated these two very different experiences because of their lack of ability to relate to the idea that blood can flow, even in seemingly large amounts, and not be a cause for concern. In fact, the Rabbis may have been influenced by the Zoroastrians, who saw all uterine blood as a cause for concern. My guess is that the Rabbis' thinking went something like this: Wouldn't we men be better off if all women wait a week before we enter their dark, bloody places again? Let's wait until we are sure the coast is clear and all blood is gone before we even go near them again!

But women live with this blood. We know the difference.

Then what does it mean when we are told in the Talmud[2] that it was the "Daughters of Israel" who took this stringency upon themselves? In this same Talmudic source, we learn that it was Rabbi Yehudah HaNasi, the compiler of the Mishnah, who initiated this move toward conflating *nidah* with *zivah* when he made the timing of the blood flow a non-issue. With his edict, it no longer mattered whether the flow occurred when a woman was expecting her period; all blood was treated as the strictest scenario. In fact, the *gemara* also refers to "the Rabbis" as being the ones who put all bleeding women into the category of *safek zavot*, "presumed *zavot*."

But it was the women themselves, *B'not Yisrael*, "the Daughters of Israel," who took upon themselves the final stricture that they would wait seven clean days even for a drop of blood. According to this source, it was the women who made the amount of blood and number of days of the flow a non-issue.

I can understand how women may have wanted to make their lives easier by cooperating with an approach that creates one rule for all bleeding. Convenience is a strong motivating factor when it comes to ritual and law. Alternatively, perhaps these women saw this act as a form of birth control. At the time of the Talmud, the common belief was that a woman was most fertile right after she stops bleeding. In their eyes, tacking on seven more days of abstinence would have decreased the chances of conception. Or this could have been an act of independence in another way: lengthening this period could have been a way for these women to abstain from sexual relations with their husbands at a time when women did not have much power or free choice in their marital relationships.

This is all conjecture, of course. We can never know why the Daughters of Israel cooperated with the Rabbis in their move toward stricture in this area, or even if it is true historically that the women cooperated at all. In any case, treating all women today as presumed *zavot* takes this matter out of women's hands. It is a way of saying that women cannot be trusted to judge when their blood flow is normal or abnormal. Even if the rabbinic model is simpler to follow, it disempowers women and creates a situation in which all uterine blood—whether or not the result of a normal menstrual period—is treated as an infirmity. Even if women in Talmudic times did, in fact, see a benefit in adding an extra seven clean days after a normal menstrual period, it is difficult for women in the twenty-first century to relate to this move. The question therefore is this: Must we continue to toe the rabbinic line in this area, or can we take back the power to identify our own blood?

Early on in my married life I decided I could live with the rabbinic version of these laws. I could tolerate in all cases waiting the extra seven days in order not to break with this long-standing rabbinic tradition. I could even find benefits in keeping a longer period of sexual abstinence. After all, absence does make the heart grow fonder. So, if our sex life would be enhanced by one week of abstinence, how much more so would it be by a two-week waiting period!

But mostly my decision to stay within the rabbinic framework was because I did not feel that straying from the tradition and the communal norm was justified in my case. I did not consider it an unbearable sacrifice to wait those extra seven days, and I had convinced myself that perhaps the women did indeed cooperate for a good reason.

But that was before I discovered the shocking phenomenon called "halakhic infertility," in which a woman who keeps the extra seven days ovulates before the time when she is eligible to go to the *mikveh*, therefore missing her chance to conceive. As women age, their periods generally tend to be shorter and their ovulation time earlier. Therefore halakhic infertility is even more common now, since today women are having children later in life than ever before.

The common "treatment" of halakhic infertility is to delay ovulation with hormones. If that doesn't work, artificial insemination is used; the rationale is that sexual intercourse is forbidden, not inserting sperm into a woman's cervix. On the one hand, these seem the easiest, most practical solutions to the problem. On the other hand, however, these women are not sick; there is nothing wrong with them. Their menstrual cycle simply does not jive with the requirements of rabbinic law. Here, the crucial question is whether it is the women's cycles or the *halakhah* that is the problem.

Apparently rabbinic authorities prefer manipulating a woman's cycle with hormones, or even inserting her husband's sperm in a medical procedure, rather than creating a halakhic solution. With the biblical principle of *pru urvu* ("be fruitful and multiply") pitted against the rabbinic principle of treating normal menstruation like abnormal bleeding, how can rabbinic authorities make the latter a higher priority—especially when the Torah makes a clear distinction between *nidah* and *zavah* and how each should be treated?

Why do modern-day rabbinic authorities like Rabbi Moshe Feinstein maintain the rabbinic conflation of *nidah* with *zivah* even in a case where the woman would not be able to conceive naturally otherwise? The reason Rabbi Feinstein gives in his own responsum[3] is that in a case like this one where the punishment for transgressing the biblical prohibition of having intercourse with (or as) a *nidah* or *zavah* is so serious—*karet* (being cut off from the Jewish people or death at the hands of God)—we do not wave even a rabbinic aspect of this set of regulations, even when it clashes with a strong biblical commandment like "be fruitful and multiply!" Is this formalistic answer what is truly at the heart of his decision? What can we read between the lines of his answer? What is he really saying as he protects this law so vehemently, even at the expense of these women? It seems that he is afraid that if this rabbinic enactment falls, all of tradition, all of Torah as we know it, will fall. But why? What is so precious about these seven clean days? Why are legal decisors today so attached to treating all bleeding women as *zavot*?

Perhaps our modern-day rabbis are still uneasy about the idea of having intercourse with a woman right after she has stopped bleeding. They want those seven extra clean days as a safety net to ensure that she is indeed blood-free before they enter her; or perhaps they still can't relate to the idea that menstruation is a totally natural phenomenon that is not a reflection of something wrong with a woman or her body.

Or maybe rabbinic decisors are unwilling to bend on this issue because it means trusting women to differentiate between normal and abnormal bleeding, and they are unwilling to put that power into women's hands—especially because the biblical punishment for both the women and their husbands is so severe if they do end up having intercourse at the wrong time.

Or, could it be that they are simply protecting the status quo in general? They may be assuming that if they bend on this issue, the whole hierarchical system, which places rabbis at the top, laymen below them, and women below them, will fall apart, and with that, the entire religion will crumble. It is also possible that they feel that a change such as this in Jewish practice would create too much of a rupture with the past, with tradition, and with the textual sources, and would therefore create an atmosphere of *laissez faire halakhah* that could end up destroying Torah as we know it.

As I examined all these possible explanations, I wondered if I could continue to keep the seven clean days. Perhaps these rabbis are correct. Maybe instituting such a change could threaten Torah as we know it. Was I prepared to preserve the halakhic system at all costs? Was I willing to cooperate with a halakhic system that claims the need to preserve tradition by sacrificing its women? And is this even a system worth preserving?

I believe that both the Rabbis and the women in Talmudic times would have seen things differently had they known what we know today: that many women have short menstrual cycles and therefore ovulate within the seven days after their bleeding stops. A woman's chances to conceive are limited to only about three to five days a month—the day (or two) before ovulation, the day of ovulation, and the day (or two) after ovulation.

If women actually took this stricture upon themselves as a form of birth control at a time when birth was a life-threatening experience, then our reality has changed significantly enough in this area for this stricture to no longer apply. Today, with other forms of birth control, and the kind of medical care that keeps most Western women from dying in childbirth, it would be absurd to keep this stricture in place for this reason.

As much as I try to understand these Daughters of Israel, I must either believe that their experience of menstruation and childbirth was so different from mine that they were willing to push this rabbinic stricture even further, or I have to believe that this is simply untrue, that what is recorded in the *gemara* is not historical truth but rather one version of what happened—and a male version at that!

Thus I feel justified in my decision to stop keeping these seven clean days when I know I am experiencing *nidah*, normal menstruation. I tell myself that both the Rabbis and the Daughters of Israel had no idea that their strict approach would limit the number of Jewish souls brought into this world and cause women who want children to suffer as a result. Since rabbinic authorities today are unwilling to stand up for halakhically infertile women, we must take this matter into our own hands.

In fact, Jewish women in medieval Egypt did just that.[4] We don't know why, but they decided *en masse* to return to the biblical laws of *nidah* and treat their menstrual blood as the Bible stipulates. Like these medieval women, we must follow our own consciences and do the same. We must take back this woman's ritual and reclaim the right to name our own blood. In so doing, we will reinterpret the ritual, turning it into a way to connect to our biological cycle rather than being alienated from it.

The Distancing Laws

In addition to the biblical prohibition on sexual intercourse, the Rabbis developed an elaborate set of *harchakot* (literally, "distancing practices") designed to keep the husband and wife separate when she is in *nidah* so they will not be tempted into sexual intercourse. Some of these include not touching, not sitting together on a couch or bench, not passing things to each other, not eating from the plate of a *nidah*, and not sitting on her bed.

Even when my husband and I were passionate newlyweds, the idea that we needed these rules—imposed from the outside—to keep our passions in check was difficult for us to accept. It made sense to refrain from intimate physical contact. But the notion that we would not touch at all, not pass objects to each other, that my husband would not eat from my dish, drink from my cup, or sit on my side of the bed—those restrictions seemed extreme and even irrelevant or inappropriate to us and our relationship. We knew how to draw the line between loving intimacy and sex.

Moreover, these laws offended me as a woman. Aside from their underlying assumption that people could not control their sexual appetites, the distancing of the menstruating woman had, in my view, misogynist connotations. These *harchakot* felt like *tumah*-avoidance practices, even though the Temple has long been gone and contracting *tumah* should no longer be of concern. For while the Bible explicitly forbids sexual intercourse with a *nidah*, necessitating that a woman is conscious of her status vis-à-vis *tumah* and ritually immerses after experiencing a uterine flow if she wants to be sexually active, there is no reason for others to avoid contracting her *tumah*.

With no Temple, there are no practical ramifications to contracting *tumah* in general. The sexual prohibiton aspect of *tumat nidah* applies only to the woman herself—the original source of the *tumah*. These distancing practices reminded me of cootie games we used to play in elementary school.

Certain of these practices brought out these negative feelings in me more than others. Among them was the idea that the husband is forbidden to sit on the wife's bed but not vice versa, and that the husband is forbidden to eat from the wife's dish but not the other way around. The proscription against the couple sitting on the same bench or couch also aroused *tumah* associations for me, because it evoked the biblical passages about how *tumat nidah* is transferred through sitting and laying.

Despite arguments in various *nidah* books and manuals I read before I got married that the *harchakot* are only about preventing sexual arousal and have nothing whatsoever to do with *tumah*-avoidance (they rationalize the one-sidedness of some of these prohibitions by saying that a man's sex drive is stronger than a woman's), I was not convinced. No matter what the official reason for these distancing practices, they sent me the message that a menstruating woman should be kept at a distance because of something negative about her—whether one calls it *tumah* or danger or her repulsive blood.

I began the research for my doctoral dissertation on the relationship between *tumah* and *nidah* and discovered that *harchakot* originated in Talmudic times. As long as the Temple was around and *tumah* was generally a practical issue, there was no need for these rabbinic *harchakot*. Natural revulsion against *tumah*, coupled with practical reasons to avoid it, kept the man away from his *nidah* wife as much as practically possible.

However, once *tumah* in general became irrelevant, the Rabbis of the Talmud felt a need to institute certain restrictions upon spousal interaction when the wife was *t'meah* from a uterine flow in order to keep the woman at bay. This was not needed before the Talmud, as *tumah*-avoidance practices had this same desired effect.

But because *nidah* was the only *tumah*-related practice still being observed *en masse*, certain communities continued to maintain some *tumat-nidah*-avoidance practices as a holdover from Temple times. In fact, some communities in the Land of Israel were keeping even stricter *harchakot* that clearly connoted *tumah*-avoidance—such as not walking behind a *nidah*, not eating from food she prepared, not letting her near holy objects—and were probably related to the fact that *tumah* continued to be of concern longer in Israel than it did in Babylonia. Further, some major medieval halakhic authorities perpetuated the forms of *tumah*-avoidance practices in order to safeguard the sexual prohibition related to *nidah*. This alone would not have been so terrible. But by perpetuating these forms, these halakhic authorities also perpetuated the notion that women in *nidah* had to be avoided because of their repulsive *tumah* status.

Layers of folk customs and reinforcement of these customs by halakhic authorities, plus a general approach that stringent behavior in this area is always commendable, resulted in our current system of *harchakot*—which most certainly can be experienced as alienating the woman in *nidah* on some level.

This relates not only to the interaction between husband and wife when she is in *nidah*; despite the clear lack of a halakhic basis, a host of strong customs are in place that distance women in *nidah* from sacred objects and sacred space. For example, it is thought that a *nidah* should not touch a Torah scroll and, in some communities, not even enter the synagogue.

These and other similar folk customs have been reinforced by major halakhic authorities—such as the *Rema*, Rabbi Moshe Isserles, who wrote the authoritative Ashkenazi gloss on the sixteenth-century law code the *Shulkhan Aruch*—and they are, surprisingly, perpetuated to this day. Reportedly rabbis of modern congregations tell their female practitioners that women can have a Torah scroll to dance with on *Simchat Torah* on the condition that menstruating women not touch it! No wonder certain *harchakot* elicited these emotions in me and reminded me of the tactics of elementary school cootie games. It was no accident that they echoed *tumah*-avoidance practices, because it was upon these practices that some of the *harchakot* were based.

While the period a *nidah* is sexually forbidden is determined by her *tumah* status, now that there is no longer a Temple standing, there should no longer exist a concern about contracting her *tumah*, since the only consequence of a man contracting *tumah* was that he could not worship in the Temple while *tameh*. Although it is important today to be aware of when a woman is *t'meah* from a uterine flow, this is only in order to determine her sexual status. There is no practical reason to avoid her out of fear of contracting her *tumah*.

As I untangled the complex nature of the system of *harchakot* and its connections to *tumah*-avoidance practices, I felt vindicated for my original intuitive reactions to these laws. However, I continued to feel that there was some wisdom in the Talmudic attempt to draw the line at a place other than actual sexual intercourse. And so although Jacob and I continue to refrain from sexual intercourse and even foreplay when I am *t'meah*, we do not keep any of the *harchakot* relating to normal daily interaction not connected to sex. In other words, anything we would feel comfortable doing in public together, we do even in private when I am in *nidah*. Anything we would feel uncomfortable doing in public we refrain from doing even in private when I am in *nidah*. That is our measure.

When counseling couples on the observance of "family purity," I encourage them to decide where they personally feel the need to draw the line in their intimate physical interaction in order to avoid being sexually aroused. I stress that this and only this consideration (not *tumah*-avoidance) should be the determining factor. I advocate that they discard any *harchakot* that imply *tumah*-avoidance, especially those that seem to be carryovers from actual *tumah*-avoidance practices, such as not eating from one's wife's leftovers when she is in *nidah* or not sitting on her bed. Enforcing such notions, and reinforcing them through practice, only perpetuates the faulty notion that *tumat nidah* and *tumat zavah* must avoided in our post-Temple reality. As long as this idea remains in the social consciousness, women will continue to be negatively associated with *tumah* and all that is antithetical, even dangerous, to the holy.

The laws of *nidah* have their basis in the laws of *tumah* and *taharah*, but this in no way implies that a woman who is *t'meah* from *nidah* should be alienated or avoided. Retaining any practices that imply otherwise will only serve to perpetuate misogynist ideology and inhibits a fully loving relationship between husband and wife. Sending a message that one's sexual partner must be avoided because of something essentially negative about her for half the couple's life together can be potentially harmful to their general physical and emotional relationship. It makes sense, therefore, not only to try and limit the period of time when she is off-limits but to try to make these periods of sexual abstinence as normal as possible.

Mikveh Immersion

Once a woman has waited the correct number of days and checked to ensure that she is no longer bleeding, she should immerse in the *mikveh* in order to reverse her *tumah* status. Immersion was always, for me, the highlight of my experience of the practice of this traditional regimen. As a "water person" who swims laps every day, I have, since my first dunk in the ritual bath, loved the feeling of total immersion in the "living waters" of the *mikveh*. The feeling of renewal and transformation that this ritual evokes for me is spiritually powerful time and time again. Yet I always felt that something was lacking in my immersion experience. Only after two successive miscarriages at the age of thirty-six, after trying for more than a year to conceive, did I discover what I was missing. Though feeling vulnerable at this time, I was also open to bringing something new to my experience of *mikveh*, something that would bring more balance into this ritual practice. I felt a need to ask my husband to immerse along with me.

This seemed an appropriate request before we resumed our sexual relationship, since, after all, he was just as *tameh* as I was—not only from contracting my *tumah* (by sitting on a chair that I had sat on, for instance) but also from other forms of *tumah*, such as *tumah* contracted from seminal emissions. This way, we could both come back together in a state of ritual purity. Although I was well aware that the sexual prohibition attached to the *nidah* applies only to a woman's *tumah* status, the notion of us reuniting in a state of mutual *taharah* appealed to my longing for balance between Jacob and me in relation to this *mitzvah*, as well as for a more general gender balance in the world.

Moreover, when I immersed alone in the *mikveh*, I had difficulty turning my intention away from my desire for another child. I had been trying to focus on my marital relationship instead of my fertility issues while immersing—a powerful change for me—but after yet another miscarriage I knew this would be more challenging.

If Jacob were there with me it would be different. His presence would help me shift the focus of my immersion from my own biology to something positive and enduring, something that went beyond my frustrations with pregnancy to my and Jacob's everlasting love.

I was not looking to replace the ritual as a celebration and mark of my menstrual cycle. This was an important aspect of my immersion experience; dunking beneath the living waters was precious to me. Yet now I was looking to add a new dimension to my monthly immersions. I wanted this ritual to take on new meanings as I felt my life moving into a new phase.

Since the men's and women's *mikvaot* are separate and not open at the same times of day—the women's is open at night, and the men's during the day—and since a major reason for asking Jacob to immerse was that I wanted us to immerse together, our only option was to go to a natural spring, pool, river, lake, or the ocean.

So on the night of the seventh clean day after my blood flow stopped (I was clearly a *zavah* in the case of a miscarriage that was certainly not a regular menstrual flow), my husband and I set out to *Ein Halavan*, literally, the "White Spring," about a fifteen-minute drive from our home, with beautiful views of the Jerusalem hills.

At *Ein Halavan* the water comes from an underground source. There are two springs, one shallow and one deep. This is one of Jerusalem's answers to a watering hole, and people flock to this and other similar pools in the heat of the summer. But this was not the heat of the summer; it was March. And although the days were warm, the nights were cold. When we arrived at *Ein Halavan*, towels in hand, it was dark. It was *Rosh Hodesh Nisan*, the beginning of the month, and though the moon was only a sliver, the stars were bright. They looked bigger than usual, giving the impression that we were closer to the heavens.

After I immersed in the nippy waters, I watched Jacob immerse. And as I watched, his immersion felt to me like a way to repair the damage that had been perpetuated throughout all the years that *tumah*-related rituals, aside from *nidah*, had fallen into disuse, and only women became associated with *tumah*. By insisting that men also immerse before a couple can sexually reunite—rather than suggesting that *mikveh* immersion be perceived as being only about the woman's purification—it can become a ritual about the couple's purification for each other, and the renewing of their romantic relationship.

It was hard for me to believe that I had been going to a regular *mikveh*, alone, for all these years. The beauty of the night and this natural source of living waters felt so clearly to be the way this ritual should be performed. I don't want to say that this is how it *was meant* to be performed: although I know the Rabbis considered a natural *mikveh* preferable to a man-made one, I am sure they did not imagine skinny dipping on *mikveh* night. But in our paradigm, this feels like the most appropriate way to carry out this ancient *mitzvah*: a reinterpretation and reapplication of its meaning in our reality.

Conclusion

An important first step toward reclaiming the rich ancient practice of periodic sexual separation within marriage is to replace previous traditional interpretations of this ritual, which focus on the woman's impure body, with interpretations that stress the ritual's potential to strengthen the marital bond.

This is not a novel approach. In fact, Rabbi Meir is recorded as imbuing the ritual with a similar meaning:

> It was taught: Rabbi Meir used to say, "Why did the Torah ordain that a woman should be a *nidah* for seven days? Because being in constant contact with his wife,[5] a husband would develop a loathing toward her. The Torah, therefore, ordained: Let her be ritually impure for seven days in order that she shall be beloved by her husband as at the time of her first entry into the bridal chamber."[6]

Of course, Rabbi Meir's interpretation is not an egalitarian one. It continues to place unhealthy stress on the woman and her body as the object of her husband's desire or loathing. However, with Rabbi Meir's approach, we can at least see the beginning of a shift toward understanding the purpose of this regimen to be the strengthening of the marital bond.

A logical conclusion of this interpretation, therefore, would be that if the regimen is not achieving that goal—or, worse yet, having the opposite effect—the couple should reexamine their practice of this ritual. Often ritual reinterpretation alone is insufficient and more serious measures are required. For instance, Rabbi Akiva promotes an approach to these sexual separations that includes a change in praxis to go along with a change in ideology:

> "And concerning she who is in her menstrual infirmity"—The earlier elders interpreted this verse as teaching us that [the *nidah*] should not wear makeup or adorn herself with jewelry until after she immerses, until Rabbi Akiva came and taught that this would cause him to lose his attraction to her, and he would seek to divorce her.[7]

Like Rabbi Meir, Rabbi Akiva seems to interpret the laws of sexual separation within marriage as being about fostering a healthy marital relationship. But, unlike Rabbi Meir, he does this not by presenting a new ideological paradigm but rather by introducing an actual change in ritual praxis that furthers the value he is promoting. He overturns the previous practice that forbids women to make themselves attractive while in their sexually forbidden period and encourages women to adorn themselves with makeup and jewelry when they are ritually impure, even if that means that the couple will have to work harder not to submit to their sexual attraction for each other.

In other words, if a couple adopts the practice of "family purity" as a way to strengthen their marital relationship, it follows that its practice should accomplish this goal, not undermine it. Therefore, if the "family purity" laws are having the opposite effect and causing tension and discord in the couple's relationship, the couple should follow Rabbi Akiva's lead and reevaluate their implementation of these laws. Perhaps they can make changes (like the ones I suggest here) that will reflect a more loving and mutual experience of this sexual regimen that will have a positive effect on their relationship in general. In this way, "family purity" can become a shared ritual that can bring the couple closer together rather than push them farther apart. I would even argue that these changes should be adopted across the board to make the observance of "family purity" a healthier religious practice that reflects our modern sensibilities about marriage, sex, and women's bodies.

NOTES

1. See Leviticus 18:19 and 20:18.
2. Babylonian Talmud (BT) *Nidah* 66a.
3. Igrot Moshe, Yoreh Deah, 1:93.
4. See Teshuvot HaRambam 242, 434–444.
5. The following is a more literal translation: "because she [i.e., sexual relations with her] will become habitual [and thus boring]."
6. BT *Nidah* 31b.
7. Sifra Metzorah, Parashah 5.

9

The Goy of Sex

A Short Historical Tour of Relations between Jews and Non-Jews

Wendy Love Anderson

IN HIS FAMOUS Hebrew-English Torah edition of 1936, Rabbi Joseph Hertz quotes approvingly from his countryman Morris Joseph's 1903 work, *Judaism in Creed and Life*: "Every Jew who contemplates marriage outside the pale must regard himself as paving the way to a disruption which would be the final, as it would be the culminating, disaster in the history of his people."[1] As Hertz realized, Joseph spoke for normative rabbinic Judaism when he depicted marriage and sexual relations outside Judaism as "outside the pale," destructive to the future of the Jewish people as a whole, and historically unprecedented. Since 1990, when the (U.S.) National Jewish Population Survey showed recent Jewish intermarriage rates hovering just over 50 percent, the rhetoric against intermarriage within the American Jewish community has only grown more strident. A quick browse through the whymarryjewish.com Web site (one of several similar sites) reveals that intermarriage will "utterly cut yourself and your children off from belonging to anything beyond your immediate family." It is "breaking the chain of tradition, passed down from father to son, mother to daughter for the past two hundred generations." It is, most damningly, a "silent holocaust." Even "interdating" is discouraged, as it leads inevitably to intermarriage and to non-Jewish children.[2]

But the historical record suggests that although sexual relations between Jews and non-Jews were often considered "outside the pale" by *both* sets of communities, nevertheless they happened—frequently, enthusiastically, and even creatively during every period of Jewish history. How can we explain the persistent and widespread incidence of Jewish-Gentile sex in the face of nearly universal condemnation? Like many other rabbinic regulations concerning sex, the restrictions on interfaith sex seem to have existed more to define a "pale"—a community, in fact—than to effectively regulate the behavior *of* that community.

Holy Seed and Unholy Alliances

Even before there were Jews and non-Jews, in fact, the Book of Genesis portrays inappropriate, boundary-crossing sex as a fundamentally human trait. In a passage that may have borrowed from Ugaritic or other Near Eastern myths, Genesis 6 explains that the *b'nei elohim*—usually rendered "sons of God"—had sex with the *b'not adam*, the daughters of men, leading God to send a flood to destroy most of humanity. This initial effort to end exogamy worked about as well as subsequent initiatives did, which is to say that the families of postdiluvian biblical narrative continue to display a marked tendency toward exogamy.[3] For example, four of Jacob's thirteen children (Simon, Judah, Joseph, and Dinah) are explicitly or implicitly described as forming sexual connections with non-Israelites; extrapolated at the rate of U.S. "intermarriage," in fact, Jacob's family clearly belongs in the 1970s!

But later interpretation and midrash worked ceaselessly to modify the scandalously exogamous Tanakh, substituting increasingly unpleasant alternatives: after Dinah's disastrous union with Shechem, one tradition marries her off to her brother Simon, and another argues that eleven of Jacob's sons married their twin sisters (not Canaanites!) and that Joseph married his niece (not an Egyptian!).[4] Similarly, the Book of Esther, with its cheerful endorsement of Esther's union with the Persian king Ahasuerus, is revised by some midrashic sources to make Esther a reluctant adulteress who suffers Ahasuerus's attentions for the sake of her people.[5] But why would incest or adultery—both prominently outlawed in the Torah—be seen as preferable to intermarriage, banned only in connection with the seven Canaanite tribes (Exod. 34:11–17, Deut. 7:1–4) and seemingly sanctioned under other circumstances, such as the captive woman in Deuteronomy 21:10–14?

The answer lies at the end of the Tanakh: just before Ezra famously demands that the now "Jewish" Babylonian returnees send away their non-Jewish wives, his officers explain that the wives' "abhorrent practices are like those of the Canaanites . . . so that the holy seed has become intermingled with the peoples of the land" (Ezra 9:1–2). This rationale took two novel steps: first, it argued that *all* foreign wives could be viewed as "Canaanites" because of their "abhorrent practices." Second, it suggested that the newly universal ban on intermarriage was linked to the notion of Jews as a uniquely holy people so that exogamy implied not only bad influences but also moral or ritual defilement.

And the purity-obsessed Judaisms of the Second Temple seem to have taken Ezra's prohibitions to their logical conclusion, extending the Torah's prohibitions against intermarriage to cover not only non-Jews in general but also interreligious sexual relations outside marriage. The Babylonian Talmud mentions a Hasmonean-era enactment prohibiting the union of Jewish men with *any* non-Jewish women—not merely because the non-Jewish women might be considered idol-worshipers but because they could be presumed to be both ritually unclean (classed with menstruants from the moment of their birth!) and adulterous (BT *Avodah Zarah* 36b). The Talmudic tradition also debates whether the famous Eighteen Decrees of the schools of Hillel and Shammai merely reiterated the Hasmonean ban (albeit apparently including both genders of non-Jews), whether they forbade extramarital sex as well as intermarriage per se, and whether any of these decisions could be traced back to a legendary (and hence irreversible) "court of [Noah's son] Shem" (BT *Avodah Zarah* 36b; BT *Sanhedrin* 82a; BT *Shabbat* 17b; and Y *Shabbat* 1:7).

Although there is some rabbinic effort to argue that the expanded ban can be considered a Torah law, a position attributed by the final editors of the Babylonian Talmud to the conveniently second-century R. Simon bar Yohai (BT *Kiddushin* 68b; BT *Yevamot* 23a), the social reality underlying Exodus 34 and Deuteronomy 7 is absent; instead, charges of defilement and idolatry based on Ezra's language are repeatedly adopted in order to justify what seems to have been limited but vehement Second Temple–era revulsion at Jewish-Gentile unions. For instance, the thirtieth chapter of the apocryphal book of Jubilees (second century BCE) borrows the Levitical laws against giving one's seed to Moloch (Lev. 18:21, 20:2) as prooftexts for its teaching that Jewish-Gentile intercourse is both a capital crime and a cause of divine wrath against the entire Israelite nation.

But the sentiments of Jubilees were clearly not universal: the Qumran text *Miqsat Ma'ase ha-Torah* (QMMT), usually dated to the early Hasmonean period, asserts disapprovingly that "some of the priests and the people intermarry, and mix and defile the holy seed, and even their own, with female outsiders" (4QMMT 80–82).[6] Similarly, Second Maccabees

(14:3) describes the priest Alcimus as having "voluntarily sullied himself in the times of their [Jews' and Greeks'] intermingling," using language which strongly suggests that Alcimus's sexual relations with Gentiles had impaired his priestly functions.[7] It is probably no accident that these two descriptive texts involve priestly protagonists and are set several centuries before the destruction of the Second Temple: despite strenuous Pharisaic and rabbinic efforts, constructions of ritual purity were peripheral to the lives of non-priestly Jews even when the Temple cult flourished. Once the Temple was destroyed, many of the remaining concerns about purity lacked any practical basis. At the dawn of the classical rabbinic period, the Jewish community sought a new vocabulary to express its continued dismay at the (apparently continued) incidence of Jewish-Gentile sexual relations.

The Beast with Two Backs

Throughout classical and medieval rabbinic texts, it seems, the metaphor of choice to describe Jewish-Gentile sex is that of a more obviously forbidden union: either bestiality or adultery, depending on the circumstances. In BT *Berakhot* 58a, for instance, the third-century Rav Shila punishes a Jewish man with lashes for having sexual relations with an Egyptian woman but then avoids Roman censure by comparing the woman to a female donkey and the man's crime to bestiality. Meanwhile, in Yerushalmi *Berakhot* 3:4, the (Gentile) female slave of Rabbi Judah the Prince defends herself against the sexual advances of a Jewish man by comparing *herself* to an animal! And thanks to the Apostle Paul's canonized suggestion that being "bound together" or "misyoked" with unbelievers was undesirable (2 Cor. 6:14), another probable reference to the mixing of species, the same metaphor appeared in Christian texts, where it rapidly came to describe sex between Christians and non-Christians in general.[8]

Medieval Jewish jurists, including the Rambam and Rabbenu Tam, explicitly compared sex with a Gentile to sex with an animal; ironically, their medieval Christian counterparts used the same analogy (and equivalent punishments) to describe Christians who had sex with Jews.[9] Since the bestiality metaphor failed to distinguish between sex and marriage, however, moralistic and legal sources on both sides of the Jewish/Christian divide also described interfaith sexual relations in terms of adultery. Christian legal opinion on the matter reached its logical conclusion as early as the Theodosian Code of 388 CE, which described Jewish-Christian marriage as equivalent to adultery and specified execution as the penalty for both.[10] A similar equivalence between Jewish-Christian sex and adultery (albeit with lesser punishments) was proposed by the twelfth-century Ashkenazic pietist Eliezer of Worms.[11]

Perhaps the most hyperbolic prescription comes from a sixteenth-century Yiddish ethical tract from western Poland which insists that "the sin of lying with a Gentile woman is more grievous than adultery with a Jewess, and anyone who finds a man lying with a Gentile woman may freely kill him. Indeed, it is a great *mitzvah* to slay him immediately."[12] (Perhaps fortunately, there is no indication that this prescription was ever put into practice.) It was even possible to reason from bestiality and adultery to other unequivocally forbidden combinations: a passage in the minor Talmudic tractate *Derekh Eretz Rabbah* claims to identify a total of fourteen negative biblical commandments being transgressed when a Jewish man has sex with a Gentile woman, including prohibitions against mixing different species of animals, different types of seeds, and different types of cloth![13]

More generally, rabbinic Judaism tended—and arguably still does —to see boundary-crossing sexual relationships as indicative of systemic moral failure. The Talmudic account of Miriam bat Bilgah's desecration of the Temple altar includes, perhaps by way of explanation, the datum that she had married a Greek officer (BT *Sukkah* 56b), and Josephus records unions with non-Jews among the many titillating exploits of the corrupt Herodian dynasty. In Yerushalmi *Taanit* 3:4, a plague in the late-first-century Jewish community of Sepphoris is explained by divine wrath at the presence of *many* "Zimris"—presumably Jews coupling with non-Jewish partners, as per the Torah's account of an Israelite prince whose union with a Midianite woman provoked both divine and human retribution (Num. 25:6–15). And in the relatively tolerant Golden Age of Judaism in the Iberian Peninsula, Jewish preachers and moralists issued an unbroken stream of condemnations concerning the promiscuity of both men and women in seeking out non-Jewish lovers.[14]

Perhaps the clearest example of equating non-Jewish sex and overall sinfulness comes from the Kabbalist R. Hayyim Vital's record of an incident in which the spirit of a deceased Jewish Sage allegedly possessed a rabbi's daughter and proceeded to explain—in detail—why almost the entire Jewish community of sixteenth-century Damascus was excluded from the World to Come. Among many other sins, the spirit explains, "your wives go about brazenly with garments and jewelry of shame . . . to show the nations their beauty. . . . And now forty-eight [male] people perform transgressions with Gentile women, and married women, and sodomize, aside from other transgressions."[15] If the women's "transgressions" remain vague, the men's are anything but, as the spirit goes on to name names and offer details about the most prominent members of the community. R. Israel Najara, for instance, is said to have sinned "when a Gentile woman came into his house and roasted fresh figs on the fire on the Sabbath, afterward he slept with her. . . . His young son also copulated with a Gentile and is a total sinner."[16] In Vital's account, as in the minds of many contemporary Jews, sex with non-Jews is not only a believable accusation but also a symptom of pervasive moral decay.

Exotic Others

If most premodern (and some modern) Jews viewed Jewish-Gentile sex as a moral failing, it comes as no surprise that some Jews tended to the opposite extreme of fetishizing the exotic other as a sexual expert. For instance, the late-thirteenth-century Jewish poet Todros Abulafia recommends that "one should love an Arab girl" because "she knows all about fornication and is adept at lechery," but should "stay far away from a Spanish girl" only because "she is so ignorant of intercourse."[17]

More recent examples come from a succession of twentieth-century authors who looked to non-Jews as a solution for what they saw as stunted Jewish sexuality: Vladimir Jabotinsky's *Samson* emphasizes the sexual vigor and national pride of the Philistines, depicts Samson's various relationships with Philistine women as a positive reclamation of these same values for Zionist Judaism, and eventually reveals Samson himself to be a product of a Philistine/Jewish union. On a less epic scale, Amos Oz's *My Michael* features an Israeli woman fantasizing about sex with Arab brothers as an escape from her unsatisfying marriage, and Jewish-Gentile relationships in American Jewish novels ranging from Philip Roth's *Portnoy's Complaint* to Erica Jong's *Fear of Flying* also feature a Gentile bringing his or her Jewish partner to hitherto unequaled sexual heights before the relationship ends.

Perhaps the most extreme Jewish treatment of the benefits of sex with non-Jews (in this case, Christian men) combines both condemnation *and* eroticization with a side of animal metaphors. In a thirteenth-century commentary on *Numbers Rabbah* 12:8, the southern French Maimonidean R. Isaac ben Yedaiah offers a truly remarkable description of the benefits of circumcision which can only be appreciated at length:

A man uncircumcised in the flesh desires to lie with a beautiful-looking woman. . . . He vexes his mind to be with her day after day, growing weary in his attempt to fulfill his desire through lovemaking with her. She too will court the man who is uncircumcised in the flesh and lie against his breast with great passion, for he thrusts inside her a long time because of the foreskin, which is a barrier against ejaculation in intercourse. Thus she feels pleasure and reaches an orgasm first. When an uncircumcised man sleeps with her and then resolves to return to his home, she brazenly grasps him, holding on to his genitals, and says to him, "Come back, make love to me." This is because of the pleasure that she finds in intercourse with him, from the sinews of his testicles —sinew of iron—and from his ejaculation—that of a horse—which he shoots like an arrow into her womb. They are united without separating, and he makes love twice and three times in one night, yet the appetite is not filled. And so he acts with her night after night. The sexual activity emaciates him of his bodily fat, and afflicts his flesh, and he devotes his brain entirely to women, an evil thing. His heart dies within him; between her legs he sinks and falls. He is unable to see the light of the King's face, because the eyes of his intellect are plastered over by women so that they cannot now see light.

But when a circumcised man desires the beauty of a woman, and cleaves to his wife, or to another woman comely in appearance, he will find himself performing his task quickly, emitting his seed as soon as he inserts the crown. If he lies with her once, he sleeps satisfied, and will not know her again for another seven days. . . . As soon as he begins intercourse with her, he immediately comes to a climax. She has no pleasure from him when she lies down or when she arises, and it would be better for her if he had not known her and not drawn near to her, for he arouses her passion to no avail, and she remains in a state of desire for her husband, ashamed and confounded, while the seed is still in her reservoir. She does not have an orgasm once a year, except on rare occasions, because of the great heat and the fire burning within her. Thus he who says "I am the Lord's" will not empty his brain because of his wife or the wife of his friend. He will find grace and good favor;

his heart will be strong to seek out God. He will not fear to behold that which is beyond, and when He speaks to him, he will not turn away.[18]

Although R. Isaac's description of uncircumcised intercourse is not necessarily indicative of real-world sexual mores, it *does* indicate the extent to which medieval Jewish men might have alternately feared or fantasized about their wives being satisfied by their Christian neighbors. It also indicates the exclusively male and tacitly misogynistic "community" for whom such a titillating description is intended. In fact, R. Isaac sees no problem in bartering away the Jewish woman's chance at sexual satisfaction—a process which he seems to understand surprisingly well, under the circumstances—in favor of the Jewish man's opportunity to apprehend God's presence intellectually.

R. Isaac's endorsement of unsatisfying sex went mercifully unheeded in later sources, but his imaginative approach to sexual relationships between Jews and non-Jews did not suffer the same fate. Non-Jewish European sources show a fascination with the other side of this paradigmatically forbidden relationship: like R. Isaac, oddly enough, they focused on the doomed relationship between the non-Jewish (usually Christian) man and the beautiful "Jewess," or *belle juive*. The *belle juive* herself was heavily sexualized but sympathetic, and the love between the Jewish woman and her Gentile suitor was often genuine; however, her literary role ensured that she would be victimized by tragic misunderstanding or, more frequently, by her evil, scheming Jewish family or community.

The beautiful Abigail in Christopher Marlowe's *The Jew of Malta*, for example, upon finding that her father has manipulated her two Christian suitors into killing each other, flees to a convent and is ultimately poisoned, along with the other nuns, by her father; her final confessor, a friar, helpfully adds that what "grieves [him] most" is her death as a virgin![19] By the nineteenth century, the literary *belle juive* had a few more choices: sometimes she could survive by separating forever from her Gentile lover, as does Rebecca of York in Walter Scott's *Ivanhoe*, or she could convert to Christianity and then waste away from neglect, as does Sara/Anna in Anton Chekhov's *Ivanov*. Once in a great while she could even find a happy ending with her lover after abandoning Judaism, as Rebecca does in *Rebecca and Rowena*, William Thackeray's riposte to Scott. But the European *belle juive* tradition was as strict as its mainstream rabbinic counterpart in its insistence that sexual or romantic relationships between Jews and non-Jews were fascinating but ultimately impossible.

Ordinary People

The overwhelming weight of historical evidence suggests that, in most times and places, sexual relationships between Jews and non-Jews were indeed possible, despite legal or religious barriers or both. Most early examples are individual rather than collective, but an archive of papyri from an Egyptian Jewish colony in the fifth century BCE includes records of several marriages and divorces between Jewish and non-Jewish partners, some with apparent sanction from the Jewish community.[20] One begins to suspect that the "intermingling" of Second Maccabees, the "Zimris" of first-century Sepphoris, and the Theodosian Code's banned intermarriages could not *all* have been exceptional! Moving later in history, one of the strongest testimonials for the continuity of interfaith relations in the religiously fraught atmosphere of medieval Europe comes from Canon 68 of the Fourth Lateran Council (1215), which states:

> A difference of dress distinguishes Jews or Saracens from Christians in some provinces, but in others a certain confusion has developed so that they are indistinguishable. Whence it sometimes happens that by mistake Christians join with Jewish or Saracen women, and Jews or Saracens with Christian women. In order that the offence of such a damnable mixing may not spread further, under the excuse of a mistake of this kind, we decree that such persons of either sex, in every Christian province and at all times, are to be distinguished in public from other people by the character of their dress.[21]

As this Christian regulation tacitly admits, "mistake" was more likely to be a post facto defense than a genuine explanation. Legal records from medieval Aragon, where Jews, Christians, and Muslims lived together in relative harmony for centuries, provide not only cases in which various individuals claimed ignorance of the precise credal status of their sexual partners (often in defiance of the obvious anatomical evidence borne by Jewish and Muslim men) but also cases in which interreligious affairs were a matter of common knowledge despite the severe legal penalties attached to them by all the faiths concerned.

For instance, a petition from the mid-thirteenth century presents us with a Jewish female moneylender petitioning King James I for an *extension* of the privilege of living with her Christian lover, because they were still "burning in their love for each other."[22] Another document accuses a

Jewish man of sleeping with women of all three faiths (including prostitutes and married women) and then bragging that he could pay his way out
of any punishment.[23] There are innumerable cases of Jewish men sleeping
with their Muslim female slaves—with predictable confusion as to the
status of their offspring—and one isolated but fascinating description of
a Muslim female slave who converted (or was converted) to Judaism after
a sexual relationship with her Jewish owner's daughter, precipitating a law-
suit from the local Muslim community.[24] While these accusations could
and sometimes did lead to physical violence (or, more frequently, quasi-
legal extortion), their combined weight gives the sense that Jewish-Gentile
relationships were more scandalous than unusual.

In the modern period the reality underlying these legal circumlocu-
tions began to change. Jews and Christians in Europe and North America
were beginning to identify themselves by nationality as much as by religion, and even in those European countries where civil marriage did not
yet exist, it had become relatively easy for a Jew to convert to Christianity
in order to marry his or her Christian partner. This seemed to apply especially when the (originally) Jewish partner was female: English and German records from the eighteenth, nineteenth, and twentieth centuries indicate that although the vast majority of converts from Judaism were men, it
was mostly *female* converts from Judaism who listed a planned marriage to
a Christian as their primary reason for conversion.[25] Indeed, this phenomenon was briefly highlighted by the very public cases of a few dozen "salon
Jewesses"—most famously Dorothea Mendelssohn, Henrietta Hertz, and
Rahel Varnhagen—who converted to Christianity in order to wed their
Christian lovers in late-eighteenth-century Germany.

Of course, frontier areas allowed some of these formalities to be sus-
pended: the first Jewish-Christian intermarriage in what would become the
United States took place in New Amsterdam in 1656, but no record exists
of Solomon Pietersen's conversion, only that of his daughter's baptism.[26]
Indeed, relatively few colonial America's Jewish-Christian intermarriages
(at least 10% of all marriages involving Jews) seem to have involved formal
conversion to Christianity; although most of these intermarried Jews were
marginal to or eventually left their Jewish communities, a sizable handful
(mostly men) remained involved in synagogue and community life.[27] And
an increasing number of Jews were willing to recognize civil marriages, at
least on some front. As early as 1806 Napoleon's "Grand Sanhedrin" responded to their emperor's question about whether marriages between
Jews and Christians were allowed by admitting that "marriages between

Jews and Christians which have been contracted in accordance with the laws of the civil code are civilly legal," along with the more shocking (and perhaps not altogether voluntary) concession that "although [Jewish-Christian intermarriages] may not be capable of religious sanction, they should not be subject to religious proscription."[28] A new, nationally oriented sense of community was now replacing religious community as a means for defining "appropriate" sexual partners, and, as a result, Jewish-Gentile sexual relationships were losing much of their shock value for Jews and Gentiles alike.

Keeping the Faith

Naturally interfaith relationships continued to exist in both literature and everyday life; it was simply that in both cases they wielded a significantly diminished level of potential tragedy or scandal. As respectable marriage became a real possibility, Jewish-Gentile sexual relationships lost some of their tragic weight in the non-Jewish world: instead of dying horribly, the beautiful Jewish prostitute in Guy de Maupassant's "Mademoiselle Fifi" is eventually rewarded for her defiance of France's lecherous Prussian occupiers by a happy marriage to "un patriote sans préjugés." In Jewish literature, on the other hand, depictions of relationships between Jews and non-Jews were more likely to end unhappily, although usually for ideological as much as strictly religious reasons. Hayyim Nachman Bialik's short story, "Behind The Fence," features a relationship between a Jewish boy and a Christian girl that is doomed by its inability to overcome the conventions of either community; the boy winds up unhappily married to a Jewish woman and the girl is left pregnant with a new generation of anti-Semites.

On the rare occasions in contemporary fiction when an explicitly Jewish-Gentile couple does last, the non-Jewish partner is likely to convert either in effect or in fact; Kitty Fremont in Leon Uris's *Exodus* becomes a passionate Zionist as a result of her relationship with Ari Ben-Canaan, and Anna Reilly in the movie *Keeping the Faith* turns out to be studying toward conversion even during her brief breakup with Rabbi Jake Schram. Jews could still define themselves as a community by opposition to *permanent* relationships between themselves and non-Jews, but increasingly these relationships appear in literature less as tragedy or taboo than as one of many possible plot elements.

At the same time, Jewish-Gentile relationships have become significantly less taboo in everyday life. Here at last there exists firm statistical ground: in virtually every country where Jews have been granted full civil rights along with freedom to marry non-Jews, their rates of marriage (and, one assumes, extramarital sexual relationships) with non-Jews have risen dramatically over the past hundred years. In the years immediately preceding the Holocaust, Jewish intermarriage rates in countries throughout Western Europe went from double to quintuple their late-nineteenth-century levels, topping out at 44 percent in 1933 Germany (just before the passage of the Nuremberg Laws) and outnumbering marriages between two Jews in countries such as Sweden.[29] Eastern European intermarriage (as well as its legal feasibility) remained relatively low during these years, but with the mass migration of Eastern European immigrants into the United States between roughly 1880 and 1920, it took only a generation or so to adapt to their new American setting.

Although the first half of the twentieth century featured rates of American Jewish intermarriage of 7 percent or lower, thanks in large part to immigrants and immigrants' children marrying inside their communities, these numbers began to climb precipitously, doubling by 1970 (13%) and exceeding 40 percent by 1985. The 2000 National Jewish Population Survey revised some of the numbers from its 1990 counterpart downward, but its rate of Jewish intermarriage in the U.S. between 1996 and 2001 still came in at 47 percent.[30] Over the past several decades, a whole range of Jewish community organizations have also developed "outreach" programs designed to inspire Jewish identification in those Jews who have become involved with non-Jews: these range from the intermarriage-positive Jewish Outreach Institute to the intermarriage-negative Aish HaTorah.

On balance, however, the American Jewish community seems to have made some peace with intermarriage: as of 2000, 80 percent of all Jews surveyed by the American Jewish Committee agreed that "intermarriage is inevitable in an open society"; 56 percent were either neutral or positive about marriage between a Jew and a Gentile, while 50 percent felt that opposition to Jewish intermarriage was "racist." The American Jewish Committee concluded that "the Jewish taboo on mixed marriage has clearly collapsed."[31]

This collapse, however, would come as news to all the major rabbinic organizations in America, as well as the overwhelming majority of Jews who self-identify as either "Orthodox" or "observant." These groups continue to in-marry at high rates and to support the venerable rabbinic tradition of unwavering opposition to interfaith relationships, even as their views seem further than ever from social reality. Although Reform Judaism is generally perceived as most friendly to intermarried couples, and although many Reform rabbis will perform certain types of interfaith weddings or commitment ceremonies, its Central Conference of American Rabbis has nevertheless affirmed repeatedly that "mixed marriage is contrary to the Jewish tradition and should be discouraged."[32] The Rabbinical Assembly of Conservative Judaism takes an even stronger stance, forbidding its members from participating in or attending an intermarriage ceremony on penalty of expulsion from the Conservative rabbinate. And most Orthodox rabbinical associations seem to assume that such prohibitions go without saying.

Not surprisingly, the only Jewish arguments that disturb this united front posit alternative and sometimes extra-halakhic formulations of Jewish community. For instance, Mordecai Kaplan, the father of the Reconstructionist movement, wrote that intermarriage among American Jews should be viewed not only as an "expected development" but as an opportunity to expand the Jewish community: "with a belief in the integrity and value of his own civilization the Jewish partner to the marriage could achieve moral ascendancy, and make Judaism the civilization of the home."[33] For Kaplan, and for many following in his ideological footsteps, "Jews" are not merely those halakhically defined as such but include any family willing to create a Jewish home. A similar approach has been taken more recently by an informal group of Conservative rabbis and laypeople, who argue that the Jewishly committed but non-Jewish partners of Jews should be identified as *k'rovei Yisrael* and brought into synagogue and community life as far as halakhically possible.[34]

Morris Joseph's century-old prediction of "the final . . . [and] culminating disaster" in Jewish history has, in some sense, come true. Many contemporary Jews do indeed contemplate, and most of those achieve, sexual relations with non-Jews; whether this is indeed disastrous for Judaism remains to be seen. From a historical standpoint, the gap between normative *halakhah* and practice on this point is nothing new, although its extent is perhaps unprecedented. Profound ambivalence about the advantages and disadvantages of non-Jewish sexual partners is also not a novel development within the Jewish tradition. It is possible that rabbinic Judaism will come to welcome the opportunity—indeed, the necessity—of rethinking precisely who and what constitutes "the" Jewish community. It is also possible that the Jewish community that identifies itself by opposition to intermarriage will simply define any disagreement with that dictum as non-Jewish and so avoid the issue (for multiple senses of that term). The safest prediction would seem to be that sex and marriage with non-Jews is unlikely either to disappear or become entirely unremarkable as a phenomenon within rabbinic Judaism. Over more than three thousand years of Jewish sources, there is simply too much historical evidence testifying to the enduring attraction between Jews and non-Jews.

NOTES

1. Joseph Hertz, ed., *The Pentateuch and Haftorahs*, 2nd ed. (New York: Soncino Press, 1960), 774.

2. From the Web site: http://www.whymarryjewish.com, March 30, 2007.

3. For more on biblical exogamy, see chapter 5 in this volume: Esther Fuchs, "Intermarriage, Gender and Nation in the Hebrew Bible."

4. On Dinah's marriage, cf. Bereshit Rabbah 53:10; and on the other daughters of Jacob, 82:8.

5. As in BT *Megillah* 15a.

6. This translation follows the suggested revisions offered by Christine Hayes in *Gentile Impurities and Jewish Identities: Intermarriage and Conversion from the Bible to the Talmud* (Oxford: Oxford University Press, 2002), 84.

7. See ibid., 51–52.

8. Paul's Greek verb ετεροζυγειν is used in contexts such as the Septuagint Leviticus 19:19 to describe the (prohibited) act of breeding two different species of animals together.

9. Rambam, *Hilkhot Issurei Bi'ah* 12:1; Rabbenu Tam in Tosafot to BT *Ketubot* 3b. Several Christian examples are offered in Joshua Trachtenberg, *The Devil and the Jews: The Medieval Conception of the Jew and Its Relation to Modern Anti-Semitism* (Philadelphia: Jewish Publication Society, 2002), 187.

10. Cf. *Codex Theodosianus* 3.7.2 and 9.7.5.

11. Eliezer—who is, of course, writing for a male audience—also distinguishes between the lesser crime of sex with one's own Christian servant versus sex with an independent Christian woman. In Eliezer's *Sefer ha-Rokeach Ha-Gadol* Hilkhot Teshuvah 12; discussed in David Biale, *Eros and the Jews* (Berkeley: University of California Press, 1997), 75.

12. From Isaac ben Eliakum's *Sefer Lev Tov*, as excerpted in Israel Zinberg, *Old Yiddish Literature from Its Origins to the Haskalah Period*, trans Bernard Martin

(Jersey City, N.J: Ktav Publishing House, 1975), 164. For a critical Yiddish text, see Rubin Noga, "Sefer Lev Tov by Rabbi Isaac ben Eliakum of Posen, Prague, 1620," Ph.D. diss., Hebrew University, Jerusalem, 2006.

13. Discussed in Shaye J. D. Cohen, *The Beginnings of Jewishness* (Berkeley: University of California Press, 1999), 302 n. 131. (*Derekh Eretz Rabbah* is probably Amoraic or early Gaonic in origin.)

14. A good sampling of these can be found in the article by Yom Tov Assis, "Sexual Behaviour in Mediaeval Hispano-Jewish Society," in *Jewish History: Essays in Honor of Chimen Abramsky*, ed. Ada Rapaport-Albert and Steven J. Zipperstein (London: Peter Halban, 1988), 25–59.

15. R. Hayyim Vital, *Sefer Ha-Hezyonot*, excerpt translated in J. H. Chajes, *Bertween Worlds: Dybbuks, Exorcists, and Early Modern Judaism* (Philadelphia: University of Pennsylvania Press, 2003), 174.

16. Ibid., 175. (It is important to note that Vital and Najara clashed over the latter's religious poetry, so the details of this anecdote should be given even less gravity than one might normally accord a third- or possibly fourthhand spirit message.)

17. Translated in Brann, *The Compunctious Poet: Cultural Ambiguity and Hebrew Poetry in Muslim Spain* (Baltimore, Md.: Johns Hopkins University Press, 1991), 145.

18. Translated by Marc Saperstein in *Decoding the Rabbis: A Thirteenth-Century Commentary on the Aggadah* (Cambridge, Mass.: Harvard University Press, 1980), 97–98. Saperstein also provides the Hebrew on pages 294–297 of I. Twersky, ed., *Studies in Medieval Jewish History and Literature*, vol. 1 (Cambridge, Mass.: Harvard University Press, 1979).

19. Christopher Marlowe, *The Jew of Malta*, ed. David Berington, Revels Student Editions (New York: Manchester University Press, 1997), 3:vi.

20. Translated in Bezalel Porten et al., *The Elephantine Papyri in English: Three Millennia of Cross-Cultural Continuity and Change* (Leiden: Brill, 1996).

21. Translated in Norman Tanner, ed., *Decrees of the Ecumenical Councils* (London: Sheed and Ward; Washington, D.C: Georgetown University Press, 1990), 1:266.

22. As discussed in David Nirenberg, *Communities of Violence: Persecution of Minorities in the Middle Ages* (Princeton, N.J.: Princeton University Press, 1996), 140.

23. Ibid., 163.

24. Ibid., 191.

25. As discussed in Todd M. Endelman, "The Social and Political Context of Conversion in Germany and England," in *Jewish Apostasy in the Modern World*, ed. Todd Endelman (New York: Holmes and Meier, 1987), 83–107.

26. As discussed in Jonathan Sarna, *American Judaism: A History* (New Haven, Conn.: Yale University Press, 2004), 8.

27. Ibid., 27.

28. Translated in W. Gunther Plaut, *The Rise of Reform Judaism: A Sourcebook of Its European Origins* (New York: World Union for Progressive Judaism, 1963), 73.

29. More detailed statistics appear in Milton Barron, "The Incidence of Jewish Intermarriage in Europe and America," *American Sociological Review* 11, no. 1 (February 1946): 9–11.

30. These numbers can be found in the 2000 National Jewish Population Survey, available online at http://www.ujc.org/ (accessed 10/26/08). (Comparable numbers have been introduced for Jewish communities in North America and Europe.)

31. These results come from the American Jewish Committee's 2000 "Annual Survey of American Jewish Opinion," published in *Responding to Intermarriage: Survey, Analysis, Policy* (American Jewish Committee, January 2001).

32. This wording was originally adopted in 1909 and reaffirmed by resolution in 1973. In the 1973 form, it can be found online at http://data.ccarnet.org/cgi-bin/resodisp.pl?file=mm&year=1973 (accessed 10/26/08).

33. Mordecai M. Kaplan, *Judaism as a Civilization: Toward a Reconstruction of American Jewish Life* (New York: Reconstructionist Press, 1934), 418–419.

34. See Mark Bloom et al., *A Place in the Tent: Intermarriage and Conservative Judaism* (Oakland, Calif.: EKS Publishing, 2005).

10

A Jewish Perspective on Birth Control and Procreation

Elliot N. Dorff

Foundations

The American and Jewish sides of the identity of American Jews complement each other in, for example, their mutual concern for individuals, education, and the rule of law (even over heads of state), although the two traditions come to those stands for different reasons. At the same time they disagree in ways that directly affect their views of sex, birth control, and whether married couples are obliged to have children—and how many.[1]

Specifically, in the American way of looking at things, I own my body. I may therefore use it in any way I wish, as long as I do not hurt others. American pragmatism dictates that I should take care of my body so that it can continue to provide me with pleasure, and that means that I need to pay attention to my diet, exercise, hygiene, sleep, and sexual habits to avoid illness and keep fit; but if I choose to take risks and endanger myself, that is my business. So, for example, it may not be smart to engage in unprotected sex, but there is no law prohibiting me from doing so.

According to Jewish sources, on the other hand, my body belongs to God. I have a fiduciary relationship to God during my lifetime and even in death; God trusts me to take care of my body. It is as if I were renting an apartment; I have the right to reasonable use of my body, but I do not have the right to destroy it because it is not mine. I must therefore take care of my body through proper diet, exercise, hygiene, and sleep because God sets such care as one of the conditions for my use of my body that belongs to Him. I also owe it to God to avoid endangering myself any more than the usual activities of life do;[2] in fact, as the Talmud understands it, "avoiding danger is more obligatory than avoiding other forbidden acts" (*sakkanta hamira m'issura*).[3]

The Duties to Provide Sexual Pleasure and to Procreate

Regarding God as having dominion over our use of our bodies also has the potential to affect our sexual activities. In addition to defining and prohibiting adultery and incest,[4] the Torah has two positive commandments related to sex: the duty to procreate, which is embedded in the commandment given to the very first man and woman in the first chapter of Genesis (1:28) to "be fruitful and multiply"; no less obligatory is the commandment in Exodus 21:10 that a man must provide for his wife "her food, her clothing, and her conjugal rights."[5]

1. *Children.* The Rabbis, who shaped what we know as Judaism, define exactly what is entailed in these two commandments. Even though a man and woman are both necessary for procreation, and even though God addresses them both in commanding procreation, the Rabbis assert that the legal duty devolves on the man alone.[6]

Various theories attest to why they so ruled. One, for example, maintains that the woman could not be commanded to procreate because pregnancy represents a real danger to her, which is still true today but much more true before safe Caesarian sections became possible in the 1950s. In contrast, the man incurs no physical danger in begetting a child. Another reason may have been biologically based, given that, anatomically, a man has to offer to have sex with a woman. Another possible explanation is economic: the man is obligated in Jewish law to support his children, and so it is against his economic self-interest to procreate and so he must be commanded to do so.[7] A fourth rationale is exegetical: as the Talmud notes, the verse in Genesis reads "be fruitful and multiply, fill the earth and conquer it." Whose nature is it, the Talmud asks, to conquer people and things? It is the man's, it answers, and so he is also the one who is addressed in the first part of the verse.[8]

Whatever the reason for restricting this duty to the man, the Rabbis determine that he is understood to have fulfilled it when he produces a boy and a girl, thus modeling his procreation after God, who created the first human beings male and female (Gen. 1:27).[9] Even then, however, the man, according to Jewish law, is required to produce as many children as he can. The Rabbis derive this commandment from Isaiah 45:18, who says, "Not for void did He create the world, but for habitation [*lashevet*] did He form it," and from Ecclesiastes 11:6, who says, "In the morning, sow your seed, and in the evening [*la'erev*] do not withhold your hand," where they interpret "morning" to mean one's youth and "evening" to mean one's older years.[10] Subsequently Maimonides affirms these precepts in his code of Jewish law: "Although a man has fulfilled the commandment of being fruitful and multiplying, he is commanded by the Rabbis not to desist from procreation while he yet has strength, for whoever adds even one Jewish soul is considered as having created an entire world."[11]

The Jewish tradition sees having children not only as a duty, but also as a great blessing. God's promise to all the patriarchs and matriarchs includes children "as numerous as the stars in the heavens and the sands on the shore."[12] Children figure prominently in the Bible's descriptions of life's chief goods.[13] Infertility, however, was well known in the tradition, for Abraham and Sarah, Isaac and Rebekah, Jacob and Rachel, and Elkanah and Hannah all had trouble having children.[14]

2. *Sexual satisfaction.* The Rabbis also defined how often a man was required to offer to have conjugal relations with his wife in order to fulfill his sexual duties to her. This is remarkable, given how many other societies and religions presumed that only men have sexual appetites and that women acquiesce to their husbands' sexual advances only because they want children and economic support. Judaism, however, understood women to have sexual desires just as much as men do, and so the Mishnah defines the minimal frequency of the husband's offer for sexual relations as a function of how often his job would make it likely that he would be home:

> If a man put his wife under a vow to have no connubial intercourse, the School of Shammai says [he may maintain the vow] for two weeks, but the School of Hillel says only for one week. Students may leave their wives at home to study Torah without their wives' permission for thirty days; laborers for one week. The time for marital duties enjoined in the Law are: for men of independent means, every day; for workmen, twice weekly; for ass-drivers, once a week; for camel drivers once every thirty days; for sailors once ever six months. This is the opinion of Rabbi Eliezer.[15]

On the other hand, the man has rights to sexual satisfaction, too. The Rabbis were again remarkable in recognizing and prohibiting marital rape,[16] a feature of American law in most states only since the early 1990s.[17] Jewish law forbids the man to force himself on his wife to satisfy his sexual needs. If she refuses to have sex with him, his recourse is to reduce the amount he must pay her in a divorce settlement by a certain amount per week until he ultimately can divorce her without paying her anything:

If a woman is refractory against her husband [in not letting him have sex with her], he may reduce her marriage settlement by seven *denars* every week. Rabbi Judah says: seven half-*denars*. How long is the reduction to be continued? Until it reaches the full amount of her marriage settlement. Rabbi Yose says: He may continue to diminish it [even after that time] in case an inheritance may fall to her from some source and he can then claim [the amount beyond the marriage settlement] from her. Similarly, if a man rebels against his wife [by not offering to have sex with her], they [the Rabbis] may add to her marriage settlement three *denars* each week. Rabbi Judah says: three half-*denars*.[18]

Thus the Jewish tradition understands sex to have two purposes, procreation and providing sexual satisfaction for both members of a married couple. We shall now probe what this means in modern times, when the desire for both sexual satisfaction and children do not differ much from the past, but both social realities and medical technology are radically different.

Sexual Satisfaction in Modern Times

Undoubtedly the most important social difference between ancient times and our own is the amount of time we spend on education. Until the mid-twentieth century people simply could not afford to send their children to school for very long, for the children were needed to help the family earn a living. Girls rarely received any formal education at all, and the lyrics the boys sing in the opening number of *Fiddler on the Roof* reflect historical realities: "At three I started Hebrew School, at ten I learned a trade." This means, as the Mishnah asserts, that men were expected to get married by age eighteen,[19] presumably to women aged sixteen or seventeen. Hormonal development was probably much the same as it is now, and so teenagers were undoubtedly tempted to engage in sex, but social norms prevented boys and girls from being together alone until they were married, and they knew they did not have long to wait. Furthermore, marriages were arranged; my own grandparents did not know each other until they stood under the wedding canopy. This reduced the anxiety that teenagers have in our society about mating, and it also made it clear that marriages were not only about sex.

One of the problems we have in contemporary America, in fact, is that movies and television programs portray sex as the equivalent of love and the primary purpose of marriage. If, for example, the song "Some Enchanted Evening" from *South Pacific* is right, not only the time that a couple meets but marriage itself is supposed to be one enchanted evening after another. When couples discover that some evenings are indeed enchanted and that most are just so-so and some are downright unenchanted, they think they must be wrong for each other and all too often they divorce. Compare that scenario to the song "Do You Love Me?" in *Fiddler on the Roof,* where Tevye and Golda have created a family together and supported each other for twenty-five years, and only then ask whether they love each other; when they affirm that they do, "after twenty-five years it does not change a thing, but it's nice to know." They certainly had conjugal relations, and one can presume that they enjoyed them, but that was only part of what it meant to be married.

In our own time, when people (and especially Jews)[20] go to school long past the age of ten, often into their late twenties and even early thirties —and when they therefore commonly postpone marriage for a long time, they need to find ways to satisfy their sexual urges. The fact that, except in some Orthodox circles, men and women see one another in classes, social events, and many other settings not only intensifies their desires to have sexual relations but presents opportunities to do so.

This is accompanied by new technology that makes it possible for couples to engage in sex without worrying too much about having children. The introduction of the Pill caused a sexual revolution in the 1950s, and other birth-control devices have added to couples' assurance that sex and children can be decoupled. If they do get pregnant, *Roe v. Wade* made it possible for them to abort the fetus simply because the mother wants to do so.

The Jewish tradition evinces a strong preference for intercourse within marriage. Still, even though men and women lived in more sexually separated communities, Jewish sources know of couples having sex before marriage, and those situations are treated much less seriously than incest or adultery. The Torah pronounces the death penalty for people who commit incest or adultery but demands that singles engaged in consensual sex either marry without the possibility of divorce or the man must pay the woman's father a fine.[21] Even though nonmarital sex is treated much less seriously than adultery or incest, it still occasions a punitive response, albeit a lighter one.

In contemporary times, Orthodox Jews know about "the *tefillin* date," when the man brings his *tefillin* with him so that he can pray the morning service after spending the night with a woman. Early marriages, however, are much more common in the Orthodox world, with many men in their late teens or early twenties marrying women a few years younger, and the writings of Orthodox rabbis still maintain that couples should wait until marriage before engaging in sexual relations.[22] Many years ago the Reform Rabbi Eugene Borowitz wrote *Choosing a Sex Ethic,*[23] which has become the primary Reform approach to nonmarital sex, recognizing that people will choose what to do regardless of traditional norms and informing them about how to choose thoughtfully. Within the Conservative Movement, I wrote *"This Is My Beloved, This Is My Friend": A Rabbinic Letter on Human Intimacy*[24] for the Rabbinical Assembly's Commission on Human Sexuality, in which the Commission takes the position that waiting until marriage is the ideal but Judaism is not only for those who can live up to ideals. If a couple is going to engage in sexual relations before marriage, the *Letter* asserts, they need to abide by the same values that apply to sex within marriage, including mutual respect, honesty, modesty, health, safety, and holiness. As the *Letter* points out, it is much harder to accomplish these values in a nonmarital context than in marriage, which, in fact, may be why Jewish sources prefer that sexual intercourse be confined to marriage. Jewish sexual ethics, however, are not "all or nothing" —either you wait until marriage or anything goes—if couples are going to engage in sex before marriage, they can still strive to fulfill Judaism's values as much as possible.

This is especially important in our times, when another factor has entered couples' considerations about their sex lives—namely, sexually transmitted diseases, including lethal ones such as AIDS. As noted above, health and safety are core values of Judaism, and this includes taking steps to avoid danger and illness to the extent that we can. This means, minimally, as I assert in my *Letter,* that fulfilling this duty in our age requires all the following:

(a) full disclosure of each partner's sexual history from 1980 to the present to identify whether a previous partner may have been infected with the HIV virus;

(b) HIV testing for both partners before genital sex is considered, recognizing all the while that a negative test result is only valid six months after the last genital contact;

(c) careful and consistent use of condoms until the risk of infection has been definitively ruled out either by the partner's sexual history or results of HIV testing; and

(d) abstinence from coitus where there is demonstrated HIV infection in either partner.

If any of these requirements cannot be met, because of discomfort with open communication, lack of maturity, a partner's reticence to disclose his or her history, or doubts about the trustworthiness of the partner's assurances, then abstinence from genital sex with this partner is the *only* truly safe choice. The use of a condom in sexual intercourse with an HIV-positive person is a second-best alternative, given that condoms provide some protection against sexually transmitted diseases, but condoms can slip off or break, removing the protection that the non-affected partner needs and that the Jewish tradition requires.

The Torah is silent about masturbation; the often-cited story of Onan (Gen. 38) is about interrupted coitus, not masturbation. The Talmud, however, prohibits masturbation as "wasting of the seed" (*hashhatat zera*). (This applies only to men, who emit semen. It is quite possible that the male rabbis did not even know that women masturbate, and even if they did, they might well have been less concerned about it because they did not know that women had eggs, a fact that scientists did not recognize until the nineteenth century. Instead, people around the world thought that the woman was effectively an incubator for the only necessary genetic materials [the "homunculus"] that the man implanted in her.) The Talmud does not explain why it prohibits wasting seed, but Maimonides, arguably the most significant Jew of the Middle Ages, who was a physician as well as a rabbi and philosopher, maintained that a man who masturbates puts himself in danger of losing his hair, his sanity, and his potency.[25] Kabbalistic sources went even further, maintaining that men who masturbate kill their own (potential) children and create demons besides.[26]

We now know that a man's body will emit semen regularly, whether through masturbation or in the midst of a nocturnal dream, and that masturbation has none of the negative medical effects that Maimonides and doctors as late as the 1950s assumed (as reflected in the *Boy Scout Handbook* of that period). On the other hand, we do have very good evidence that the use of condoms significantly reduces the spread of sexually transmitted diseases.

Thus, even though the Jewish tradition did not approve of condoms since using them meant that the man intended that his seed not be used for procreation, I maintain that current medical knowledge and the current circumstances in which unmarried people engage in sexual relations mandate that a man use a condom whenever he has sexual relations with a woman to whom he is not married. In this I am simply applying the tradition's commitment to saving lives over almost all the other commandments.[27]

For the same reason I maintain that masturbation, which is harmless, is preferable to nonmarital sex, which can involve the spread of sexually transmitted diseases as well as misunderstandings about exactly what commitments the two partners are making to each other in having sex together and the hurt feelings that result. Masturbation, of course, like all sex acts, should be done only in private. Furthermore, because teenage males feel strong hormonal pressures, they should be reminded that there are important things in life besides sex. (Hormonal pressures in women peak later, usually in the late twenties.) Masturbation clearly does not bring with it many of the pleasures of sexual contact, including intercourse, with someone else, so I have no illusions that most people will let it substitute for sexual relations. Nevertheless, masturbation has an important role in helping people avoid medical risks as much as possible to the extent that it can relieve hormonal pressure and reduce the number of sexual encounters that unmarried people have. It is an important component for women as well as men in a healthy sex life.

In recent times, a vaccine has been developed that helps to prevent women from contracting cervical cancer caused by some strains of the human papilloma virus (HPV), which may colonize in the cervix as a result of sexual intercourse. Physicians recommend, therefore, that girls be injected with the vaccine around age twelve, presumably before they begin having sexual intercourse. This raises hard questions for parents; it forces them to acknowledge that their daughter may have sexual intercourse in the near future, and their decision to vaccinate a daughter risks the interpretation that they are permitting her to have sex as a teenager. It is important for parents to emphasize to a daughter that in having the family doctor or gynecologist administer the vaccine the parents are neither expecting nor permitting her to engage in sexual activity now; this discussion should include a frank talk with both boys and girls of that age (and also in the mid-teenage years, as a kind of booster) about not only the biology of sex but the values that Judaism brings to sex. If parents are embarrassed or feel unskilled to have such a conversation, they should have their rabbi conduct this discussion, perhaps together with a physician and with the aid of the *Rabbinic Letter* that I wrote[28] or some other presentation of Jewish sexual values. Given that cervical cancer is often lethal, however, we must give our daughters the protection afforded by the new vaccine, just as we vaccinate our children against other devastating diseases.

A more difficult issue concerns the distribution of condoms at youth group events, especially those involving overnight stays. Even though condoms do not guarantee against either an unwanted pregnancy or the prevention of a sexually transmitted disease, they diminish the risk of both. It is certainly better for a couple to use them—and for women to use contraceptives—than to abort a fetus after the fact. Yet parents and youth leaders are squeamish about distributing condoms to high school students or even having them available for students who ask for them, lest condoms communicate the message that sexual intercourse is both expected and permitted. In the mid-1990s the Conservative Movement's Committee on Jewish Law and Standards considered a rabbinic ruling that would have endorsed distributing condoms at youth events and camps associated with the movement, but the overwhelming majority of committee members was against that, and so the proposed ruling was withdrawn. Whether that is the right stance for educational institutions is arguable. Parents of teenagers, however, surely need to have frank discussions with their children about sexual values and activities, and if they endorse or suspect that their sons or daughters plan to have sex, they should give them condoms and urge that they use them. Given that approximately 90 percent of college students engage in sexual intercourse, however, Hillel Foundations on college campuses probably should have them readily available, and it is not too late to schedule frank discussions of sexual ethics with college and graduate students.

Procreation in Modern Times

Jewish sources from as early as the second century describe methods of contraception. A rabbinic ruling from that time prescribes the use of contraception when pregnancy would endanger either the woman or the infant she is nursing.[29] Subsequent rabbinic opinion splits between those who sanction the use of contraception only when such danger exists and those who mandate it then but allow it for other women, too.

If couples are going to use contraceptives, Jewish law prefers those that prevent conception in the first place over those that abort an already fertilized egg because in most cases Jewish law forbids abortion. For most of gestation, the fetus is considered "like the thigh of its mother," and, because our bodies are God's property, neither men nor women are permitted to amputate their thigh except to preserve their life or health.[30] Jews are often misinformed about this because they have heard, correctly, that Jewish law requires abortion when the woman's life or health (physical or mental) is threatened by the pregnancy and that Jewish law also permits abortion when the risk to the woman's life or health (physical or mental) is greater than that of a normal pregnancy but not so great as to constitute a clear and present danger to her.

"Mental health" as a ground for abortion, however, has not been interpreted nearly as broadly in Jewish sources as it has been in American courts; it would not include, for example, the right to abort simply because the woman does not want to have another child, even because of economic pressures. According to most rabbinic authorities, however, permission to abort on the grounds of the woman's mental health would include cases where the child will be malformed or afflicted with a lethal or debilitating genetic disease, and it also includes pregnancies that result from rape or incest.

Abortion, in any case, according to Jewish law, is not a legitimate *post facto* form of birth control. The most favored contraception from a Jewish perspective is the diaphragm, for it prevents conception and has little, if any, impact on the woman's health. The contraceptive pill and the intrauterine device are the next most favored forms of contraception if they are not contraindicated by the woman's age or body chemistry. Couples like these forms of birth control because they are easy to use and are quite reliable; Jewish authorities recommend them because their success rate minimizes the possibility that couples will later consider an abortion as retroactive birth control. RU486 and any other contraceptive that retroactively aborts an embryo is, from this understanding, considered only when pregnancy would threaten the mother's physical or mental health, as defined above.

The only nonpermanent, male form of contraception currently available is the condom. As noted above, in Jewish law the male is legally responsible for propagation, and that argues against the man using contraception at least until he has fulfilled that duty.[31] Condoms, moreover, sometimes split or slip off,[32] and even if they remain intact and in place they do not always work. Nevertheless, condoms must be used if unprotected sexual intercourse poses a medical risk to either spouse, as condoms do offer some measure of protection against the spread of some diseases, and the duty to maintain health and life supersedes the positive duty of the male to propagate.[33]

It should be noted, however, that even rabbis who permit contraception for nontherapeutic reasons never anticipated that Jews would postpone having children as long as many Jewish couples now do and that, even with modern medical advances, the late teens and the twenties are biologically still the best time for the human male and female to conceive and bear children.[34] Age is not the only factor in infertility, but it makes all the other factors more likely to be present and more difficult to fix. Furthermore, a third of infertile couples are so because of a problem in the woman; a third because of a problem in the man; and a third because of a problem in both or for reasons that are unclear.[35] Couples who wait until their thirties to begin their families will most likely be able to have only one or two children, and all too many couples beyond their twenties find that when they are ready to have children, they cannot. Because Jews attend college and graduate school in percentages far beyond the national norm and postpone marriage and the effort to have children until their late twenties, thirties, or even forties, they are more prone to infertility than the general population. This is an excruciating problem for the couples themselves, for all the techniques to overcome infertility impose substantial financial burdens and tensions on their marriage, sometimes even leading to divorce over this issue.

There are, of course, good reasons why so many Jews wait so long. In addition to long-term schooling, most women in our society find that they must earn money to support themselves and their families, just as their husbands do. Moreover, many people who would love to find a mate and get married in their early twenties may not be so fortunate. This means that parents should ensure that their teenagers choose a college attended by many Jews, for social as well as religious and educational reasons, and point out that the college years are not too early to look for a spouse; young people who find a mate in college might marry in graduate school and begin having their children at that point so as to increase the probability that they will have the number of children they want and that the Jewish tradition hopes they will have. Meanwhile, the older Jewish community must contribute the funds to make day care and Jewish schooling and camping affordable. It also means that even if young couples choose to use contraceptives for a time, they are well advised, medically and from a religious standpoint, not to wait too long.

Another factor must be mentioned. We Jews numbered approximately 18 million before the Holocaust, and a third of our numbers were lost during those terrible years. Counting everyone who identifies as a Jew, we are now slightly more than 13 million.[36] Even if we forget about replenishing the numbers we lost, we are currently not replacing our numbers. To do that requires a reproductive rate of 2.1, that is, 2.1 children, on average, for every two adults. It must be more than 2.0 to account for those who never marry, those who marry and cannot have children, those who have only one child, and those who have two or more children who themselves do not reproduce. The present reproductive rate of Jews in North America is less than 1.9.[37] This means that we are endangering ourselves demographically as a people. The contemporary, demographic problem of the Jewish people is another factor that should figure into the thinking of Jews using contraception.

The dwindling population of Jews also must be a factor in communal planning. If the Jewish community is seriously attempting to replenish its numbers, policies and programs must be developed to enable and encourage young Jews to have larger families. Grandparents should be told that the Talmud imposes a duty on them, just as it does on parents, to educate their grandchildren,[38] and so grandparents should contribute to the tuition for their grandchildren's Jewish education. Greater discounts should be given to each added sibling in Jewish day schools, camps, and youth group programs. Jews, acting out of their own best interests and out of Jewish values, should support pro-family legislation such as laws that provide family leaves for both mothers and fathers and for high-quality, affordable day care. We must, in a phrase, "put our money where our mouths are."

Jews who use contraception for family planning, then, are advised to give serious thought to having children earlier in their lives than is now common; the pressures of graduate school are not necessarily greater than, and are often less than, those of the first years of one's career. People can always find reasons to postpone childbearing—until they finish their education, until they have more money, or until they get started in their careers—but by then it is often too late.

Couples who can propagate should seriously consider having three or four children. As noted earlier, the obligation in Jewish law to propagate is fulfilled when one has a minimum of two children, but one is not supposed to stop there. In our current demographic crisis, this is all the more imperative. Thus, although a couple's first two children fulfill the commandment (*mitzvah*) to procreate, the Conservative Movement's Committee on Jewish Law and Standards has approved a rabbinic ruling urging couples to have one or more additional children who are also "*mitzvah* children," both in the sense that Jewish law requires couples who can to have more than the minimum number of two, and also in the sense of *mitzvah* as "good deed," in that they are helping to make Jewish physical continuity, and therefore Jewish religious and cultural continuity, possible.[39]

Once again, those who cannot have children through sexual intercourse may try assisted reproductive techniques or adopt children, but Jewish law would not require them to do either. Those who can procreate, however, should do so, both for their own self-fulfillment and for the sake of the Jewish people. To avoid the heartache of infertility, young marrieds, especially those who marry in their late twenties or later, should use contraceptives for family planning purposes only for a very short time, if at all. In the end, we must all be reminded that the Jewish tradition thinks of children as a true blessing from God.

NOTES

1. For a more thorough comparison of American, Jewish, and Christian views of life, see Elliot N. Dorff, *To Do the Right and the Good: A Jewish Approach to Modern Social Ethics* (Philadelphia: Jewish Publication Society, 2002), chap. 1. See also idem, *Love Your Neighbor and Yourself: A Jewish Approach to Modern Personal Ethics* (Philadelphia: Jewish Publication Society, 2003), 19–31.

2. The level of risk that is acceptable is that which most people assume: BT *Shabbat* 129b.

3. BT *Hullin* 10a.

4. Leviticus 18 and 20.

5. Some biblical scholars think that the Torah's word here, *onata*, means "conjugal rights"; others believe it means "housing"; and still others define it to mean "ointments." See Nahum Sarna, *The JPS Torah Commentary: Exodus* (Philadelphia: Jewish Publication Society, 1991), 121. The Rabbis, however, understood it to mean "conjugal rights" (M *Ketubbot* 5:6), and that is what is controlling for Judaism.

6. The duty to procreate devolves on the man: BT *Yevamot* 65b; BT *Kiddushin* 35a. The Talmud (BT *Yevamot* 65b–66a) brings conflicting evidence as to whether a woman is legally responsible for procreation and ultimately does not decide the matter. That is left for the later codes (MT *Laws of Marriage* 15:2;

SA *Even Ha-Ezer* 1:1, 13), which rule that the duty falls only on the man but the woman must enable him to fulfill it.

7. See Dorff, *Love Your Neighbor*, 277 n. 69; and Elliot N. Dorff, *Matters of Life and Death: A Jewish Approach to Modern Medical Ethics* (Philadelphia: Jewish Publication Society, 1998), 39–40, 335–336 nn. 9 and 10; and, on using artificial techniques to procreate, see chaps. 3 and 4, passim.

8. BT *Yevamot* 65b; BT *Kiddushin* 35a.

9. That a man fulfills his duty to procreate by producing one boy and one girl: M *Yevamot* 6:6 (61b); MT *Laws of Marriage* 15:4; SA *Even Ha-Ezer* 1:5. There was some debate about this, however, with some claiming that two boys would also suffice and with the School of Hillel, on whom the law is based, maintaining that *even* a boy and a girl would suffice. See Dorff, *Matters of Life and Death*, 336 n. 9; and idem, *Love Your Neighbor*, 275–276 n. 61.

10. BT *Yevamot* 62b.

11. MT *Laws of Marriage* [*Ishut*] 15:16.

12. God promises Abraham, Isaac, and Jacob children as numerous as the stars in the heavens (or the sand on the shore or the dust of the earth): Gen. 15:5; 22:15–18; 26:4–5; 28:13–15; 32:13; see also 17:4–21; 18:18.

13. See, for example, Leviticus 26:9; Deuteronomy 7:13–14; 28:4, 11; and Psalms 128:6.

14. Sarah, Rebeccah, Rachel, and Hannah all have trouble having children: Gen. 15:2–4; 18:1–15; 25:21; 30:1–8, 22–24; 35:16–20; 1 Sam. 1–20.

15. M *Ketubbot* 5:6.

16. BT *Eruvin* 100b; *Leviticus Rabbah* 9:6; *Numbers Rabbah* 13:2; MT *Laws of Ethics* 5:4; MT *Laws of Marriage* 14:15; MT *Laws of Forbidden Intercourse* 21:11; SA *Orah Hayyim* 240:10; SA *Even Ha-Ezer* 25:2, gloss.

17. In Common Law, in force in North America and the British Commonwealth on many matters, the very concept of marital rape was considered impossible. Thus Sir Matthew Hale, the Chief Justice in seventeenth-century England, wrote in his classic treatise, *Historia Placitorum Coronae*, that "the husband cannot be guilty of a rape committed by himself upon his lawful wife, for by their mutual matrimonial consent and contract the wife hath given up herself in this kind unto her husband, which she cannot retract." In December 1993 the United Nations High Commissioner for Human Rights published the Declaration on the Elimination of Violence Against Women (www.unchr.ch/huridocda/huridoca. nsf/(Symbol)/A.RES.48.104.En?Opendocument [accessed 12/20/07]). This establishes marital rape as a human rights violation. As of 1997, however, the United Nations Children's Fund (UNICEF) reported that just seventeen nations had criminalized marital rape. In 2003 the United Nations Development Fund for Women (UNIFEM) reported that more than fifty nations had done so. In the United States, in 1975, South Dakota was the first state to remove the husband's protection from prosecution; by 1993 all fifty states had done so, but in thirty of

them the husband still was exempt from prosecution if he did not have to force his wife to have sex—if, for example, she was unconscious or asleep or if she was mentally or physically impaired. See Raquel Kennedy Bergen, "Marital Rape: New Research and Directions," http://new.vawnet.org/category/Main_Doc.php? docid-248 (accessed October 29, 2007); and "Spousal Rape," *Wikipedia*, http:// en.wikipedia.org/wiki?Spousal_rape (accessed October 29, 2007).

18. M *Ketubbot* 5:7.

19. M *Avot* (*Ethics of the Fathers*) 5:23. According to the Talmud, if a man does not marry by the time he is twenty, God says, "Blasted be his bones!" (BT *Kiddushin* 29b).

20. "More than half of all Jewish adults (55%) have received a college degree, and a quarter (25%) have earned a graduate degree. The comparable figures for the total U.S. population are 29% and 6%." *The National Jewish Population Survey 2000–01: Strength, Challenge, and Diversity in the American Jewish Population* (New York: United Jewish Communities, 2003), 6; available at http://www.ujc. org/page.html?ArticleID=33650 (accessed 12/20/07).

21. Deuteronomy 22:28–29. The Mishnah's refusal to allow men in Judah to complain in court that their new wives were not virgins because the women lived in the man's household during the year between engagement and marriage also indicates that the Rabbis understood that the man in the marriage may well be the reason that she is no longer a virgin; see M *Ketubbot* 1:5; BT *Ketubbot* 9b, 12a.

22. See, for example, Maurice Lamm, *The Jewish Way in Love and Marriage* (New York: Harper and Row, 1979), 92, 116–117, 149–150, 171–172; Shmuley Boteach, *Kosher Sex: A Recipe for Passion and Intimacy* (New York: Doubleday, 1999), pt. 3; and Gershon Winkler, *Sacred Secrets: The Sanctity of Sex in Jewish Law and Lore* (Northvale, N.J.: Jason Aronson [now Rowman and Littlefield], 1998), 78–79, 86–98.

23. Eugene B. Borowitz, *Choosing a Sex Ethic: A Jewish Inquiry* (New York: Schocken for B'nai Brith Books, 1969). For more recent writings on sex ethics within the Reform and Renewal movements, see Paul Yedwab, *Sex in the Texts* (New York: Union of American Hebrew Congregations [UAHC] Press, 2001); Mark Washofsky, *Jewish Living: A Guide to Contemporary Reform Practice* (New York: UAHC Press, 2001), 317–319; and Arthur Waskow, *Down-to-Earth Judaism: Food, Money, Sex, and the Rest of Life* (New York: William Morrow, 1995), pt. 3.

24. Elliot N. Dorff, *"This Is My Beloved, This Is My Friend": A Rabbinic Letter on Human Intimacy* (New York: Rabbinical Assembly, 1996); reprinted with minor changes in idem, *Love Your Neighbor and Yourself: A Jewish Approach to Modern Personal Ethics* (Philadelphia: Jewish Publication Society, 2003), chap. 3.

25. MT *Laws of Ethics* (*De'ot*) 4:19. For the ban on masturbation, see BT *Nidah* 13a; MT *Laws of Forbidden Intercourse* 21; SA *Even Ha-Ezer* 23.

26. Men who masturbate kill their children: Zohar *Vayehi* 219b. They also

create demons: Zohar, *Genesis* 19b, 54b. On masturbation generally, see Dorff, *Matters of Life and Death*, 116–120; and David M. Feldman, *Birth Control in Jewish Law* (New York: New York University Press, 1968 [later republished as *Marital Relations, Birth Control, and Abortion in Jewish Law*]), pt. 3.

27. BT *Yoma* 85a–b; BT *Sanhedrin* 74a–b.

28. See note 22 above.

29. BT *Nidah* 2; BT *Yevamot* 12b, 100b; *Ketubbot* 39a; *Nidah* 45a; *Nedarim* 35b. On this entire topic, see Feldman, *Birth Control in Jewish Law*, chaps. 9–13. (The subsequent, paperback edition, published by Schocken in 1973, is titled *Marital Relations, Birth Control, and Abortion in Jewish Law*, as is the revised 1996 edition published by Jason Aronson, now Rowan and Littlefield.) On the question of assessing the dangers posed to the woman or child by sexual intercourse such that contraception is, according to that Baraita, permitted or required, see Feldman, *Birth Control in Jewish Law*, 185–187.

30. BT *Hullin* 58a and elsewhere. According to BT *Yevamot* 69b, during the first forty days of gestation the zygote is "simply water," but even then the Rabbis required justification for an abortion based on the mother's life or health. On this topic generally, see Feldman, *Birth Control in Jewish Law*, chaps. 14–15.

31. The language of the Mishnah (M *Yevamot* 6:6) suggests that the man may use contraceptives after fulfilling the commandment with two children. It reads: "A man may not cease from being fruitful and multiplying *unless* he has children. The School of Shammai says: two males; the School of Hillel says: a male and a female." This, however, was not the position of later Jewish law (BT *Yevamot* 62b), which encouraged as many children as possible on the basis of Isaiah 45:18 and Ecclesiastes 11:6, as indicated above (MT *Laws of Marriage* [*Ishut*] 15:16).

32. British researchers, citing World Health Organization statistics and their own study of three hundred men at a south London clinic, have suggested that the failure of condoms may largely result from only one size being available for all men, a size too small for one-third of the men in the world. See "One Size of Condom Doesn't Fit All," *Men's Health* (March 1994): 27.

33. For more on the Jewish imperative of safe sex, see Michael Gold, *Does God Belong in the Bedroom?* (Philadelphia: Jewish Publication Society, 1992), 112ff.

34. The optimal age is twenty-two. See *The Columbia University College of Physicians and Surgeons Complete Guide to Pregnancy*, as quoted in Beth Weinhouse, "Is There a Right Time to Have a Baby? The Yes, No, and Maybe of Pregnancy at 20, 30, 40," *Glamour*, May 1994, 251, 276, 285–287. Infertility increases with age: 13.9 percent of couples where the wife is between thirty and thirty-four are infertile; 24.6 percent where the wife is between thirty-five and thirty-nine; and 27.2 percent where the wife is between forty and forty-four. See U.S. Congress, Office of Technology Assessment, *Infertility: Medical and Social Choices*, OTA-BA-358 (Washington, D.C.: U.S. Government Printing Office, 1988), 1, 3, 4, 6.

35. "Infertility," www.womenshealth.gov (accessed 12/20/07) (National Women's Health Information Center of the U.S. Department of Health and Human Services, Office on Women's Health), esp. 5.

36. The best estimate of the current number of Jews in the world is 13,089,800. See Sergio Della Pergola, "World Jewish Population," *American Jewish Yearbook 2006* (New York: American Jewish Committee, 2006), 106:559–601, esp. 571. With the world's population at 6,477 million, Jews are 2.02 per 1,000 of the world's population—that is, approximately 0.2 percent of the world's population.

37. *National Jewish Population Survey 2000–01*, 4.

38. On grandparents being obligated to educate their grandchildren, see BT *Kiddushin* 30a. On the duty to educate children and its costs today, see Dorff, *Love Your Neighbor*, 143–150.

39. Kassel Abelson and Elliot N. Dorff, "Mitzvah Children," available at www.rabbinicalassembly.org (accessed 10/18/08) under the link "Contemporary Halakhah."

11

Not Like a Virgin

Talking about Nonmarital Sex

Sara N. S. Meirowitz

"DON'T WORRY, YOU can still marry a *kohen.*" Thus spoke my well-meaning college boyfriend as part of our seduction ritual. I was twenty years old and wrestling with "going too far" in my first serious relationship, shouldering the baggage of *yeshiva* day school and overzealous safe-sex education. We were bending over the *Shulchan Aruch* volume of codes in the library, with hormones and Torah stories cascading through us in equal parts, as this *frum*-from-birth boy tried to calm our guilt over wanting to have sex by appealing to Rabbi Yosef Karo. "In this day and age, *bi-yah*[1] (sexual intercourse) doesn't constitute marriage," he told me. "Even if you're not a virgin, you'll still be able to marry a *kohen.*"[2]

As immersed in the intensity of the moment as I was, even then I thought that it was funny, bizarre, that we'd appeal to a fifteenth-century code as a way to justify something that felt totally right to us in our twentieth-century morality. Making the decision to be sexually active is a normal part of a committed adult relationship, a decision we undertook with love and respect. And despite the pressure of our traditional upbringings, I don't think we seriously considered *not* becoming sexually active because of Torah law. That said, when this well-meaning boy told me that I'd still be able to marry a *kohen*, a part of me was relieved, grateful that even when transgressing this biggest taboo of sexual behavior, I would not be constrained in future relationship choices or considered forever tainted. It may have been absurd to think that a relationship at twenty could prohibit a marriage ten years later—but it was a real concern for the world I lived in.

What is this story that we tell ourselves about sex in the unmarried world? For many traditionally observant Jews making their way in the adult dating world, the decision to be sexually active is filled with inconsistencies and contradictions. With the age of first marriage rising, few observant Jews in long-term committed relationships choose to remain abstinent, knowing that years may pass in a relationship before marriage. In college and afterward, my friends and I agonized over these questions, having internalized teachings of parents and rabbis that good Jewish kids don't do what all those *other* college kids do. You don't stay over in your boyfriend's dorm room, you don't live together, and you *certainly* don't have sex. And yet we did, and we lied about it, and we felt guilty.

It was easier for our parents. Until the sexual revolution of the 1970s, American Jews (and middle-class white people in general) would find their prospective spouses in high school or college, wed as soon as possible, and promptly begin having children. The narrative is familiar: "Don't graduate college without your M.R.S. degree." But with the expansion of professional opportunities for women (and for men as well) and the easy availability of reliable contraception, many more people choose to delay settling down in marriage until their later twenties and thirties. So the question arises: What do you do in the bedroom? And how do you justify it to your community and, more important, to yourself, while remaining true to a coherent vision of Jewish practice?

Although our current standards of sexual behavior that discourage premarital sex can be traced clearly through the years of Jewish tradition, we can also see parallel strands of understanding that speak to continued engagement with this issue. By articulating these unspoken assumptions in traditional texts and comparing them to our modern sexual norms, we can construct a modern ethic of sexuality that embraces the transient and varied behaviors in our society and sanctifies the flexibility of youth and possibilities.

Of Cows, Milk, and Barren Women: Traditional Texts on Nonmarital Sexuality

As Jews connect to millennia of tradition, we find the sources of our philosophy and ethics in the laws of the Torah.[3] Although the lessons in the traditional teachings on respecting strangers and honoring parents are still relevant today, it is much harder to learn sexual values from the desert-dwelling Israelites, constrained as they were by the societal morality of their times. While biblical Judaism did not forbid premarital sex per se— as do traditions of other religions—a woman's virginity was still seen as the marker of a suitable bride, worthy of transfer from father to husband. As the Torah states:

> Do not degrade your daughter and make her a harlot [*zonah*], lest the land fall into harlotry and the land be filled with depravity.[4]

> If a man seduces a woman [*betulah*, virgin] for whom the bride-price has not been paid and lies with her, he must make her his wife by payment of a bride-price. If her father refuses to give her to him, he must still weigh out silver in accordance with the bride-price for virgins.[5]

In these and other biblical laws,[6] a woman's father essentially owns her virginity, a commodity purchased by her husband in marriage or, if ruined, compensated for. A woman with her virginity intact would be transferred from father to husband and evaluated for her suitability; if her sexual practices placed her in the category of *zonah*, harlot, her marriage could be annulled—or she could even be stoned.

How do we modern women and men relate to these laws? My first instinct is to discount their relevance, reread them as constructs of a bygone society in which women were merely considered their husbands' possessions. Yet, with our postmodern eyes, we can try to read premodern feminism into these laws, to see how they protected a woman from being sold into sexual slavery. By putting the onus for protecting virginity onto a woman's father and husband, the biblical lawgiver could limit the exploitation of women and construct a society in which marriage and protection of women were values. Despite this optimistic reading, it is still hard for us to view an understanding of women as "objects not to defile" as a positive value that we can use to construct a modern ethic. Indeed, the traditional division of women into *betulah* and *zonah* remains with us today, even as twin packs of lip balm, labeled "sweetheart" and "slut," are sold to teenage girls at cosmetic counters.

Rabbinic thought took these two categories and explicated them in depth, attempting to define the parameters of *zonah* so as to preserve a marital society and prevent otherwise moral non-virginal women from becoming unmarriageable. A woman's sexual status, in particular, becomes most relevant should she wish to marry a member of the priestly caste, a *kohen*, whose ritual purity is connected to his wife's untouched status.[7] In Talmudic discussions, the Sages hashed out which women are considered *zonot*, and thus forbidden to marry *kohanim*:

Rabi Yehudah said: A *zonah* is one who is infertile.

And the Sages said: No one is considered a *zonah* save a convert, or a liberated slave, or one who has had forbidden sexual relations [i.e. engaged in a forbidden sexual partnering, such as incest]. . . .

Rabi Elazar said: If a single man comes to a single woman [for sexual relations] without the intention of marriage, he makes her into a *zonah*.

Rav Amram said: The law is not according to Rabi Elazar.[8]

These three definitions of *zonah*—an infertile woman, a licentious woman, and an unmarried non-virgin with a problematic past—can illuminate our modern discussion of sexual permissiveness. On the one hand, only a woman who is either known or assumed to have had forbidden or licentious sexual relations—converts assumed to have been licentious in their former lives—must be seen as a harlot; the average Jewish woman who may have indulged her sexual appetites before marriage is not punished or even censured. But, according to Rabi Elazar, even consenting single adults can be seen as licentious when they couple without the sanctity of marriage. Rabi Elazar's opinion can be seen as idealistic, hopeful for a society secure in marriage; yet the Sages are realists about sexual desires. Thankfully for Jewish women everywhere, the law is not according to Rabi Elazar.

Rabi Yehudah's definition sheds light on another question: Why encourage sexual coupling and marriage, if not for the purpose of procreation? Indeed, the broader Talmudic debate in this section concerns whether the *Kohen Gadol* is permitted to marry a woman who is not fertile, whether she is a child or postmenopausal. Underlying the concerns about virginity and bride-prices is the important *mitzvah* of "being fruitful and multiplying." Judaism is often praised as a religion that encourages nonprocreative sexual pleasure, but Rabi Yehudah's opinion reveals the strain of thought that it is preferable for procreation to, at least, be a *possibility* in a marital liaison. Modern laws do not follow his opinion—postmenopausal and pregnant women are allowed to have as much sex as they want—but this preference for procreative sex has been retained in the discouraging attitude toward contraception in the ultra-Orthodox world.

Another key area where sexual relations are proscribed is the laws against sexual relations with a menstruating woman, called *nidah*. This chapter touches on the laws only briefly, as they are examined in depth in chapter 8 of this volume. The laws of *nidah* hold an undeniably central place in constraining and defining permissible sexual relations. Biblically, relations with a menstruant are in the category of *gilui arayot*, forbidden sexual relations, which also includes incest and adultery.[9] Later rabbinic laws expand the fence around the time of *nidah* to include all women who have not gone to the *mikveh*, the ritual bath, since the time of their last periods. The concept of *nidah* becomes linchpin of rabbinic restrictions against nonmarital sexual relations, inextricably linked with restrictions against sleeping with a *zonah*. Indeed, in order to protect unmarried people from having premarital sex, medieval rabbis discouraged unmarried women from going to the *mikveh*, lest they lose their *nidah* status and seem permitted to their partners.[10] These laws of *nidah* and *mikveh* are important for our understanding of the complications surrounding nonmarital sex, and they are somewhat less ambiguous than the prejudices and interpretations of the *zonah*: the laws state that if you menstruate, you go to the *mikveh*, and then you become permitted to your (permissible) partner. But even when we tackle these issues of *nidah*, the restrictions against premarital sex remain.

What are the underlying values behind these categories and prohibitions? A woman's virginity is valued, yes, but so is her fertility, and the categories are steeped in notions of purity and impurity somewhat obsolete since the Temple's destruction. Although women are encouraged to be monogamous, preserving their virginity and procreative years for marriage, the man's concern is with his wife's purity status, not *his* sexual behavior or monogamy. Polygyny is biblically accepted, but polyandry is punishable by death. And although a woman's immersion in the *mikveh* renders her pure for her husband for the next few weeks, there is no ritual immersion that can make a licentious woman permitted to a *kohen*. The woman's virginity status is permanent, marked on her *ketubah*, marriage contract; the man's past history is entirely irrelevant.

Saving It for Marriage: And in Our Day?

Where do we stand in our modern world? Years of Jewish education and modern sex ed have drilled into my head that premarital abstinence is not only divinely ordained but the commonsense strategy. "Why buy the cow when you can get the milk for free?" my mother continues to say, even as I find myself in yet another long-term, nonmarital relationship. The structures of monogamy, marriage, and procreation are what move and motivate social interactions in both the traditional and less traditional Jewish world. We find the markers of rootedness and commitment to a community to be tied to partnership: buying a home, joining a synagogue, declaring "this is where I live." Over and over, we hear stories of single people feeling disenfranchised from their Jewish communities, and gay and lesbian couples feeling that their partnerships are unrecognized without commitment ceremonies. The marriage plot is alive and well in modern Judaism, and underlying it are these teachings about *betulah* and *zonah,* the *halachic* categories that divide relationships into the sacred and the profane.

But despite these years of Jewish education that we've all had, there's something very unusual in traditional Jewish communities where everyone is otherwise observant: they do not worry about these prohibitions. In communities where everyone keeps *Shabbat* and *kashrut,* the Jewish dietary laws, twenty- and thirty-somethings sleep at their partners' houses, consummate relationships, and move in together. The legendary *"tefillin* date" is no myth: bring your *tefillin* on the date tonight so you can pray with them tomorrow morning when you wake up in your date's bed. People who would never think about eating vegetarian food at nonkosher restaurants have no problem breaking some of the strictest blood taboos in the Torah. What is it about the laws of sexual behavior that make them seem more difficult, more outdated, than laws about carrying in public space on *Shabbat* or daily davenning?

I write this chapter as a sometimes-member and observer of a few specific communities; I do not purport to speak for the majority of Orthodox young adults. I know of many people who keep the laws of *negiah,* abstaining from any potentially erotic touch or even any touch at all before marriage, as a way to keep these sexual restrictions. But as we go from high school to college to the post-college dating years, it becomes less and less common to find people who manage to keep their impulses in check. Many people think they are sinning by having intimate encounters, giving every sexual experience a veneer of guilt and blame that can poison a relationship. Others draw perhaps specious borders around forbidden encounters, consigning vaginal intercourse alone into the definition of sex, as President Clinton did before them. I hear of couples who have anal sex to preserve technical virginity, and I've been told that "oral sex is ok as long as you swallow." If our parents heard these stories, they'd certainly blush.

So why is it so much harder for otherwise observant people to keep these prohibitions, or why do we choose to reject them outright? In one sense, I think these prohibitions fail to find value in our society because they have been fenced in, expanded until their inner truths are obscured by layers and layers of forbiddenness. Perhaps the Torah restrictions against sex with a woman during her period could be kept, and most of us have little trouble avoiding incest, prostitution, or other obviously licentious behavior. But when all unmarried women are considered to be menstruating and thus impure, or when nearly any non-marital sex can make you into a harlot, it's very hard for us to take these prohibitions seriously. In a modern world, where we are not married off in our teen years but spend significant years single, dating, and forging independent identities, these ever-so-strict prohibitions are no longer akin to the annoyance of separating milk and meat; they become insurmountable obstacles.

But I don't want to just say that we are lazy or hungry or unwilling to chain our baser appetites. In a deeper sense, most liberal Jews understand instinctually the misogynist values underlying the marriage plot. When thinking about *kashrut* or *Shabbat*, it's nice to support touchy-feely values of making time to think about God, restraining physical urges, and so forth. But it's hard for liberal Jews to see the moral worth of said prohibitions when they are so one-sided, restraining a woman's sexual contact while permitting a man's promiscuity. Even in our day, when polygamy has been outlawed, the traditional wedding ceremony remains an acquisition of the bride by the groom, and we remain more concerned about a woman's virginity and promiscuity than we ever are about a man's. The most repulsive instance of this thinking comes from a proverb whispered by Orthodox men: "*Shiksahs* are for practice." Many men still see their own sexuality as somehow less valuable or less defilable than a woman's; sleeping with a non-Jewish woman (and referring to her derogatorily) would in no way hurt a man's marriageability. I posit that even as traditional Jews try to reclaim the spirituality of *mikveh* and the *nidah* laws, we have much work to do to move away from these relationships of inequality, where a woman's sexuality is somehow impure and a man is forgiven, even admired.

Deformities and All: New Paradigms

One of the first of my parents' books that I ever read was Herman Wouk's 1950s novel, *Marjorie Morningstar*. In the book's denouement, the heroine, Marjorie, confesses a former love affair to her traditionally-minded fiancé: "The fact was, she had passed herself off as a good Jewish girl. Twentieth century or not, good Jewish girls were supposed to be virgins when they married. . . . He took her as she was, with her deformity, despite it. For that was what it amounted to in his eyes and in hers—a deformity: a deformity that could no longer be helped; a permanent crippling, like a crooked arm."[11]

Although the hyperbolic language of "deformity" may seem judgmental and archaic, the lessons of this quaint yet moving story still stand in our modern age as emblematic of the dilemmas of modern women (and men, to a lesser extent) in the Jewish community. Despite no explicit prohibition, we are nurtured on values of virginity until marriage; if we break these taboos, we feel guilty. Despite the changing norms of secular approaches to marriage—not every Jewish girl nowadays feels the way that Marjorie did—these values still stand strong in the observant communities.

So, as grandchildren of the sexual revolution concerned with *halakha* and creating observant communities, how do we build norms of sexual behavior that make sense? One traditional response to the problematics of the category of *zonah* is the category of *pilegesh*, the concubine. A *pilegesh* is an unmarried woman in a one-way exclusive relationship; her partner, on the other hand, can be in other exclusive couplings (marital or not). Monthly immersions in the *mikveh* are mandatory, to prevent violating prohibitions against sleeping with a menstruating woman, but she does not need a marriage contract or ceremony to make her permitted to her male partner. The concept of *pilegesh* is regarded as biblical in origin, with the foremothers Bilhah and Zilpah serving as primary examples, and the Talmud discusses its prevalence in its time as well.[12] Among medieval scholars, Rabbi Moshe ben Nachman, the Ramban, was a particularly outspoken supporter of the permissibility of a *pilegesh* relationship, although it is unclear whether people actually used this legal category in his day.[13] The eighteenth-century scholar R. Yaakov Emden later wrote a long responsum attempting to reinstate this category, in the hopes of broadening the range of permitted sexual relationships.[14] I see these rabbinic discussions of *pilegesh* as attempts to wrestle with the problematics of assuming that all nonmarital sexual relationships are somehow immoral.

Some contemporary scholars in the Orthodox community have also begun looking toward the category of *pilegesh* as a means of finding halachic legitimations for nonmarital sexual relations. In particular, a recent scholarly article by Zvi Zohar posits that rabbinic prohibitions against sexuality outside marriage can and should be dismantled to permit sex in monogamous and *nidah*-observant relationships.[15] When an unmarried couple follows the laws of *nidah* and behaves in "mutually respectful" ways, Zohar posits that they should be able to follow the Talmudic category of the *pilegesh,* declaring the woman a concubine only permitted to her male partner. Although the one-sided nature of a concubine relationship still leaves something to be desired for feminists, Zohar's attempt to legitimize what our community already accepts as moral behavior is a first step that could be valuable to many in the observant community.

Implicit in Zohar's reasoning, however, is yet another unspoken assumption: only monogamous relationships can have holiness. The *pilegesh* construct can be used to build a lower-stakes marriage, a bond with enough commitment for a monthly *mikveh* visit and not enough for a wedding canopy to make the grandparents happy. While I do see the value for rejuvenating this legal category for those who need the *halakhic* loophole, I don't think it goes far enough in addressing the modern-day sensibilities of nonmarital sexuality. What can traditional Judaism do with the preponderance of nonmonogamous, "non-serious" sexual relationships? Can only long-term relationships have sexual holiness? I posit that traditional Judaism has a thing or two to learn from more radical feminist and Jewish scholars who see that holiness in sexual relationships can come from recognizing the spark of divinity in one's partner and creating respectful norms.

A recent article that brought forth new principles of sexual practice is in Judith Plaskow's recent book, *The Coming of Lilith.* In her chapter on the forbidden relationships in Leviticus 18, she writes of crafting a new code of sexual ethics with the gay and lesbian study group Or Zarua. Using the biblical commandment to "be holy as [God is] holy"[16] as a starting point, they propose ethical principles that include the following:

> We believe that we honor the image of God by honoring the body. Through our bodies we can connect with each other, the world, and the sacred. . . .
>
> We affirm that each human being must be taught that the awakening of sexual feeling and the desire for sexual activity are natural and good, and that an understanding of how to express sexuality must also be taught. . . .
>
> We affirm human sexuality in all its fluidity, complexity, and diversity. . . .
>
> We affirm the goodness of sexual pleasure independent of the goal of procreation.[17]

Although Plaskow's study group uses the Torah text as a springboard rather than a guidepost, I found something powerful in their using the biblical framework to create a modern ethic. As a modern observant Jew, I would hope that we could see positive principles of respect in sexual relationships as just as divine as the negative ones espoused in the Talmud.

Plaskow's ethic gives us some broad ideas about how to reconstruct our texts. The main problems with the categories of *zonah* and *betulah*, in Jewish and secular contexts, are that these living categories still teach us that women's sexuality is more judged and less free than a man's. College kids throw around the phrase "boy slut," implying that the term needs the gendered modifier to make it *male:* the very nature of promiscuity is somehow gendered as female. In constructing an ethic of sexual holiness in a modern age in which biblical polygyny is no longer acceptable, we need to dismantle these double standards of sexual behavior. Men may not fall into traditional categories of *zonah* and *betulah,* but they are equally obliged to recognize the divinity in all sexual interactions and maintain standards of morality; male promiscuity should be no more praiseworthy or shameful than a woman's.

I would even contend that the very notion of nonmonogamy as equivalent to promiscuity, with its accompanying judgmental tones, is problematic for a community of nonmarried, sexually active adults. As we decide to experiment with different sexual partners, forming more—and less —significant relationships and connections, we should rethink the traditional idea that one long-term partner is the most ethical way to live one's romantic life. Indeed, one advantage of the reinvigorated *pilegesh* custom is its acknowledgment that not all relationships need to be sanctified with a permanent legal and financial transaction to have meaning. Although it is always important to treat sexual partners with respect for the other's *tzelem Elohim,* spark of divinity, we no longer must think that one needs to commit to a long-term relationship to forge an intimate connection that is moral and respectable.

Safe Sex

One aspect of creating holiness in modern relationships is an open discussion of safe sex and contraception. Statistics show that in Christian communities, where abstinence pledges are faddish and teens see premarital sex as sinful, condom usage rates among the so-called sinners are much

lower than in secular communities.[18] Similar stories are told about Orthodox kids experimenting sexually for the first time; we certainly didn't learn
about condom usage in my Modern Orthodox high school. All sexually active observant Jews should take seriously platitudes about *pikuach nefesh*,
the responsibility to save lives and act safely, and practice safe sex by using
condoms, by open communication, and by respectful behavior that honors
the divinity of the body. Condom use is often frowned on in the Orthodox community because of the prohibition against "spilling seed,"[19] but I
would argue that unmarried and sexually active people should prioritize
saving lives with safer sex over this prohibition. Further, to train us to be
respectful of the power of our bodies to both give life and transmit deadly
illnesses, Jewish day schools need to teach safe-sex education, not merely
laws of marital purity, as my school did.

In thinking about holiness in nonmarital relationships, we can also
learn from Plaskow's work regarding how lesbian and gay relationships can
be integrated into concepts of holy sexuality. This chapter focuses on heterosexual relationships, but a key characteristic of younger communities of
traditional Jews is their acceptance of gay and lesbian sexuality as normative. Accompanying the marriage plot of earlier generations is an insistence
on heterosexuality as the only acceptable option for partnership. In the
liberal observant communities of which I've been a part, queer sexuality
is respected and celebrated, despite religious injunctions to the contrary.
Traditional communities that may privately recognize and respect lesbian
and gay couples need to also recognize them publicly with the same communal honors that straight couples receive.

We can also recognize that these very constructs of marital and
nonmarital sexuality exclude many members of our community, gay or
straight, who may not ever plan on heterosexual marriage. Indeed, we can
expand the communal boundaries of what is acceptable to include not only
straight and gay couples but also people who are (gasp) single by choice.
The Orthodox feminist Hagit Bartov recently wrote on the invisibility of
unmarried women in traditional communities, documenting how traditional communities view unmarried women as subversive for denying the
established social order that demands marriage.[20] Women and men who
are encouraged to join synagogues as individual members and are invited
to Shabbat meals and holiday celebrations tend to find value and community in their Judaism, and, not surprisingly, those who are shunned for
lacking a romantic partner tend to leave our gates. By recognizing that not
all Jews wish to marry, and acknowledging the narratives of single people

as equally valid, we can create communities where multiple views of sexuality can be seen as contributing to the fullness of our Jewish vistas.

Beneath these alternative texts and new forms of *halachic* recognition is an underlying emotional issue: how to stop seeing our own sexuality as somehow impure, guilt-ridden, only acceptable within the bounds of marriage? I wonder whether the secret to *halachic* comfort is societal normalization: coming out of the closet, so to speak. When friends who live together stop putting a single name on a wedding's response cards, when we remove the language of *betulah* from the wedding contract, when we stop pretending that "all single Jewish women are virgins," we can begin to think of nonmarital sexuality as containing within it the potential for holiness. We create holiness in every interaction with another human being, when we connect with the spark of divinity in emotional, spiritual, or sexual ways. In our times, when life is long but childbearing years are few, we should empower ourselves to connect deeply with others and feel the range of experiences that come from different intimate connections.

Many years ago I heard a *dvar Torah* (sermon) on the divine aspects of creation.[21] We humans are created in the image of God: What are the most divine things that we can do to mirror this image? God creates other people: thus, by procreating, we can create other people and be connected to God's *yetzirah*, creating by uniting the divine substance of our bodies. But God also creates by speaking, and we as human beings are uniquely privileged to have the intelligence to create new ideas and form emotional connections. I look forward to the modern world we're creating where all our capacities for connections can be cherished and valued.

NOTES

1. *Biyah* is the mishnaic Hebrew word for sexual intercourse. In the initial rabbinic conception of the marriage ceremony, sexual intercourse was one of three ways to consummate a marriage, along with writing a document and the exchange of an item of value with the groom's recitation of, "With this ring I consecrate you to me according to the laws of Moses and Israel." Current rabbinic thought (in Orthodox as well as liberal circles) holds that *biyah* alone will not create a marriage, although the marriage does need to be sexually consummated to stand as valid.

2. According to traditional Jewish caste rules, those of the priestly caste, known as *kohanim*, are forbidden to marry licentious women, including divorcees. The details of what constitutes a licentious woman are discussed later in this essay.

3. For the traditional sources and liberal approach of this essay, I am indebted to my Talmud teacher, Rabbi Richard (Shmuel) Lewis.

4. Leviticus 19:29. All biblical translations are from *The JPS Hebrew-English Tanakh: The Traditional Hebrew Text and the New JPS Translation*, 2nd ed. (Philadelphia: Jewish Publication Society, 2000).

5. Exodus 22:15–16.

6. See also Leviticus 21:9; and Deuteronomy 22:28–29 and 23:18–19.

7. According the laws of priestly conduct, the restrictions on the sexual practices of a *kohen's* partner rest somewhat on a sliding scale. Although the high priest, the *Kohen Gadol,* must marry a virgin, your everyday *kohen* may marry a non-virginal women whose sexual history does not put her in the category of *zonah*. This essay is mostly concerned with the restrictions on everyday *kohanim*, since today we have no *kohen gadol* and worry less about his purity restrictions.

8. Babylonian Talmud (BT) *Yevamot* 51b. Talmudic translations are my own. For other Talmudic sources on *zonah*, see BT *Yoma* 18b and BT *Yevamot* 37b.

9. Leviticus 18:19.

10. *She'elot U'Teshuvot Ha'Riva''sh* (*R. Yitzchak b. Sheshet Perfet)*, Responsum 425 (Constantinople, 1546). Thanks to Haviva Ner-David for help in finding this reference.

11. Herman Wouk, *Marjorie Morningstar* (Boston: Back Bay Books, 1992) (reissue), 552–553.

12. Talmud Bavli *Yoma* 18b and *Yevamot* 37b.

13. Ramban, Responsum 105. Cited by Rabbi Yaakov Emden, *She'elot Ya'avetz* 2, no. 5. Translated in Gershon Winkler, *Sacred Secrets: The Sanctity of Sex in Jewish Law and Lore* (New York: Jason Aaronson, 1998).

14. Ibid.

15. Zvi Zohar, "Halakhic Positions Permitting Nonmarital Sexual Intimacy" [Hebrew], in *Akdamot*, vol. 17 (Jerusalem: Beit Morasha, 2006).

16. Leviticus 19:2.

17. Judith Plaskow, *The Coming of Lilith: Essays on Feminism, Judaism, and Sexual Ethics, 1972–2003* (Boston: Beacon, 2005), 176.

18. Hannah Brückner and Peter Bearman, "After the Promise: The STD Consequences of Adolescent Virginity Pledges." *Journal of Adolescent Health* 36, no. 4 (April 2005): 271–278.

19. This is based on the story of Onan in Genesis 38:9, who ejaculates on the ground rather than impregnate his brother's widow. This story is used as the basis for the prohibition against many forms of barrier birth control, although generally oral contraception is permitted by Modern Orthodox rabbinic authorities.

20. Hagit Bartov, "The Challenge of Unmarried Women: Does Defining Them as a 'Problem' Meet a Social Need?" *Edah Journal* 4, no. 2 (2005): 6–13.

21. Credit for the nuggets of these ideas goes to Rabbi Robert (Aryeh) Klapper.

12

Reconsidering Solitary Sex from a Jewish Perspective

Rebecca T. Alpert

WE LEARN A lot about something by examining the words we use to describe it, where they come from, how they sound, what they evoke. Things
related to sex usually have many descriptive terms, and the act of stimulating our own genitals for sexual satisfaction is no exception. I use the term
"solitary sex," but there's also the slightly more sexy technical term "auto-
eroticism" and the many slang terms that may also come to mind (I'll spare
you the list, but you can look it up). The most common English word to
describe these acts is, perhaps, "masturbation," from the Latin, and the
least common is "onanism," but both terms came into use around the same
time, at the end of the seventeenth century.[1]

The term "onanism" connects solitary sex to Jewish tradition in a cir-
cuitous way. It refers to the story, in Genesis 38, of Onan, a grandson of
the patriarch Jacob, the second son of Judah. Onan's older brother, Er, was
married to Tamar. Er was in some unexplained way "displeasing to Adonai,
and Adonai took his life" (38:7). According to the custom known as levirate marriage, Onan was obligated to have sexual relations with Tamar
in order to provide a son for his brother's line and, according to the text,
was directed to do so by his father, Judah. But Onan did not want to provide his dead brother with offspring, and so, we are told, he "let his seed go
to waste" when he had relations with Tamar. This, too, displeased Adonai,
and so Adonai took his life as well (38:9–10).

What was Onan's crime? The most obvious conclusion is that it was
his refusal to comply with the task his father set for him, which was to impregnate Tamar. So although the term "onanism" should refer to a refusal
to follow orders or to take a stance against the custom of levirate marriage,
it refers instead to the method Onan used to accomplish this act, namely,
"letting his seed go to waste." Commentators disagree, however, about

what "wasting seed" means. Some argue that it refers to coitus interruptus (withdrawal of the penis from the vagina before ejaculation). The text tells us that Onan had sexual relations with Tamar, so that would seem to be a logical conclusion. But those who coined the term may also have believed that, by masturbating, a man weakens his ability to impregnate a woman, and so they assumed Onan masturbated in order to avoid his obligation.[2] Hence "onanism" is defined in the dictionary as both withdrawal before ejaculation and solitary sex, and even, in some cases, all sex that does not involve vaginal penetration.

Thinking about onanism in reference to solitary sex has strong precedent in the Babylonian Talmud, where Onan's crime is used as a proof text to support an antipathy toward male self-arousal. The deed is emphatically condemned in the Mishnah: "Every hand that frequently checks: in women, it is praiseworthy but in men you should cut it off" (*Nidah* 2:1). The text does not support female masturbation; in fact, the Gemara here assumes that women can check because they will not experience a sensation through self-examination (BT *Nidah* 13a). This viewpoint, however, is inconsistent with other rabbinic passages. One text in BT *Avodah Zarah* 44a[3] indicates an awareness that women used phalluses to masturbate, and comments about lesbian behavior indicate that the Rabbis were aware that women rubbed against one another (presumably also by themselves) to achieve orgasm (BT *Yebamot* 76a).[4]

But this text is concerned primarily with men, not women. Although it reinforces women's obligation to check their genitals for any flow that might indicate the start of their menses—defining their entrance into their monthly state of *nidah*, or seclusion—its main focus is to remind men, in no uncertain terms, of their obligation to refrain from touching their penises because, as the Gemara explains, it may lead to self-arousal. Whether that arousal is intentional or unintentional doesn't matter; the Gemara's only concern is with the resulting semenal emission. But although the Rabbis warn against all possible emission of semen, they take particular notice of self-arousal with intent to achieve pleasure.

The Gemara that focuses on intentional self-arousal (BT *Nidah* 13b) makes it clear that this is unacceptable because it will result in terrible and dangerous consequences, including having one's hand cut off. According to Rav, "anyone who willingly causes himself to have an erection will be banned by the community." Rabbi Ami calls such a person a "renegade" (*avaryen*) and blames the *yetzer ha ra* (the evil inclination) for inducing a temptation that the masturbator cannot resist. Rabbi Ami assumes that self-arousal will ultimately lead a man down a slippery slope that ends in idol worship. The connection to Onan is attributed to Rabbi Yosi, who suggests that "anyone who incites himself lustfully is not brought into the precinct of the Holy One, blessed be He" (in other words, one who arouses himself will not be welcome in the World to Come) because he, like Onan, "did what was displeasing to the Lord." Death, Onan's fate, would also be the fate of the lustful inciter. Finally, Rabbi Eliezer is credited with accusing masturbators of "committing adultery with their hand," citing Isaiah 1:15 ("Your hands are full of blood") in support.

The discussion in the Gemara concludes by considering whether the mishnaic punishment, to cut off a man's hand, is a law or merely a curse. According to Rabbi Tarfon, it is better to be without a hand than to end up "descending into the pit of destruction." Although it is unlikely that masturbation was a crime that was actually punished, and the Gemara is inconclusive as to whether cutting off the hand is a law or simply a curse that serves as an admonition, the text gives us a sense of how strongly the Rabbis felt about the evils of male self-arousal and the lengths to which they would go to warn against it.

So, according to Jewish tradition, solitary sex is unthinkable for men and rarely considered for women. Men who masturbate are doing wrong because they should work to control their impulses. A man's *yetzer ha ra* needs to be managed through appropriate sexual engagements with his wife. It is important to remember that, unlike Onan's obligation simply to produce an heir for his dead brother, those sexual encounters were supposed to result both in procreation and sexual pleasure for both partners, as concretized in the law that a man is required to satisfy his wife sexually, known as *onah*. As long as sex was channeled properly, it was not viewed negatively. Just about any sexual position was considered acceptable in marriage, as was contraception in certain circumstances. But orgasm, even if viewed positively, was to be experienced only within the context of appropriate relationships, and certainly not by individuals in solitary exercises that encouraged sexual fantasy or had the potential to turn them away from their social obligations.

To understand the rabbinic view of solitary sex with the goal of moving Jewish thinking beyond negative pronouncements, it may be instructive to look at the parallel case of homosexuality.

The most obvious similarity between these two phenomena is the way the differences between same-sex desire is described in men and women. In the Hebrew Bible there is no same-gender sexuality for women and no allusion to female masturbation, whereas lying with a man as with a woman is famously prohibited twice in the Torah. Although later rabbinic texts pay little attention to the possibility that women indulge in solitary sex, they do approach lesbianism negatively. The transgression is still minor, however, compared to male homosexuality, and is not taken seriously.

Much speculation surrounds the question of why the Rabbis did not take women's sexual desires seriously, since women's reproductive capacities are of great import in ancient Jewish texts. It is surprising in part, given the existence of *onah*, which demands that men satisfy their wives' sexual desires. Of course, these laws may have emerged because of the link the Rabbis make between sex and reproduction, and the concern may not be at all about a man satisfying his wife's desire for sex but, instead, her desire to have children. It is also possible that in ancient Judaism sexuality was only "real" if it involved a penis, which is also assumed necessary in the brief mention of female masturbation in *Avodah Zarah*. But then the prohibition against women rubbing their clitorises against one another for sexual satisfaction, as found in BT *Yebamot* 76a, would also make no sense. We simply do not know why women's sexuality wasn't of concern to the Rabbis. Whether they believed that women really did desire men and motherhood to the exclusion of other possibilities or what women did in private was of no concern or interest to them, it remains our legacy that only what men do matters, for better and worse.

We are left, in any case, with a gender divide that does not speak to our present reality. As Jewish lesbians began to become vocal, demanding a presence in the community, the world of traditional Judaism responded by emphasizing the few negative statements in our ancient texts about female same-sex love. However, no such effort has been made either to redeem or condemn solitary sex for women.

The reasons given in opposition to solitary sex and same-sex love are also similar. As we saw in the discussion of BT *Nidah* 13a–b, the Rabbis were concerned that male self-arousal would lead a man down a slippery slope: if a man can't control his urge to give himself an orgasm, the thinking goes, how can he avoid the greater temptations of idol worship or nonkosher food or the gymnasium? The Rabbis also may have held to the notion that frequent masturbation would weaken the man's capacity (or interest) in satisfying his wife. The same argument is made on the subject of homosexuality. In explaining why male homosexual sex is considered *toevah* (generally translated as "an abomination"), the Rabbis pun on the term and suggest that in fact it means to say *toeh ata ba*, "you will go astray because of it." Again, the temptation to be involved in homosexual or solitary sexual experiences are not necessarily bad in themselves, but they are understood as leading a person in evil or destructive directions and away from the goals of a well-lived life.

The last similarity between solitary sex and homosexuality brings us back to the term "onanism" and the related derivation of the term "sodomy." Both are based on stories in the Book of Genesis, and on surprising interpretations of the relevant texts. Although the Rabbis adopted the story of Onan as their proof text for solitary sex, they did not for the most part attribute homosexual behavior to Sodom; many Christian commentators did, however, and hence the prevalence of the term in European thought prior to the modern era. It is important for us to remember that, just as Western culture has been influenced by stories from the Hebrew Bible, Jewish teachings have also been deeply influenced by ideas of the host societies in which Jews have lived—Muslim, Christian, and secular. Not only do negative views defined by the terms "sodomy" and "onanism" have roots in Jewish tradition, but Jewish views on masturbation and homosexuality in modern times have also been influenced by the negative Western attitudes (both religious and medical) toward these acts. Throughout the modern era, sodomy and onanism were given broad public discussion and approbation in European thought. The historian Thomas Laqueur has argued that the term "onanism" was coined in 1712 in response to a growing social acceptance of sexual pleasure in marriage, as well as concomitant concerns that masturbation might appear to be acceptable and, because of its private nature, uncontrollable. It is in that era when the idea that masturbation caused warts, syphilis, and blindness (to name only a few imagined consequences) began. Sigmund Freud shifted the nature of the concerns about solitary sex from the physical to the psychological, but he also argued that, like homosexuality, masturbation was an immature sexual response that was harmful if not outgrown.

In our own world today, we have witnessed a significant change in attitude regarding same-sex desires as the movement for LGBT (Lesbian, Gay, Bisexual, Transgender) rights has had a powerful impact on public behaviors and policies. The women's movement has made it clear that both women and men have same- and solitary-sexual desire and participate in same and solitary sexual behaviors. The sexual revolution has also helped rehabilitate solitary sex. Those who write about the topic today note a shift from earlier eras. Beginning in the 1980s, they argue, masturbation came to be seen as a valid way for people to express themselves sexually, and a healthy habit.[5] But even with these changes, sexual self-arousal is still considered by many to be immature, harmful, even dangerous. Mentioning masturbation in public certainly was dangerous for Joycelyn Elders, the Surgeon General who was dismissed from her post in 1994 for recommending that schools teach about solitary sex as a positive outlet and a means of preventing sexually transmitted diseases.

When I taught an undergraduate course on religion and sexuality, I gave students the assignment to write a paper about any issue of sexuality from the perspective of three of the world's religions. The students who wished to write about masturbation (and there were several) were unable to do the assignment because they couldn't find sufficient information to write viable papers, beyond the book by Thomas Laqueur from which I draw the title for this article.[6] It's time to reconsider the value of this widely practiced activity that "dare not speak its name."

To rehabilitate solitary sex from a Jewish perspective, it makes sense to return to the perspective of the Rabbis. They presented strong arguments to suggest that solitary sex should not be judged as an end in itself but because it is a means to a (harmful) end and leads its practitioners to danger. Given contemporary perspectives, however, rather than seeing masturbation as a means to harmful ends, we can find in this activity a way to achieve valuable goals.

Self-care is an important Jewish value. Maimonides was a strong proponent of "maintaining physical health and vigor so that the soul may be upright and in a condition to know God" (Mishneh Torah *Hilchot Deot* 4:14). Though once considered an unhealthy practice, studies today show that masturbation has advantages for sexual well-being.[7] As boys and girls learn to give themselves orgasms, they learn an important technique to relieve stress. They also develop the capacity to engage in fantasy and learn what arouses them sexually.[8] At the same time, encouraging young people to engage in solitary sex may help them avoid the real physical dangers of other forms of sexual experimentation that can lead to harmful ends like unwanted pregnancy and sexually transmitted diseases. But it is also important to remember that solitary sex can have value for adults, both in and out of relationships. For the adult in a long-term committed relationship, solitary sex may also provide opportunities for relaxation, experiencing sexual variety without going outside the relationship, developing a capacity for fantasy, and understanding what he or she desires. For the adult who is not in a relationship, masturbating has the advantages described above and can also be an empowering way to satisfy sexual needs. This is particularly the case for older people, who should be encouraged to masturbate to keep their sex drive alive, as achieving orgasm has been shown to have long-term health advantages;[9] further, sexual response needs regular stimulation to stay in shape in the same way that our other muscles and nerve endings do.

Preparation for sexual activity with others is another goal of solitary sex. Solitary sex has the potential to lead to more comfort with one's own sexuality, and that extends to making sexual connections beyond oneself. The command to "love your neighbor as yourself" (Lev. 19) can be understood as an injunction to love yourself so that you can learn how better to love others. In this paradigm, solitary sex provides an avenue of discovery for enhancing and improving sexual intimacy for partners. If you understand your own sexual desires and how to achieve orgasm effectively for yourself, it is not unlikely that in the process you will also discover how to please your partner and how to teach your partner to please you. Solitary sex is limited because it does not create actual opportunities for intimacy or the possibility of pregnancy. However, it can lead one in the direction of understanding how achieving mutual sexual pleasure enhances the prospects of achieving these other goals as well, on the principle that self-love leads to love of others.

Privacy is also an important Jewish value and can be fostered by solitary sex. We are taught that modesty (*tzniut*) is fundamental to Jewish ethics. Solitary sex is modest because it happens in solitude, away from public consideration. Jewish teachings encourage us to behave modestly, to hold private that which we value as sacred. I am reminded of the scene in the (very Jewish) film *Borat* where the protagonist becomes enraged when he finds his business partner masturbating while looking at a photograph of Borat's "sacred" love object, Pamela Anderson. This scene describes the antithesis of the values that properly modest masturbation aims toward. Borat is right to be angry; masturbation and its attendant fantasies are private matters. Jewish values encourage us to keep certain matters out of public discourse and attention. Solitary sex can lead to an understanding that certain things in one's life should not be shared with others. This is particularly valuable in today's society, where everything is on display and under surveillance. In this way solitary sex is unlike homosexuality. For gay and lesbian people, making sexual orientation visible is crucial, as it has created opportunities for political and social rights unknown in prior eras.

What I offer here is a tentative effort to bring attention to a valuable, safe, and potentially enriching activity that is often disparaged and ignored. Rather than remaining tied to an ancient (or contemporary) negative perspective, it is my desire that this new Jewish approach to solitary sex, which is open to its positive consequences, may increase possibilities for sexual health and pleasure.

NOTES

I am grateful to Sarra Lev and Danya Ruttenberg for their helpful editorial comments on this essay.

1. For a full discussion of the history of the definitions used to define the practice, see Martha Cornog, *The Big Book of Masturbation: From Angst to Zeal* (San Francisco: Down There Press, 2003), 3–14; for a list of slang terms in all languages, see 15–22. Cornog distinguishes solitary sex from masturbation that is a component of sexual activity involving others, as do I throughout this essay.

2. See Michael Satlow, "'Wasted Seed': The History of a Rabbinic Idea," *Hebrew Union College Annual* 65, no. 1 (1994): 159.

3. R. Jose answered them: "But has it not been stated, And also Maacah the mother of Asa the king, he removed her from being queen, because she had made an abominable image . . . he made dust of it, and burnt it at the brook of Kidron! . . . What means *miplezeth* [abominable image]? Rab Judah said: [An object which] intensifies licentiousness [*maphli'lezanutha*] as R. Joseph taught: It was a kind of phallus with which she had sex every day."

4. Greco-Roman civilization was also aware of similar practices of female masturbation. See Vern L. Bullough, "Masturbation: A Historical Overview," *Journal of Psychology and Human Sexuality* 14, no. 2/3 (2002): 22–23.

5. See Arne Decker and Gunter Schmidt, "Patterns in Masturbatory Behavior: Changes between the Sixties and the Nineties," *Journal of Psychology and Human Sexuality* 14, no. 2/3 (2002): 35–48.

6. Thomas Walter Laqueur, *Solitary Sex: A Cultural History of Masturbation* (New York: Zone Books, 2003).

7. See Eli Coleman, "Masturbation as a Means of Achieving Sexual Health," *Journal of Psychology and Human Sexuality* 14, no. 2/3 (2002): 5–16. Coleman cites research which indicates that masturbation is an early marker of healthy sexual development. It has also been used as a technique to help those with hypoactive sexual desire disorder. See Brian Zamboni and Isiaah Crawford, "Using Masturbation in Sex Therapy: Relationships between Masturbation, Sexual Desire, and Sexual Fantasy," *Journal of Psychology and Human Sexuality* 14, no. 2/3 (2002): 123–142.

8. Zamboni further argues that sexual fantasies are necessary in many cir-

cumstances to stimulate desire, which in turn is necessary to achieve arousal in single and dyadic sexual encounters (Zamboni and Crawford, "Using Masturbation in Sex Therapy," 139).

9. A recent biological study suggests that sexual satisfaction through the production of prolactin is much greater (400%) in intercourse than through masturbation, thus limiting, though not entirely, the value of masturbation for health (Stuart Brody, "The Post-Orgasmic Prolactin Increase Following Intercourse Is Greater Than Following Masturbation and Suggests Greater Satiety," *Biological Psychology* 71 [March 3, 2006]: 312–315).

We-Thou: Visions

13

"Created by the Hand of Heaven"

Sex, Love, and the Androgynos

Elliot Rose Kukla

An androgynos is in some respects legally equivalent to men, and in some respects legally equivalent to women, in some respects legally equivalent to men and women, and in some respects legally equivalent to neither men nor women. How is the androgynos legally equivalent to men? The androgynos conveys impurity with white [penile discharge] like men, dresses like men, marries but is not taken in marriage like men.

—Mishnah *Bikkurim* 4:1–2

"The Androgynos Marries"

The first time I read this text I was stunned because the question was not *if* the androgynos could marry but *how* the androgynos marries. Not only is a person who is neither male nor female allowed to be a fully sexual being worthy of companionship in Jewish sacred texts, the androgynos is *presumed* to be one. The inclusion of transgender and gender nonconforming people within loving relationships, and community and family life, is still a hotly contested issue in the twenty-first century, but the Rabbis of the Mishnah writing in the first century CE were merely debating the details!

The Rabbis of the Mishnah identify at least four possible genders/sexes:[1] the *zakhar* (male) and the *nekevah* (female), as well as two sexes which are beyond male and female: the *tumtum* and the *androgynos*. The Talmud sees the tumtum as a person whose genitals are obscured, making it difficult to discern whether he/she should be classified as male or female. The androgynos is a person who has both male and female sex traits. All these sexes appear frequently in classical Jewish texts[2]—the *androgynos* appears more than one hundred times in the Babylonian Talmud alone.

The tumtum and androgynos are often held up as anomalous examples to test the limits of traditional rabbinic understandings of sex and gender. In other words, they often function to bolster the dichotomy between men and women, and the primacy of men within *halakha*. However, they are also always seen as fully human and integrated into the social life of the Rabbis. Mishnah *Bikkurim* 4, for example, explores the various civil and ritual laws that apply to the androgynos. Throughout this chapter, care is taken to describe the ways in which the life of the androgynos is protected, sanctified, and embedded within Jewish communal life.

At the end of this chapter of Mishnah, Rabbi Yossi offers the startling opinion that the androgynos is *"Bri'a b'ifnei atzmah hoo."* This phrase is hard to translate into English, but the best equivalent is probably "he is a created being of her own." This Hebrew phrase blends male and female pronouns to poetically express the complexity of the androgynos's identity. *Bri'a b'ifnei atzmah* is a classical Jewish legal term for exceptionality. The *koi*, an animal neither wild nor domesticated, is referred to by the same phrase (Tosefta *Bikkurim* 2). Rabbi Yossi is a minority opinion in the Mishnah, but his view that the androgynos is a unique being of its own beyond male and female categories frequently guides the way the androgynos is treated in later Talmudic and *halakhic* texts.[3]

That the androgynos marries in the Mishnah is no small matter. It raises a series of questions that the twenty-first century is just beginning to tackle.[4] If the androgynos is a created being of its own and not (or not only) a male being, then how does the androgynos's presence in marriage impact the way we have understood the gender hierarchy between husband and wife in traditional Judaism? Once the androgynos marries a woman, does that mean that the couple is permitted to engage in all forms of sexual intimacy, with all possible combinations of genitalia? If so, how does this impact Jewish law prohibiting homosexuality? More generally, how does the presence of a gender-nonconforming sexual being disrupt the heterosexual and misogynist assumptions underlying a traditional Jewish view of sex and love?

The Disappearing Hermaphrodite

Over the past few years I have had the opportunity to offer workshops on gender diversity in Jewish sacred texts at a number of synagogues, universities, and communal organizations. I have found that progressive people are often (quite rightly) offended by the lower-class and ambiguous status that the androgynos seems to hold in ancient society. The androgynos, certainly, is not afforded the same rights and privileges as men and is denied some of the protections of women. However, it often takes someone of transgender or intersex experience to get the radical meta-point—our existence is recognized. We are seen as full human beings in Jewish sacred texts!

Sadly, the humanity of people who do not fit into binary genders is not nearly so clear in our time. Each year upwards of 30 transgender and gender-nonconforming people are murdered worldwide, and most of these crimes go unsolved and unpunished.[5] Not only is the androgynos protected from violence in Jewish texts, but the androgynos is presumed to be part of a loving family and community life. The sexuality of the androgynos in Jewish texts is troubling and difficult to classify, but it is never effaced. This is an uncomfortable fact for a modern society that denies the very existence of gender multiplicity, much less acknowledges that we might be desirable, loving partners. The first time I encountered the tumtum and androgynos in a text, I was learning in an ultra-orthodox yeshiva. My teacher told me that they were mythical creatures, kind of like a unicorn.

Modern society holds that there are two (and only two) ways of being human. Before we are born, people ask: "Is it a boy or a girl?" From the moment of birth onward, most facets of our life—the clothes we are told to wear, the activities we are supposed to like, the careers and hobbies we are encouraged to pursue, the loving relationships we are expected to have—are guided by the answer to this crucial question.

The past few decades of feminist organizing have deeply questioned whether we can (or should) see gender as an essential way to divide up humanity. Yet most of us twenty-first century people have still been raised to believe that whether we are a girl or a boy is a simple, unchangeable fact. The less than two centimeters of body tissue that lies between a medically "acceptable" clitoris and a passable penis will still consign someone to a life of earning less on the dollar, a one in three possibility of being sexually abused, as well as a rational fear of walking home alone at night. "If three decades of feminist theorizing about gender has thoroughly dislodged the notion that anatomy is destiny, that gender is natural, and that male and female are the only options," asks the contemporary queer theorist Judith Halberstam, "why do we still operate in a world that assumes that people who are not male are female, and people who are not female are male (and even that people who are not male are not people!)."[6]

According to the Intersex Society of North America, the primary organization that advocates for intersex people, one in every one thousand to two thousand infants is born with physical traits that cannot easily be classified as male or female.[7] Many more people discover at the onset of puberty that they have ambiguous hormonal or chromosomal status. Intersexuality is quite common. But the twenty-first century (from locker rooms to census forms) is structured to allow two, and only two, sexes. In our times, if visible anatomy does not identify the sex of a baby, in most cases a surgeon operates to transform the infant into an unambiguous boy or girl. If an individual's body takes an alternate route to maturity at puberty, we offer hormone therapies to stimulate conformity.

The exceptional bodies that richly populate the Mishnah, as well as the Hellenistic ancient world, have almost vanished in modernity. This is not because sex is any less variable in the twenty-first-century United States than it was in first-century Palestine, but because cultural authority figures such as doctors, scientists, and scholars have found ways to make individuals who do not conform to binary sex assignment disappear.

Michel Foucault argues that in modernity, human sexual embodiment changed.[8] Until that point, sex difference was generally seen through the prism of a single normative sex. Galen, a Greek physician of the second century CE, held that women were simply men who lacked an essential form of inner heat. This coolness led women to be less perfectly formed than males. Hence organs that reached their full external development in the male remained "inverted" in the female.[9] This single gendered view of sexual embodiment persisted in colloquial speech even after it had begun to be replaced by the modern science of binary sex assignment. A nineteenth-century doggerel verse betrays traces of this sentiment when it rhymes: "Though they of different sexes be / Yet on the whole they are the same as we / For those that have the strictest searchers been / Find women are but men turned outside in."[10]

A single-gendered view of human sexuality persisted through the medieval period. Maleness represented the pinnacle of human perfection with femaleness as its nadir. This framework is certainly misogynist and hierarchical, but it allowed for the open, if begrudging, social acknowledgment of sexual individuality. As Anne Fausto-Sterling has described in her book, *Sexing the Body*, throughout medieval and early modern Europe, determining the sex of a body rested on the authority of religious institutions, thus differing religious concerns led to divergent approaches to gender variance. Referring to a number of case studies of hermaphrodites in the early modern period, Fausto-Sterling writes: "The Italians seemed relatively nonplussed by the blurring of gender borders, the French rigidly regulated it, while the English, although finding it distasteful, worried more about class transgressions."[11] What all these approaches have in common is their recognition of gender diversity, regardless of their responses to it.

Rigid binary categories for the human experience grew in popularity in the eighteenth and nineteenth centuries as a way to regulate and control society. The Victorian science of difference discovered "evidence" of dichotomous physiological differences between men and women, working and owning classes, and white people and people of color. This evidence was used to justify and reinforce fundamental social and economic hierarchies at a time when these power structures were under siege by various emancipation movements.[12] "People of mixed sex all but disappeared," writes Fausto-Sterling, "not because they had become rarer, but because scientific methods classified them out of existence."[13]

Beyond Binary

Jewish sacred texts speak in a different voice. Although Jewish Sages often tried to sort the world into binaries, they also acknowledged that not all parts of God's creation can be contained in orderly boxes. Distinctions between Jews and non-Jews; Shabbat and the days of the week; purity and impurity are crucial to Jewish tradition. However, it was the parts of the universe that defied binaries that most interested the Rabbis of the Mishnah and the Talmud. Pages and pages of sacred texts are occupied with the minute details of the moment between fruit and bud, wildness and domestication, innocence and maturity, the twilight hour between day and night.

The Mishnah and the Tosefta, compiled in the first few centuries of the Common Era, explore all the ways that genders beyond male and female fit into all aspects of civil and community life, including with regard to inheritance, purity, earning a livelihood, and ritual participation, as well as sex and love.[14] The Sages of the Talmuds, dealing with the tumtum and androgynos nearly five hundred years later, also see them as persons who are fully integrated in society—including as sexual beings. In the Babylonian Talmud we learn the story of a tumtum who becomes a parent of seven children (BT *Yevamot* 83b). In the same tractate, the radical claim is made that the first ancestors of the Jewish people—Abraham and Sarah

—were actually originally *tumtumim*. According to this text, they only later transitioned genders to become male and female (BT *Yevamot* 64a).

These texts reveal a tension in classical Jewish thought. Homosexuality between men is prohibited, and a gender hierarchy that places men above women is fundamental to human relations and Jewish law. However, the openly acknowledged presence of gender-nonconforming figures in sex and marriage implicitly questions the solidity of both compulsory heterosexuality and the subjugation of women. This tension is particularly clear in a fascinating text in BT *Yevamot* that deals with the (in)famous verse: "A man should not lie with a man as he would with a woman" (Lev. 18:22). In modern Western culture, this is perhaps the most common verse used as a weapon against the LGBT community and interpreted as a blanket ban on queer sex of all varieties. In Jewish tradition, this verse has primarily been understood much more narrowly as a prohibition on anal intercourse between men.

In an obscure passage of the Talmud, this verse is understood to be even more specific: "Said Rava: 'Bar Hamduri used logic to explain to me the verse: *A man should not lie with another man in the lying-places of a woman* (Lev. 18:22). Who is this man who has within him two-lying places? Aha . . . that is the androgynos!'" (BT *Yevamot* 83a). In this text the Hebrew word "lying-places" is understood literally to mean orifices capable of receiving penetration. Who is this male-like person (i.e., someone with a penis) they ask, who has two orifices? The answer is the androgynos, who can be penetrated both anally and through a vagina. In other words, according to Rava/Bar Hamduri's reading, this verse is not referring to male homosexuality at all! Instead, it is specifically teaching that men are forbidden to have vaginal sex with the androgynos as this is the "lying-place" of women. This often-ignored little text destabilizes one of the most central Torah bases for prohibiting homosexual sex.

The majority of the Sages in this debate reject Rava and Bar Hamduri's narrow reading of the verse from Leviticus. Instead, they understand it as referring to sex between men. However, they go on to discuss whether men are liable to death by stoning for sex with an androgynos just as they would be for sex with another male. The opposing view is put forth that a man incurs the penalty for lying with a man only "when he comes upon the androgynos in the way of males, but if he does not come upon him in the way of males, he is not liable."[15] In other words, according to the majority opinion, only receiving penetrative anal sex with the androgynos is prohibited.

This text is certainly homophobic: it reinforces the penalty of stoning for homosexual acts. It also reinforces rabbinic misogyny, as the central concern seems to be treating a person with a penis in a "feminine" and therefore degrading fashion. However, by including the androgynos–who is understood in this text as neither male nor female—in the conversation, it also (perhaps unintentionally) undermines the a priori assumptions of heterosexuality and gender hierarchy. The openly acknowledged presence of a gender-nonconforming person within sexual acts makes it clear that it is much harder to define the line between sexes than we might have thought. It also challenges the law's capacity to describe the limits around sanctioned heterosexuality.

Despite the problematic nature of this perplexing text, it can be seen as a significant disruption of normative understandings of gender and sexuality. The feminist theorist Judith Plaskow, in an article called "Judaism Beyond Gender," writes that the very existence of the tumtum and androgynos potentially destabilizes gender binaries, and hence heterosexuality within Judaism. She writes:

> The figure of the hermaphrodite plays a paradoxical role in rabbinic thought, as it does in other cultural contexts. On the one hand, the hermaphrodite poses a problem that binary gender logic must find a way to erase; it is a "necessary irritant" that ultimately serves to consolidate and stabilize the two-gender system. On the other hand, the hermaphrodite is the "vanishing point" of the gender binary; it embodies the dissolution of male and female as absolute categories.[16]

The presence of gender-nonconforming partners in sex and marriage makes it clear that the line around sex differences and the boundaries around sexual identities are constantly shifting and difficult to define. Therefore, it is far more difficult than most of us have supposed to make sweeping statements about the dominance of "men," the subjugation of "women" in traditional Jewish sexual relations, or the compulsory nature of heterosexuality in classical Jewish life and law.

Contemporary Implications

The boundaries around sexual identities have shifted throughout history. Names for gender and sexual identities cannot be translated between languages and eras without also importing an entire set of preconceptions. An exact equivalence cannot be made between premodern gender diversity and contemporary transgender and intersex identities, but it is important to note that bodies and identities beyond male and female have existed across millennia and that discussions of premodern gender diversity can inform and enrich contemporary gender nonconforming lives.

The presence of the androgynos in Jewish sacred tradition as a "uniquely created being of its own" intertwined in loving sexual relationships makes it clear that sex is complicated. Today we confront those who do not "fit" into binary sex assignment and endeavor to change them. Our rabbis took people as they really were and went on from there. These texts may be read in many ways, and the Sages' approach is far from perfect. They certainly do not advocate the overthrow of binary systems; they do not argue for sex and gender liberation, as some of us might wish that they had. But they also never question whether gender diversity really exists or whether gender-nonconforming people should be included in romantic and social life. They do not advocate operations to transform an infant's body to better fit a gender category or assume that transgender adults are the objects of fetish but never genuine love.

The inclusion of the androgynos in discussions of sexuality and love in Jewish sacred texts opens more space in society for men, women, transgender, intersex people, and everyone else. The image of the androgynos as a lover, partner, and parent forces the tradition to acknowledge that not all of creation, and not all of our relationships, can be understood within binary systems. It is also a theological statement, a proclamation that God creates a diversity of bodies and an abundance of desires far too complex for human beings to understand. It conveys an understanding that all people are created *al y'dei shamayim*[17]—by the hand of Heaven—and that every Divine creation is entitled to be seen, loved, and desired.

ACKNOWLEDGMENT

Most of these ideas and many of these sentences were written in collaboration with my *chevruta* (study partner) Reuben Zellman. Thank you!

NOTES

1. The term "gender" has been used to denote social roles and behaviors, whereas "sex" indicates physiological differences. Both terms can be complex for

transgender and gender-nonconforming individuals. In recent years theorists such as Michel Foucault and Judith Butler have pointed to the shifting nature of sex, as well as gender, across lines of history and geography. Butler and other contemporary feminists have suggested that the borders around sex have been drawn and redrawn in various times and places to meet a variety of social and cultural needs. This view posits that the sexing of our bodies, as much as the gendering of our roles, is culturally and historically construed. This contemporary feminist position is where I situate myself. I do not mean to deny that there are sexual characteristics that unite and divide bodies in every epoch, but I believe that it is impossible to say anything about sex difference that does not also encode messages about gender relations and power. For more information, see Judith Butler, *Gender Trouble: Feminism and the Subversion of Identity* (New York: Routledge, 1990); and Michel Foucault, *The History of Sexuality*, trans. Robert Hurley (New York: Vintage Books, 1985).

2. The tumtum appears 17 times in the Mishnah; 23 times in the Tosefta; 119 times in the Babylonian Talmud; 22 times in the Jerusalem Talmud, and hundreds of times in midrash, commentaries, and *halacha*. The androgynos appears 21 times in the Mishnah; 19 times in the Tosefta; 109 times in the Babylonian Talmud; and countless times in midrash and *halacha*.

3. See, for example, BT *Yevamot* 83a.

4. In 1978 the Union for Reform Judaism (URJ) passed a lukewarm responsum allowing transsexuals to marry, but it explicitly excludes individuals whose gender is not clearly established and only permits marriage between individuals where it is clear "that this in no way constitutes a homosexual marriage." See "Conversion and Marriage after Transsexual Surgery," CCAR Responsum 5750.8.

5. For a complete list of the victims of hate crimes against gender-nonconforming individuals each year, see http://www.gender.org/remember/index.html (accessed 10/22/07).

6. Judith Halberstam, *Female Masculinity* (Durham, N.C.: Duke University Press, 1998), 20.

7. http://www.isna.org (accessed 10/22/07).

8. This position, which is followed by Laqueur and others, is most fully associated with the work of Foucault. See Foucault, *The History of Sexuality*.

9. See Galen, *De semine*, 2.1, in *Opera omnia*, ed. William Teffler (Philadelphia: Westminster, 1955).

10. Cited in Thomas Laqueur, *Making Sex: Body and Gender from the Greeks to Freud* (Cambridge, Mass.: Harvard University Press, 1992), 6.

11. Anne Fausto-Sterling, *Sexing the Body: Gender Politics and the Construction of Sexuality* (New York: Basic Books, 1990), 35.

12. For a fuller discussion of the nineteenth-century science of difference and the enforcement of social power, see Fausto-Sterling, *Sexing the Body*, 30–45.

13. Ibid., 39.

14. See Mishnah *Bikkurim* 4; Tosefta *Bikkurim* 2; Tosefta *Megillah* 2, Tosfeta *Rosh HaShana.*

15. BT *Yevamot* 84a.

16. Judith Plaskow, "Judaism Beyond Gender."

17. The Maggid Mishnah on Maimonedes, *Mishnah Torah, Hilchot Shofar.*

14

Toward a New *Tzniut*

Danya Ruttenberg

ON MY THIRD day of rabbinical school, a male colleague ran his finger slowly up my arm to my shoulder and said, in a voice that was somewhere between flirtatious and downright creepy, "You'll be wanting to cover up, then." I was dressed in a tank top—a sleeveless T-shirt—and a skirt. Where I came from, upper arms were not considered obscene. This, then, was the beginning of my formal religious education.

Much is made about *tzniut* (modesty) in contemporary religious Judaism, particularly in Orthodoxy. Although *tzniut* is a broad concept that traditionally addresses many different ways that a person should be humble and unassuming, in today's context it refers almost exclusively to female dress, and sometimes to female behavior. As women's increased roles in the broader culture threaten to encroach upon a traditionally gendered society, placing special emphasis on *tzniut* reframes discussions of gender roles in terms of a woman's humility, the importance of knowing her place, and staying away from the influence of Western secular culture and sexual norms. Increasing numbers of popular books on modesty are being published by the religious Jewish world, describing in obsessive detail the ways in which proper women ought to attire themselves—featuring lists of acceptable fabrics and explicit measurements of skirt lengths, as well as extensive debates about whether or not patterned tights might be considered acceptable. One such tome, *Oz Vehadar Levusha* (the English edition is titled *Modesty: An Adornment for Life*), makes the stakes and boundaries clear: "Even a minor exposure is provocative and a serious shortcoming in *tzniut*. It is therefore *asur* [forbidden] for the neckline of the garment to extend even half a centimeter beyond the permitted level."[1]

Although the focus on this issue relative to other *halakhic* concerns is relatively recent, the Jewish impulse to cover women's bodies—and the reason why—has been explicit for a long time. The Talmud in Tractate

Brachot discusses the aspects of a woman's body (from her little finger to her hair and voice) that might be considered *erva*, a word that can be translated, variously, as "nakedness," "sexually forbidden," or "intimate." The Talmudic commentator Rashba explains why this would be the case in his comment on Rav Hisda's statement, "A woman's leg is *erva*,"[2] explaining that it is specifically forbidden "to men because of sexual thoughts."[3] A woman's leg is not problematic in and of itself, but the thoughts it arouses in men are problematic—to the men. Therefore, according to the *halakha* derived from this passage, women need to cover up. (It's worth noting that the Talmud passage itself deals with the question of what is in one's view while reciting the Shema, a prayer that requires particular concentration, and not with legislating female dress in a general sense. Still, many later legal statements on modesty use BT *Brachot* 24a as their textual foundation.) Tova Hartman sums up the situation neatly: "What we find at the end of the day is that the full-time job of managing male sexuality has been displaced onto women, freeing their counterparts to more noble pursuits."[4]

This job has been extended further and further as of late. *Oz Vehadar Levusha* encapsulates its ideals in a clever little catch-phrase: "What Torah does for men, tzniu[t] does for women." The author explains that, just as study is the corrective that saves men from temptation, so, too, are women kept at their holiest through scrupulous attention to proper covering of clothing and hair. Ironies abound; one might even cheekily ask if this formulation intends to suggest that women don't need Torah at all but, rather, just a long skirt. As Rabbi Yehuda Henkin observes, "This ideology prohibits a woman from standing out—and from being outstanding. She must not act in a play, paint a mural, play an instrument or otherwise demonstrate special skills in front of men, lest she attract attention and her movements excite them."[5]

This is, of course, unacceptable. At its most benign, this fixation on the modesty of women's dress fosters hypocrisy (check the women's section of many Modern Orthodox synagogues in Manhattan on a Friday night, and you'll find legions of young women whose clothes, though reaching comfortably past the knee and elbow, are I-can't-breathe-and-I-bet-you-can-see-every-single-curve-on-my-body *skin tight*) and at its most sinister, demands (as R. Henkin suggests) the absolute erasure of female potential.

A common feminist response to this sort of oppression is to assert female sexual agency by revealing exactly the body parts (and perhaps a few more) that the Modesty Police are so intent on keeping covered. I certainly agree that each body is its owner's to do with as she pleases. Yet, in our current context, women traverse a fraught and complex path in which the decision to reveal is as loaded as the decision to cover. Given that babes in bikinis are used to sell everything from beer and cars to computers and bank accounts, even the most articulate feminist can find that her reasons for uncovering are slightly fuzzy. There's a cultural reward that comes to women who dress in minimal clothing, who facilitate the objectification of women in its secular context. Even when executed with feminist intent, this set of sartorial choices can all too easily support the patriarchal demand that the female body be, at all times, readily available for consumption. On either end of these extremes, the obsession is with revealing or covering disparate female body parts, keeping women (individually or as a collective) neatly packaged, compartmentalized, and, perhaps, more easily controlled.

In her landmark essay, "The Uses of the Erotic: The Erotic as Power," Audre Lorde writes,

> The erotic has often been misnamed by men and used against women. It has been made into the confused, the trivial, the psychotic, and plasticized sensation. For this reason, we have turned away from the exploration and consideration of the erotic as a source of power and information, confusing it with the pornographic. But pornography is a direct denial of the power of the erotic, for it represents the suppression of true feeling. Pornography emphasizes sensation without feeling.

She continues,

> The very word *erotic* comes from the Greek word *eros*, the personification of love in all its aspects—born of Chaos, and personifying creative power and harmony.... Erotic connection functions [in] the open and [is a] fearless underlining of my capacity for joy, in the way my body stretches to music and opens into response, harkening to its deepest rhythms so every level upon which I sense also opens to the erotically satisfying experience whether it is dancing, building a bookcase, writing a poem, or examining an idea.[6]

In other words, Lorde defines the erotic as that which embodies the deepest and most fundamental connection to the self (and, I suggest, to the

Divine) and the pornographic as that which cuts us off from the self, the sense of embodiment, and, I suggest, God Godself. In the erotic, we are subjects. In the pornographic, we are objects.

Can this distinction, I wonder, be useful in an examination of modesty? How can we begin to talk about women's bodies and clothing, as well as the notion of *tzniut* in a broader sense, in a way that emphasizes the importance of our erotic, integrated, Divinely connected selves rather than focusing on compartmentalized individual body parts? What would it mean to get dressed as a subject?

In several places,[7] the Talmud debates the question of whether *mitzvot tzrichot kavvanah*, whether the performance of a mitzvah requires the intention to perform it. In Tractate *Rosh Hashanah* (28a–29b), for example, the Gemara debates the status of someone who passed by a synagogue and heard the shofar being blown on Rosh Hashanah but thought that the sound was an animal braying. If he did not have the *intention* of fulfilling his obligation to hear the shofar when he heard the sound, is he considered to have fulfilled the obligation? Or, if the person who blows the shofar does not intend to use the horn to fulfill a *mitzvah*, but rather to make music, does it count for the listener? The Gemara ends this discussion with the position of R. Yose, who argues that "an ordinary individual does not perform his religious duty until both the hearer and the performer put their mind to it," intending to fulfill the *mitzvah*. *Mitzvot*, it seems, do require intention.

The *halakhic* commentator the Rema supports this notion when he suggests that cross-dressing is permitted on Purim, despite being forbidden the rest of the year, because the dresser's intention (*kavanah*) is only for the joy of the day and not, say, for the pursuit of the sexually forbidden.[8] Again, it's not what you do but how you think about it that's spiritually significant.

The erotic instead of the pornographic. Intention. What if these things were to matter in our ethics of modesty? In order to restore the self to the erotic core, the first crucial step is to cease preoccupation with superficial details. After all, the distinction between the erotic and pornographic is based on internal and interpersonal context. The same woman could be wearing the exact same shirt with two very different thoughts in her head, and the wearing might, as such, mean different things: "I'm going to wear this shirt to the bar so that a bunch of guys will think I'm desirable and will want to have sex with me," is very different from, "I'm going to wear this shirt because I feel beautiful in it and because I love feeling the sun on my shoulders." In one case, our wearer wills herself into becoming an object —she is pornographic and compartmentalized. In the other, her subject-hood is at the forefront; she is erotic and whole. Whether her skirt is long or short, it must enable her to feel the quiet but always-pulsing connection to a sense of internal sacredness and to God Godself. For different people, at different times, in different contexts, the clothes that enable that connection will vary. Cross-dressing is permitted on Purim because it is done in the spirit of joy.

Thus modesty requires intention—the intention of connection, the intention of wholeness, of subjecthood, of care for the self and of the sacred. As one piece from *The Vagina Monologues* attests, subjecthood comes in all lengths of clothing:

> My short skirt, believe it or not, has nothing to do with you. My short skirt is about discovering the power of my lower calves, about cool autumn air traveling up my inner thighs, about allowing everything I see or pass or feel to live inside. But mainly my short skirt and everything under it is mine, mine, mine.[9]

If we demand that true modesty involves a subjective connection to the erotic, if we place its definition in the hands of each individual, it ceases to be an exercise in which women constantly and vigilantly manage the male gaze. Rather, it becomes a way for the woman-as-subject (and man-as-subject; everything I propose here is meant to be relevant for everyone) to connect to her deepest sense of self and to that which enables service to the Divine.

A caveat: there is no such thing as perfect intention. For all of us, a myriad of motivations, some loftier than others, come together when we make decisions. A woman may be genuinely grounded in her sense of personal power and also be slightly self-exploitative about the very same sartorial choice. It happens. The model of erotic connection for which I advocate is an ethic to pursue, a way of relating to the self to be fostered in our communities. And, little by little, it will take root. As Lorde suggests,

> When we live outside ourselves, and by that I mean on external directives only rather than from our internal knowledge and needs, when we live away from those erotic guides from within ourselves, then our lives are limited by external and alien forms, and we conform to the needs of a structure that is not based on human need, let alone an

individual's. But when we begin to live from within outward, in touch with the power of the erotic within ourselves, and allowing that power to inform and illuminate our actions upon the world around us, then we begin to be responsible to ourselves in the deepest sense.[10]

This ethic of modesty seeks to enable empowered individuals to live in connection with the Divine. But it is also a communal value. When Maimonedes discusses modesty in the Mishneh Torah, he talks relatively little about women as a category per se.[11] He argues, instead, that the way to behave with *tzniut gedolah* (great modesty) is to be discreet in the bathroom, to refrain from talking louder than is absolutely necessary, to refrain from showing off your money, and to generally keep other people's needs and reactions in mind as you move through the world.

Care and concern for the feelings of others is at the heart of modest behavior. Even though this ethic has been exploited at women's expense in the past, its significance is real. Caring for others, after all, is a vital part of how we live an engaged life of service to God. This, then, is the core of a new *tzniut*: to dress and behave with a sensitivity both to oneself and one's deepest needs, and to one's context, to the reactions of others; to love our neighbors as ourselves in our actions and in our interactions.

However, as the feminist religious scholar Carol Lee Flinders observes, in our patriarchal culture, care for others may sometimes be fraught for women. She writes,

> Enclosure, silence, self-naughting, and restructuring of desire are proven avenues, say advocates of meditative spirituality, to resources that remain untapped in most of us. Well they might be, feminists are quick to reply, but unless a woman can choose them freely, knowing that she *could* come and go as she likes, say what she wishes, and be *somebody*, then her apparent embrace of those renunciations is relatively meaningless and surely can't be expected to bear fruit.[12]

In other words, religious practices that might have a profound effect on someone who has always had male privilege might be disastrous when foisted on a woman who has been raised with a far more tenuous relationship to her personhood, freedom, and independence. The spiritual effect of *tzniut* can be powerful, but for the woman whose selfhood was never firmly established to begin with, the *tzimtzum*—the self-contraction—demanded by adapting oneself to suit the needs of others has the potential to be quite dangerous, to make it even harder for her ever to connect with her erotic core. *Tzniut* is an important spiritual value, *but one's selfhood, subjecthood, connection to the erotic and the Divine must not be threatened.* It's a two-step process. One must have a certain amount of selfhood available before one can transcend it and give to others. There may be times in an individual woman's life when she is more able to do this, and times when she is less able to do so, times when self-care is paramount and times when generosity needs to be at the foreground. It's not static.

With this reframing of *tzniut*, the choice to adapt oneself to one's circumstances and surroundings becomes not a denial of the self, but rather a way to allow the self to flow in caring relationship to others. This does not mean that, under all circumstances, one must dress for the "most easily offended denominator" but rather that one should understand that others' reactions and impressions matter, that it is crucial to live in connection with other people as well as with God. In one sense, the length of the skirt does not matter, if it is worn with "good *kavvanah*," with the intention of subjecthood, wholeness. And yet all people are embedded in contexts, and we may not all be coming from the exact same perspective. How do we care for others without being squeezed unfairly by their expectations? A generous open-heartedness that pours forth from an open, connected, erotically engaged heart is key—a will to give of the self not because it is demanded but because it will help to foster connection. And sometimes a firm, loving "no" to requests that seek to deny or destroy the spirit is appropriate.

At other times this understanding of *tzniut* involves inner work rather than changing external reality. I think of the men who try to displace feelings of unease onto the women in their communities, asking that they change their behavior to make the men more comfortable. Perhaps these men ought to learn how to cope with their own desire in a less harmful way, so that they can deal with women as whole people rather than as body parts. *Tzniut* requires a measure of *tzimtzum*, of withdrawal of the self for the sake of others. These men, learning how to place others' needs before their own in order to connect with those people, might find the spiritual work of this *tzniut* practice valuable.

Obviously, in our culture(s), asking men to reframe old ways of thinking may seem like a formidable task, but perhaps only because of the relentless objectification of women in both religious and secular contexts. This status quo need not be maintained, however. An analogy, perhaps, is the advice most people would give someone who expresses discomfort about being around a noticeably disabled person—an individual missing a limb, for example. Many would suggest that the uncomfortable person learn how to "get over it" and focus on the person herself. Why does the same request seem outrageous regarding discomfort expressed about the mundane female body? In fact, as the gender theorist S. Bear Bergman observes,

> There's no other situation in which [placing the burden of desire onto the object desired] is culturally acceptable. We don't camouflage a doughnut shop to protect dieters from the tempting sight of a doughnut, nor shutter bars to protect alcoholics, or any other such thing—one is responsible for managing one's own cravings responsibly and appropriately. But when it comes to women's sexuality or sensuality, it is still culturally and socially appropriate to say that any display is a temptation and that men . . . cannot be expected to resist such a thing.[13]

Learning how to manage these desires effectively—committing an act of *tzimtzum* in which one deals with his or her desire in a way that does not impose upon others—can be an important aspect of a culture of *tzniut*. This, combined with the generosity of the oft-objectified party to try to connect with others and adapt to her surroundings as long as her connection to herself, to God, to the erotic impulse remains intact might have far-reaching effects. An ethos in which women are perpetually subjects and men work to relate to them as such has the potential to help transform our culture and the toxic ways in which gender is currently constructed.

In this formulation, the internal, rather than external, aspects of *tzniut* are emphasized. Living in relationship to God and to the deep well of one's own spiritual power is at the forefront, and care and concern for others is understood as a major value. If we strive to live as whole, connected beings and to regard others as such, the length of a skirt, the cut of a top, and the volume at which we speak with one another become secondary. How things look in this new modesty will vary with the players and contexts involved. Shaming, coercion, and disregarding one another's needs are unacceptable. Treating one another with love and respect—never at the expense of our own selves—will be at the forefront. It is with this love that we serve God.

NOTES

Thanks to Rabbi Haviva Ner-David, Dr. Aryeh Cohen, and Rabbi Dan Shevitz for suggestions of sources for this essay.

1. Pesach Eliyahu Falk, *Oz Vehadar Levusha: Modesty—An Adornment for Life* (Gateshead, England: Feldheim, 1998).

2. BT *Brachot* 24a.

3. Rashba on BT *Brachot* 24a.

4. Tova Hartman, in a paper presented at the conference of the Jewish Orthodox Feminist Alliance, New York, 2002.

5. Yehuda-Herzl Henkin, "Contemporary Tseni'ut," *Tradition* 38:2, 2003.

6. Audre Lorde, "The Uses of the Erotic: The Erotic as Power," in idem, *Sister Outsider: Essays and Speeches, Crossing Press Feminist Series* (Freedom, Calif.: Crossing Press, 1984).

7. BT *Rosh Hashanah* 28b–29a; BT *Pesachim* 114b.

8. *Orech Hyim* 696:8. Much may be said about the prohibition against cross-dressing and the ways that we might understand it, but it is outside the scope of this essay.

9. "My Short Skirt," *The Vagina Monologues* by Eve Ensler.

10. Lorde. "The Uses of the Erotic: The Erotic as Power."

11. I refer specifically to Mishneh Torah *Hilchot Deot* 5:6–9. Only about 28 percent of the Rambam's use of the word *tzniut* in some form is related to female behavior in particular. Of course, the Rambam does discuss proper norms of female dress and behavior (noting, in *Hilchot Ishut* 13:11, that, at the very least, norms of head coverings are culturally relative), but my point here is that he—as others before him and since—understood *tzniut* as more of a global issue.

12. Carol Lee Flinders, *At the Root of This Longing: Reconciling a Spiritual Hunger and a Feminist Thirst* (San Francisco: HarperSanFrancisco, 1998), 89.

13. Personal correspondance, February 3, 2006.

15

On the Religious Significance of Homosexuality; or, Queering God, Torah, and Israel

Jay Michaelson

WHY DOES GOD make some people gay? Notwithstanding the rhetoric of denial prevalent in some religious circles, sexual orientation is known— by those with firsthand experience and by scientists who study it—either to be genetically determined or so deeply developmentally ingrained as to be fundamentally unchangeable.[1] The reality of gay and lesbian identity thus presents a theological, as well as existential and political, question.

For many people, the question is only relevant because of the alleged prohibitions of Leviticus 18:22 and 20:13 (as well as Romans 1:26–27, 1 Cor. 6:9–11, and Tim. 1:8–10). Theologically it seems unthinkable that God would make people gay and then tell them to repress their most fundamental selves. Thus many opponents of "gay liberation" maintain that homosexuality is not fundamentally determined (what I mean by "God makes people gay"), but is, in some way, chosen. This despite the overwhelming scientific evidence, the lived experiences of gay and lesbian people, the shocking rates of suicide among gay and lesbian youth (it is odd to kill yourself for a choice, is it not?),[2] and the total ineffectiveness of so-called reparative therapy,[3] not to mention the inapplicability of categories such as natural/unnatural[4] and heterosexuality/ homosexuality to biblical concerns about purity,[5] gender,[6] and the boundaries between Israel and other nations.[7]

My purpose in this chapter, however, is not to engage these claims but to argue that the entire focus on prohibition is unfortunate.[8] First, it tends to reduce homosexuality, and queer sexuality more broadly, to questions of permission and prohibition, as if that were the sum total of its religious significance. Second, and relatedly, it implies that gays and lesbians (and *mutatis mutandis* bisexuals and transgendered persons) will essentially fall into preexisting religious and/or theological categories, with nothing new or distinctive about them: they/we are either kosher or treif, with no disruption of those categories and assumptions and nothing religiously significant about sexual variance. Indeed, it is generally only the opponents of inclusion who argue that GLBT (Gay, Lesbian, Bisexual, Transgender) people in some way challenge existing structures; there is often an implicit claim among advocates that they do not.

But homosexuality presents a deeper theological question than how we read two verses of the Torah. The question may be introduced as follows: Is being gay like having brown eyes—a biological quirk of no religious significance? Or, given the central status in Judaism of procreation, patrimony, and gender binarism, is there something more theologically significant about people who, because of their souls' anatomies, defy the traditional constructions of each? And if there is something significant about GLBT people, what is it?

This need not be the naïve, anthropomorphic, and uncritical question of why God acts in a particular way. Rather, just as we speculate today on the religious, philosophical, and ethical significance of *nova* such as genetic engineering, climate change, or bio-ethics, so, too, is it theologically appropriate to reflect on the religious significance of what we now understand about sexual diversity. By way of prologue to a much longer treatment of these themes, I explore here how three pillars of Jewish belief and practice —God, Torah, and Israel—are each affected by what we now know about sexual variance. In each case, I have explored one topic as a prelude to a more sustained discussion. I begin with sexual liminality and the boundaries of "Israel," proceed to love and the experience of Torah on exoteric and esoteric levels, and finally conclude with how queer experience can usefully inform our positive and negative theologies.

Liminality and the Boundaries of "Israel"

Of the many iterations of queer identity proposed in recent years, some of the most interesting connect homosexuality's upsetting of categories of sexual binarism and dimorphism with liminality, the state of "in-betweenness," which, beginning with Victor Turner, has been understood as a hallmark of the sacred in numerous world traditions.[9] Curiously, in both contemporary queer theory and contemporary gay spirituality—two discourses that almost never interact with each other, and which in many ways are diametrically opposed—binaries are the problem and queerness is the remedy. The queer *qua* liminal figure, who defies binaries and "walks between" conventional gender categories, is in both discourses troped as an intercessionary, sacred, and even redemptive figure—but one which, I suggest, is deeply problematic in a Jewish context.

In queer theory, gender and sexual dimorphisms are social constructions that invariably efface difference, administer power to the powerful, and subject the weak/disfavored to the rule of the strong/favored.[10] Dyads such as them/us, black/white, and female/male oversimplify actual experience and invariably subordinate one side to the other; both Levinas and Derrida have argued that even the basic dualisms of self/other and presence/absence contain within them the seed of oppression, marginalization, and subjugation; as soon as we divide, we begin to conquer.[11] Queer sexuality, by eluding the heteronormative expectations of gender and sexual roles, can serve as "a potentially privileged site for the criticism and analysis of cultural discourses."[12]

Likewise, though in a very different intellectual key, the leading writers of the half-anthropological, half-fantastical literature of "gay spirituality" seek to reclaim for queer people (primarily gay men) the ancient roles of "those who walk between," gender-variant people who often served as shamans, healers, and other intercessors with the infinite.[13] These writers draw on diverse traditions, from the gender-variant Galli of the classical world[14] to the 157 Native American traditions which held that people whom we now would label as gay or lesbian possessed two spirits, one masculine and one feminine, and accorded them special significance in society (medicine men/women, shamans, warriors, etc.).[15] Of course, our understanding of these "third-gendered" and "two-spirited" people remains greatly attenuated, but the evidence is considerable, ranging from the gender-variant *berdaches* or *winktes* of the Plains Indians (including Omaha, Sioux, Iban, and Hidatsa people) to shamans of Siberia (including the Chukchi, Yakut, and Koryak tribes), the *basir* of Borneo, and the male *isangoma* of the Zulu. In such cultures, gays and lesbians exist to be sacred priests of the liminal.

Yet the liminal is sacred precisely because it is terrifying. In the moment of in-between, that point of inflection between what was and what is becoming, there is a taste of extinction. And precisely for that reason, because such moments occasion brief transverses of the ineffable, the liminal is sacralized by ritual, symbol, and myth. Some cultures sacralize these chaotic, anarchic, and death-linked moments, but others—surely including biblical Israel—seek to circumscribe it. Biblical Judaism sanctifies not the ecstatic but the formal, not the chaotic but the ordered. Jewish biblical narrative favors the tablets of the law, not the golden calf; favors Moses's descent to the people, not his ascent to the ineffable; and favors the precise rules and regulations of Leviticus, not the "strange fire" of Nadav and Avihu. Even amid the majestic theophany, the visible manifestation of the godhead at Sinai, the biblical text spends less time on the power and glory of revelation than on what God tells Moses about tort law and damages.

This is how it must be, for in a religion of civilization, the notion of boundary is essential. One does not organize clans, tribes, and nations without a healthy respect for hierarchy, law, and propriety—and within the Jewish tradition, the respect is deified. God mandates civil and ritual law, and, notwithstanding the tendency of biblical narrative to complicate the simplifying tendency of biblical legislation, the overwhelming emphasis is on the need for order and boundary. Such binaries of pure and impure, male and female, dark and light, Israelite and foreigner, and sacred and profane are the essence of the Levitical writings, both in the body of Leviticus and in the "Holiness Code." Indeed, the injunction "to discern between impure and pure" is repeated over and over again: in Leviticus 10:10–11 ("discern between holy and secular, and between impure and pure"); 11:47 ("to discern between impure and pure"), and Leviticus 15:31 ("thus shall you separate the children of Israel from their impurity"). Taking a cue from Mary Douglas's landmark anthropological work, *Purity and Danger*, we can see these concerns as reflecting the idealized plan of Genesis itself. Dietary laws divide water creatures from air creatures, air creatures from earth's, and abhor transgression of the boundary.[16] God saw that it was good—because now it was ordered, where before it was not. Or, taking a cue from Douglas's *Leviticus as Literature*, we can see the precision of the sacrificial offerings as mirroring the precision of the design of the tabernacle, and even the structure of the biblical text itself.[17]

The borders drawn around sexual behavior are of the same type. It is not known whether the Levitical prohibitions, like the ban on *kedeshim* (cultic prostitutes), referred to actual ritual present in the Ancient Near East; nor do we know, in light of the fact that "the binary opposition between 'Israelite' and 'Canaanite' turns out, in large part, to be an effect of particular biblical discourses"[18] rather than any actual cultural or ethnic boundary, whether the sexual distinctions were invented by biblical authors seeking to demarcate pseudo-ethnic, rather than ethical-sexual, boundaries.[19] Whatever the historical facts regarding these practices, however, Israelite "border anxiety" (again, Ken Stone's term) clearly leads to a rigid creation and enforcement of sexual boundaries. Indeed, the very Hebrew word for holiness, *kadosh* (etymologically related to *kedeshah*), carries the meaning of "separate." In the biblical system, binaries are necessary; they are needed; they are holy.

Clearly there is a flat contradiction between civilizing boundaries, on the one hand, and queered or otherwise effaced binarisms, on the other (though, obviously, this structure is itself a binarism that is susceptible to critique). Nor is the tension restricted to the margins of sexual differentiation: not only men who have sex with other men but interreligious couples, single parents, and anyone following (or creating) alternative models of Jewish sexual-social life find themselves astride the boundaries of the *halachic* mainstream.[20] And so, too, does anyone who sees himself/herself/themselves as "both/and" rather than "either/or." The Levitical understanding of liminality is squarely opposed, perhaps even deliberately, to the sacralization of boundary crossing found in certain shamanic cultures, hypothesized in the Ancient Near East, and celebrated by latter-day spiritual thinkers, many of whom are themselves constructing their views in deliberate opposition to "Judeo-Christian" religious thought. Obviously, as discussed below, these structures are symbolic, not literal; poetic, not political. Yet, to the extent that they inform not merely the superficial details of religious praxis but its very form and structure, the binary-disrupting queer finds hirself in, ironically, a binary opposition to the biblical ideal.

This may be a productive opposition, however, usefully problematizing some of Judaism's more troubling boundaries. (It is also, of course, an optional one; liminality is a function of self-actualization, not essential biology.) First, it invites us to reconsider "Judaism" as being less the normative product of the priestly elite, and more of a descriptive term, including precisely those practices of the Israelites which some sought to efface; whose Judaism is it, anyway? Second, scholars tell us that sexual boundaries were largely drawn to differentiate Jew from "Canaanite"—essentially a social construction used to Other-ize aspects of Israelite practice which the priestly elite sought to name as foreign. Sexual pluralism thus leads to a much-needed corrective to parochialism and ethnocentrism, because in problematizing the rhetoric of social construction in the area of sexuality, it questions the same lines drawn, often with the same brushstrokes, between us/them, gay/straight, Canaanite/Israelite, even female/male. And, finally, embracing sexual variance reminds us of biblical multivocality; as the theologian and scholar Theodore Jennings has recently developed at some length, biblical text has far more to say about homosexuality than two troubling verses in Leviticus; homoeroticism is often utilized as a resource for exploring the dynamic between YHWH and Israel itself.[21]

In this way, embracing the deeper significance of sexual liminality leads to a useful questioning of how the notion of boundary does exactly what postmodernists worry it does: prioritize, oppress, and dominate. And here I have only described domination on the national/religious realm; let us remember that we are talking about sexuality, the zone of the most binarism, and the most domination, of all. If gays and lesbians really comprise a third (or third and fourth) gender, then perhaps they can help destabilize the assumptions of the other two as well—God willing.

"Torah" and the Experience of Love

If liminality invites an expansion of the term "Israel," then the queer experience of love invites a transformation of "Torah." Theologically, emotionally, even spiritually, love transforms, and, necessarily, the permutations in the nature of that love affect the ways in which it alters us, and our commitments to the sacred. On a spiritual level, how we experience love of humans shapes how we experience love of God. On an intellectual level, it colors how we conceive it. On a physical level, it changes how we manifest it in the world. And on an emotional level, it gives form and meaning to the yearnings of the heart. What we are doing, when we open to the reality and essential nature of love, is admitting that we learn from texts other than those found in scrolls; we confirm that the heart writes its own faith, whether in the text as received from Sinai or as received anew each day.

This understanding colors our encounter with text in at least three essential ways. First, and most obvious, our experience of sacred text is naturally shaped by our experience of love in the world. When I chant *Yedid Nefesh*, the moving, homophilic, medieval love song for God, I think I have a relationship to that poem's *Yedid*, the (male) Beloved that is distinctively flavored by my love of men.[22] When I read of the receptivity of Isaac, the effeminate beauty of Joseph, or the love between David and Jonathan, I find a resonance between my own experience and these nontraditionally gendered Jewish heroes—and an ideal which, as described in Daniel Boyarin's work on the "effeminate" Jewish man, resounds through the generations.

Second, all Western mystics express their relationship to God in erotic terms, and it is no mere metaphor; in the Oneness of the One, a great Knowing Love naturally flows. To be holy, the Kabbalists write, is to be on fire with love for God. On a superficial level, if a lesbian experiences love of "like" rather than love of "unlike," this changes how she conceives, embraces, and loves God. On a deeper level, if a gay man experiences unity not as union-with-an-opposite but as an internal embrace of his own masculine and feminine natures—which is what the Zohar calls the essence of mystical practice—that, too, reconfigures (in a provocative, nondualistic way) what *unio mystica* is really about. Love is no mere "activity," not a pastime nor a behavior; it is absolutely fundamental to our religious consciousness, whether it manifests as traditional *ahavat* and *yirat shamayim* (love and fear of Heaven, respectively), or the Shema's injunction to love God with all one's heart and one's soul, the notion that God loves each of us with an *ahavat olam*, an eternal love, or as the highly untraditional ecstatic, mystical, earthy, or otherworldly loves for the energies and essences of the Divine. Across the span from piety to heresy, love is the amplitude of religious devotion.

Third, and perhaps most important, to be a self-accepting gay or lesbian person, one generally must go through a certain process of negation and affirmation. In homophobic societies, one is told that how one loves is wrong. Yet, at some point, to live a full life, one must learn for oneself that these statements are wrong and that love is right. This inversion teaches, in an experiential way, the primacy of love. It forms a unique mode of moral conscience, and teaches in a distinctive way what it is to love God *b'chol levavcha, b'chol nafeshecha, u'v'chol meodecha*, with the whole heart, body, mind, and spirit. And it engenders the queer mysticism we read in Rumi, Hafiz, and Judah Halevy; the poems of Whitman, Wilde, Sappho, and Shakespeare; the art of Michelangelo and Da Vinci.

The process of relating to sacred text, liturgy, and *tshuvah* is indelibly colored by the same process of "coming out" morally, intellectually, and spiritually. At first, the religious lesbian or gay man loves religion and thus hates herself. Then she may either affirm the self and hate religion; continue to repress the self and "love" religion; or, somehow, reconcile religion with the reality of love and sexual expression. But even if the third option is chosen, gay religious consciousness is necessarily distrustful, because it has seen—and, more important, felt—how rules, codes, and even the operation of conscience itself can actually be tools of oppression and self-repression. Of course, straight people may come to this realization also. But religious gay people must.

There are those whose fundamental modality remains fear: fear of difference, fear of their own unexplored territory, fear of losing that which they care for by accepting that which seems threatening. But to be accepting of one's queerness means that one has moved from a place of fear to a place of love. The luxury of ignorance is not afforded to the self-accepting queer. Nor is the luxury of acceptance. Because queer love must reassert itself, re-understand itself, revalidate itself on an almost continual basis, it represents a distinctive opening to the Love of the One

When I turn to legal text, I do so with all these understandings: with my distinctive approach to the text, with my embrace of love as religiously essential, and with my appreciation of love as ultimately valid. As the recent legal wrangling in the American Conservative movement has shown, it is not difficult for clever scholars to find ways to prohibit and permit; indeed, to permit something explicitly prohibited in the Torah is said, in BT *Sanhedrin* 17a, to be a prerequisite to be admitted to the Sanhedrin. In light of the plasticity of rational reasoning, the emotive/cognitive conditions in which we first approach the text become paramount, and the legal-hermeneutical process is itself conditioned by them.

This reconfigures the legal question, which now becomes less about the particulars of interpretation than the foundations of the interpretive act itself. Are we convinced of the truth of love, or do we continue to doubt it? Do we defer to that which others, who are ignorant of this truth, have interpreted the text as saying? Or are we commanded, as the Talmudic Sages felt themselves to be with regard to the rebellious son,[23] to read radically in order to guard Torah conservatively?

God and the Queering of Theology

Finally, the existence and experience of sexual diversity has productive implications for Jewish theology. I begin with the cataphatic, immanentist, narrative-rich, erotic, and this-worldly approach to God, and then conclude with a few remarks on the apophatic, negative, transcendentalist way. The juxtaposition of the two is itself an important aspect of the fluidity of identity: God/dess is not only male, not only transcendent; S/he is not only female, not only immanent; there is a unity of sames as well as opposites. This is perhaps the great contribution of the mythic theosophical Kabbalah: not the unity of the Divine but its manifestation as multiplicity—itself an important dimorphism but one replicated on the planes of emanation, creation, formation, and action in countless ways. Of course, it may seem peculiar to select theosophical Kabbalah as a site of intervention, as Kabbalah is among the most heteronormative discourses in Western thought, with masculine and feminine shaping not only ontological, erotic, and normative structures but the nature of the Divine itself. Yet the dynamics of Kabbalah are also pervasively homoerotic, and, above all, queer, moving among dynamically evolving genders in an almost dizzying theo-erotic dance.

Let us begin with manifestation. At this moment, God is separating and reunifying, differentiating into male and female, and reuniting both opposite principles and same principles into a unity that encompasses all and loves itself. The genders of the godhead fluctuate, sometimes with an abundance of feminine potency and then, at a later time, with an abundance of the masculine. The very concept of the sefirotic tree,[24] which ascribes different qualities, and genders, to emanations of God, presupposes that the Divine, and, by analogy, the human as well, contains diverse masculine and feminine elements, each containing aspects of the other: sefirot gendered feminine also emanate; those gendered masculine also receive. As the scholar Charles Mopsik says, "the sefirot are thus called masculine or feminine because they are each, as a function of gender, androgynous in a particular way."[25] For example, the sefirah of *malchut* is sometimes described as being poised between two lovers; the (male) *tzaddik/yesod* below and the (male) *tiferet/yesod* above. *Binah* and *malchut*, two feminine-gendered *sefirot*, often interact in ways described in the same terms as the sexualized unions of other sefirot. And the sefirah of *hochmah*, generally gendered masculine, assumes the feminine gender when set in relation to *keter*.[26] The drama of the sefirot does not conform to the model of a wholly masculine male person uniting with a wholly feminine female one; rather, it is in constant flux. Gender role depends on the identity of the partner, and each of the two parties in any union already contains within hirself masculine and feminine components, which themselves need to be balanced in an appropriate way, both internally and externally.

The ideal human form, like the Divine one, is not a butch masculine and femme feminine (in popular culture, stereotypes such as Popeye and Olive Oyl, the quarterback and the cheerleader). On the contrary, since God is seen to manifest gender bending, fluidity, and multiplicity, the idealized human (sometimes figured as appearing only in the messianic period, and other times as an available mystical type) is, as in many other cultural traditions, an androgyne, in which some form of masculine and feminine are integrated.[27] This is precisely the configuration that has recently been reappropriated by the "gay spirituality" discussed above. While still re-

maining somewhat essentialist, this model does propose a radically different status for sissy boys, butch women, and other gender-nonconforming
individuals from the hegemonic Western gender-essentialism that regards
them as inferior deviations from the norm; as described earlier, "two-
spiritedness" is the redemptive ideal.

Indeed, if in queer theory it is generally understood that gender categories such as masculine and feminine are socially constructed and only
awkwardly imposed upon the more polymorphous biological-sexual reality, kabbalistic anthropology, in its way, agrees with this position. Obviously the kabbalistic literature generally understands the uniting of cos-
mic masculine and feminine as reflecting the uniting of male and female
people.[28] However, each individual contains both masculine and feminine
attributes—"male and female each include male and female," in the words
of the Gaon of Vilna.[29] As such, unifications also take place within individual people, between people in a variety of permutations, and between
individuals and God in ways that do not at all conform to heteronormative
expectation, or even to the typical categories of sex, gender, and personality. Indeed, it is even possible for a person to have a soul of an opposite
gender to his/her body,[30] a condition that, according to Joseph Karo, affected the biblical figures Sarah, Tamar, Ruth, Judah, and Boaz.

But the disjuncture between masculine/feminine and male/female
animates everyone, not just exceptions. For example, if we consider David's
role as a manifestation of *malchut*, and *malchut*'s role as courtesan of *tiferet*,
we are left with a curious situation in which the leading male poet of God
plays the female role in erotically unifying with the masculine Godhead.[31]
In fact, since it is generally understood in kabbalistic text that all of Israel
stands in relationship to God just as David does, all of (male) Israel also
stands before God as a woman, praising God's masculine nature, and seeking to unify with God in an explicitly eroticized way, much as described
in the previous section. In this model, the individual mystic's soul, gendered feminine, first takes the masculine role in an act of transgendered,
homoerotic mystical fellowship with those of hir fellow mystics in order to
communally welcome in the Divine feminine and enter into erotic union
with Her,[32] and then embodies that same Divine feminine for her congress
with the male Godhead. This act of psychic double-transvestism is abet-
ted by the kabbalistic trope that casts God and Israel as the two lovers in
the Song of Songs, or the two cherubs over the ark, in both cases with Israel taking the female role. Even as mystics enact the masculine role of the
cosmogenic coitus with their wives on the Sabbath, and even as they are

exhorted to move their bodies erotically as if making love with the Shechinah (the feminine, immanent aspect of God) during prayer, they also take the female role (with their feminine souls) in courting the Divine masculine, praising His beauty, and seeking to erotically unite with him.

Every (presumptively male) Kabbalist, then, is invited to participate in an almost comic gender play, imitating God Him/Herself, who is, via the sefirot, a kind of multigendered, transgendering, hermaphroditic drag queen, wearing the masks of different genders at different times, and seeking partners who do the same. Pious Jews beg God's sweet feminine side (*malchut*/lower) to come out on the Sabbath—but beg God's mean feminine side (*gevurah*/left) to be sweetened by the softer, masculine attributes of lovingkindness. And if we take seriously the Zohar's repeated insistence that the monistic, panentheistic Reality is the only true existent, then the entire gendered masquerade is part of a Divine dance, or perhaps strip tease, enacting concealment and revelation, dressing up and undressing, in a sort of theological carnival.[33]

Ultimately, though, that monistic Reality is homoerotic. How could the nondual be otherwise? From the Zohar's point of view, prior to the world's coming into being, God existed/not-existed in a state of delighting in Godself, in the undifferentiated unity. The word for "delight" is *sha'ashua*, which has a sexual connotation. Like the primordial masturbation of the Greek Oranos, which spills seed into Ocean and creates the world, the predifferentiated state of the *ein sof* is not what we would suppose to be a neutral one. It is one of pre-heterogenous arousal. The foundational love of the universe, then, is homoerotic, because at that moment there was no Other to love. And since the foundational moment of the universe exists outside of time, it exists through all time.

So, from the human point of view, for God to "come out," God must be awakened by us and within us, since thus God comes to know Godself, which in the Hebrew is to make love to oneself, replicating the auto-erotic delight of pre-creation. In this light, we might say (in a mythic mode, of course) that God's closet is the illusion of separation and distinction. What seems to be Other-than-us is not Other-than-us, because "it" is God and "we" are God. What appears to be the uniting of opposites is, in truth, a uniting of sames. We unmask Being for what it is: a hermaphrodite in manifestation (to use anthropomorphic language), seeking to unite with itself; ontologically prior to manifestation, only the One. Aeons of evolution have engendered higher and higher forms of complexity, each transcending and including those below. Everything manifests the One, but as complexity evolves consciousness, Being begins to have the power to know (*yada*) that it is the One, to bring about the knowledge that transcends and includes "carnal knowledge," transcends and includes mystical knowledge; is, fundamentally, the Knower and the Knowing and the Known.

It is in this transcendence that we move from the cataphatic and theosophical to the apophatic and philosophical. Apophatic theology, which colors most Jewish philosophical thinking (Maimonides, Saadia Gaon, Yeshayahu Leibowitz) as well as much kabbalistic thought (particularly as applied to the Infinite ineffability of *ein sof* or *ayin*)[34] tells us that the more we remove familiar categories and ways about thinking about God, the closer we are to God. Labels that come from our own experience—God is male, God is just, God is the source of wonder—are projections. They can reduce the ineffability of the transcendent, and flatten our experience of the immanent into categories shaped by desire and aversion. In this light, to "queer" (i.e., as rejecting the notion that binary gender and normative sexuality are natural categories) theology helps to undermine normative tendencies in theological thinking. Removing assumptions of Divine gender, speaking of permutations of gender fluidity that are quite removed from most of our experiences, denying that categories of gender even exist ultimately at all—all these are moves closer to the Infinity and Oneness of the Divine. The farther we get from our preconceived notions of what "identity" is supposed to be, the closer we are to realization.

Conclusions and Reversals

Few people ever ask, "Why did God make me straight?" Yet it has gone literally without saying that the modalities of masculine and feminine, and their unique forms of congress, have some relevance to theological thinking. But if this is so, then other modalities of sexuality and gender must as well.

At the same time, to explore these points of relevance should not be to search for an explanation. In promoting our special gifts, or our unique mission, queers should be wary both of essentialism and of believing that our existence needs to be explained if it is not to be regarded as an aberration. "I've fought all my life for the right to be boring," U.S. Representative Barney Frank once said. Thus I only ask individual questions: how do *I* conceive sexual violence, marginalization, joy, friendship, music, design, irony, morality, theology, love—and in what informative ways might these be related to my sexuality? At times there may be no difference. But at other times I find a relationship that may be useful. Queer voices have been relatively silent in the mainstreams of Western religion, even as they have been (in concealment) prominent in mysticism. Now that those voices are beginning to be heard, do they have anything distinctive to say?

Then, the door is open, to two-spirit people, and the path of the walks-between; to those who have defied gender roles, stood outside ordinary society, and become priests, poets, and healers; to lovers and theologians and mystics of all kinds. And to those who find no attraction in alterity.

Images of the ineffable are always projections, and relationships to the transcendent always carry the character of myth. Yet, to the extent we conceptualize the One at all, we have no choice but to do so from our conceptions of love, self, and world; tradition, text, and tribe. Questions of boundary, models of the soul, ideals of human behavior, experiences of love, and relationships with sacred text—these are but a few of the areas in which sexuality matters to theology, and I have stated them here only by way of introduction. Really, if theology is thinking about God, the only way sexuality *couldn't* matter would be if we really believed that how we love has nothing to do with how we think, imagine, dream, and create. What an impoverished life that would be.

NOTES

1. See Kari Balog, "Equal Protection for Homosexuals: Why the Immutability Argument Is Necessary and How It Is Met," *Clev. St. L. Rev.* 53 (2005): 545 (reviewing scientific evidence for how the legal argument of immutability is satisfied); John Kirsch and James Weinrich, "Homosexuality, Nature, and Biology: Is Homosexuality Natural? Does It Matter?" in *Homosexuality: Research Implications for Public Policy,* ed. John C. Gonsiorek and James D. Weinrich, 13–31 (Thousand Oaks, Calif.: Sage, 1991); John D'Emilio, "Born Gay," in *The World Turned: Essays on Gay History, Politics, and Culture,* ed. John D'Emilio (Durham, N.C.: Duke University Press, 2002); Chandler Burr, *A Separate Creation: The Search for the Biological Origins of Sexual Orientation* (1996); idem, "Homosexuality and Biology," *Atlantic Monthly* 271:3 (March 1993): 47.

Some of the voluminous scientific literature on the subject is discussed in D. F. Swaab et al., "Brain Research, Gender, and Sexual Orientation," *J. Homosexuality* 28 (1995): 283; Richard Pillard, "The Genetic Theory of Sexual Orientation," *Harv. Gay & Lesbian Rev.* 4:1 (winter 1997): 1–54; W. H. James, "Biological and Psychosocial Determinants of Male and Female Human Sexual Orientation," *J. Biosoc. Sci.* 37 (2005): 555–567 (suggesting a comprehensive theory of sexual orientation); and L. Gooren, "The Biology of Human Psychosexual Differentiation," *Horm. Behav.* 50 (2006): 589–601 (reviewing sex steroid studies and hormonal developments before birth).

Cross-cultural sociological studies have long found that culturally contingent environmental factors are not responsible for a person's sexual orientation. See, for example, Frederick L. Whitman, "Culturally Invariable Properties of Male Homosexuality: Tentative Conclusions from Cross-Cultural Research," *Archives of Sexual Behavior* 12:3 (1983) (finding that homosexual persons appear in stable and constant numbers in all societies, and all homosexuals express the same durable behavioral and social characteristics across cultures). In addition, a sizable literature finds homosexual behaviors also to be present in nonhuman species. See, for example, E. A. Fox, "Homosexual Behavior in Wild Sumatran Orangutans," *Am. J. Primatol.* 55 (2001): 177–181 (finding that homosexual behavior is part of the natural repertoire of sexual behaviors among primate species). These studies controlling for culture and species lend support to the belief that homosexuality is neither volitional nor environmentally conditioned.

2. Gay and lesbian youth are estimated to comprise 30 percent of completed youth suicides annually, and are two to three times more likely to attempt suicide than other young people. See Paul Gibson, "Gay Male and Lesbian Youth Suicide," in *Report of the Secretary's Task Force on Youth Suicide*, ed. Marcia R. Feinleib (Washington, D.C.: U.S. Department of Health and Human Services, 1989), 110. Incidentally the study was suppressed by the Bush (I) administration on the grounds that it "undermined the institution of the family" (Chris Bull, "Suicidal Tendencies," *The Advocate*, April 5, 1994, 37). Subsequent studies have confirmed the 30 percent figure. See Gary Remafedi, J. Farrow, and R. Deisher "Risk Factors for Attempted Suicide in Gay and Bisexual Youth," *Pediatrics* 87:6 (1991): 869–876. See, generally, Warren J. Blumenfeld and Laurie Lindop, "Gay, Lesbian, Bisexual, Transgender Youth Suicide," available at http://www.outproud.org/article_suicide.html (accessed 12/7/07).

3. For a thorough compendium of studies debunking this form of brainwashing, and a refutation of every study supporting it, see Wayne Besen, *Anything But Straight: Unmasking the Scandals and Lies behind the Ex-Gay Myth* (New York: Haworth, 2003). For a humorous account of reparative therapy in the Jewish context, see Phil S. Stein, "How I Ended Up at the Jerusalem Same-Sex Attraction Group," *Zeek*, November 2005 (www.zeek.net/spirit_0511.shtml [accessed 12/7/07]). See also testimonials and stories collected at exgaywatch.com.

4. See, for example, Rabbi Joel Roth, "Homosexuality," Committee on Jewish Law and Standards of the Rabbinical Assembly (1992), Part 2 (arguing that Talmudic word play explains *toevah* prohibitions as "unnatural"). Available at www.rabbinicalassembly.org/law/tshuvot_public.html (accessed 12/7/07).

5. Mary Douglas's *Purity and Danger: An Analysis of Concepts of Pollution and Taboo* (New York: Praeger, 1966) remains the classic study on this subject.

See also Ken Stone, *Practicing Safer Texts: Food, Sex, and Bible in Queer Perspective* (New York and London: T&T Clark, 2005), 46–50; Jacob Milgrom, *Leviticus 1–16: A New Translation with Introduction and Commentary* (New York: Doubleday, 1991); John Sawyer, ed., *Reading Leviticus: A Response to Mary Douglas* (Sheffield, U.K.: Sheffield Academic Press, 1996).

6. See Saul Olyan, "'And with a Male You Shall Not Lie the Lying Down of a Woman': On the Meaning and Significance of Leviticus 18:22 and 20:1," *Journal of the History of Sexuality* 5:2 (1994): 179–206; Michael Satlow, "'They Abused Him Like a Woman': Homoeroticism, Gender Blurring, and the Rabbis in Late Antiquity," *Journal of the History of Sexuality* 5:1 (1994): 1–25; Steven Greenberg, *Wrestling with God and Men: Homosexuality in the Jewish Tradition* (Madison: University of Wisconsin Press, 2004), 192–196; Daniel Boyarin, "Are There Any Jews in 'The History of Sexuality'?" *Journal of the History of Sexuality* 5:3 (1995): 333–335.

7. Bradley S. Artson, "Gay and Lesbian Jews: An Innovative Legal Position," *Jewish Spectator* (winter 1990): 6; Jay Michaelson, "How Can You Be Gay and Jewish?" *Zeek* (September 2004); Stone, *Practicing Safer Texts* (maintaining that "the 'Canaanite' is arguably positioned with respect to the 'Israelite' in something like the same way that the 'homosexual' is positioned with respect to the 'heterosexual'").

8. I have addressed these issues elsewhere. See Jay Michaelson, "Chaos Law & God: The Religious Meanings of Homosexuality," *Michigan Journal of Gender and Law* 15, forthcoming; idem, "Boundaries and the Boundless: Homosexuality, Liminality, Judaism," in *Jews and Sex*, ed. Nathan Abrams (Nottingham, U.K.: Five Leaves Publications, 2008).

9. Victor Turner, "Betwixt and Between: The Liminal Period in Rites de Passage," in *The Forest of Symbols* (Ithaca, N.Y.: Cornell University Press, 1967).

10. See David Halperin, *One Hundred Years of Homosexuality* (New York: Routledge, 1990), 43–48; Katz, *The Invention of Heterosexuality*; Eve Kosofky Sedgwick, *Epistemology of the Closet* (Berkeley: University of California Press, 1990); Gilbert Herdt, *Third Sex, Third Gender: Beyond Sexual Dimorphism in Culture and History* (New York: Zone, 1996).

11. See Emmanuel Levinas, "Diachrony and Representation," in *Time and the Other and Additional Essays*, trans. Richard A. Cohen (Pittsburgh: Duquesne University Press, 1987), 45–51; Jacques Derrida, "Like the Sound of the Sea Deep within a Shell: Paul De Man's War," *Critical Inquiry* 14:3 (spring 1988): 590–652.

12. David Halperin, *Saint Foucault: Toward a Gay Hagiography* (New York: Oxford University Press, 1995), 61.

13. See Randy Conner, *Blossom of Bone: Reclaiming the Connections between Homoeroticism and the Sacred* (San Francisco: HarperSanFrancisco, 1993); Toby Johnston, *Gay Spirituality: The Role of Gay Identity in the Transformation of Human Consciousness* (Maple Shade, N.J.: Lethe, 2004); Mark Thomspon, *Gay Spirit: Myth and Meaning* (New York: St. Martin's, 1988).

14. Conner, *Blossom of Bone*, 99–125; Will Roscoe, "Priests of the Goddess: Gender Transgression in Ancient Religion," *History of Religions* 35:3 (1996): 295–330.

15. Will Roscoe, *Changing Ones: Third and Fourth Genders in Native North America* (New York: Palgrave, 2000), 222–247; Walter Williams, *The Spirit and the Flesh: Sexual Diversity in American Indian Culture* (Boston: Beacon, 1986), 107–109.

16. See Douglas, *Purity and Danger*, 4–6, 59–61; Stone, *Practicing Safer Texts*, 46–50; Stout, *Ethics after Babel*, 156–161.

17. Mary Douglas, *Leviticus as Literature* (Oxford: Oxford University Press, 1999), 19–25 (refuting much of the theories of her earlier book); Stone, *Practicing Safer Texts*, 60–64.

18. Stone, *Practicing Safer Texts*, 59.

19. See Frymer-Kensky, *In the Wake of the Goddesses*, 200–202; Stone, *Practicing Safer Texts*, 58–61; Greenberg, *Wrestling with God and Men*, 177; Johanna Stuckey, "Sacred Prostitutes," *MatriFocus* 5:1 (2005); Conner, *Blossom of Bone*, 67–81; William G. Dever, *Did God Have a Wife? Archaeology and Folk Religion in Ancient Israel* (Grand Rapids, Mich.: Eerdmans, 2006); Richard A. Henshaw, *Female & Male, the Cultic Personnel: The Bible and the Rest of the Ancient Near East* (Allison Park, Pa.: Pickwick, 1994); Saul M. Olyan, *Asherah and the Cult of Yahweh in Israel* (Atlanta, Ga.: Scholars, 1988).

20. It is important not to overstate the gender dimorphism of the *halachic* system, however, which includes multiple gender and sex categories, including *tumtum, androgynos,* and, by some counts, *avlonit, saris adam,* and *saris chama.* (The term *androgynos,* for example, appears more than three hundred times in the Babylonian Talmud). See Alfred Cohen, *"Tumtum* and *Androgynous," Journal of Halacha & Contemporary Society* 38 (fall 1999); Elliot Rose Kukla and Reuben Zellman, "Created by the Hand of Heaven: A Jewish Approach to Intersexuality," *Torah Queeries,* April 21, 2007.

21. Jennings, *Jacob's Wound,* 25–66.

22. Numerous liturgical poems praise God's masculine beauty, such as the *Shir HaKavod,* or *Song of Glory,* which originated with the thirteenth-century German Pietist movement and which describes the beauty of the Divine hair and body in clearly masculine terms.

23. Deuteronomy 21:18–21 instructs that the parents of a "stubborn and rebellious son" take their child to the elders of the city at the city gate to be stoned to death, to "remove the evil from your midst." The Rabbis of the Mishnah (Tractate *Sanhedrin,* chap. 8), however, interpreted the conditions during which this trial could take place so narrowly that the ritual was functionally defined out of existence.

24. According to the theosophical Kabbalah, sefirot are the emanations from the One to the many; in one metaphor, they are like panes of colored glass

through which the Infinite light shines. Sometimes the sefirot are arrayed on the "Tree of Life," understood to be a map of creation or of the Divine realms. Popular introductions to this material include Arthur Green, *A Guide to the Zohar* (Stanford: Stanford University Press, 2004); and Daniel Matt, *The Essential Kabbalah* (San Francisco: HarperSanFrancisco 1995). As this section assumes a basic understanding of the sefirotic tree, readers unfamiliar with Kabbalah are directed to those introductory sources for explanations of the concepts used here.

25. Mopsik, *Sex of the Soul*, 27; see also 21, 24–27.

26. See Moshe Idel, *Kabbalah and Eros* (New Haven, Conn.: Yale University Press, 2005), 96–101 (describing how genders of sefirot may vary depending on the relationship and concluding that "the different versions of the sefirotic realm do not reflect a human personality"); see, too, 142–143 (describing sefirotic triads as erotic combinations).

27. On the mystical androgyne in Kabbalah and other cultures, see Idel, *Kabbalah and Eros*, 55–105. See, generally, June Singer, *Androgyny: The Opposites Within* (Boston: Sigo, 1989).

28. See Idel, *Kabbalah and Eros*, 233–237.

29. R. Elijah of Vilna, *Liqqutim on the Sidra Nisniuta,* quoted in Mopsik, *Sex of the Soul*, 35.

30. See *Tikkunei Zohar*, 132b–133a; R. Hayyim Vital, *Shaar Gilgulim*, trans. Yitzhok bar Chaim, pt. 9, introduction; Joseph Karo, *Maggid Mesharim*, 11d–12a. See also Mopsik, *Sex of the Soul*, 39–45 (discussing these texts).

31. See, for example, *Zohar III*, 84a. This is a subset of the larger homoerotic dilemma described by Howard Eilberg-Scwartz in *God's Phallus: And Other Problems for Men and Monotheism* (Boston: Beacon, 1994). Eilberg-Schwartz argues that the homoeroticism of the gaze between God and Israel is lessened by averting the gaze from God's phallus, on the one hand, and the feminization of Israel, on the other. In the kabbalistic schema, however, the former evasion is unavailable; *yichud* is unavoidably erotic, even if it is said to be with *tiferet* rather than *yesod* (see discussion infra). Thus, as Eilberg-Schwartz's framework would suggest, the trope of feminization is more prominent.

32. For example, see *Zohar I*, 49b–50a.

33. Even when male Kabbalists are unifying with the female Shechinah, their union is far from an ordinary heterosexual one. In many texts, *malchut*/Shechinah stands, as it were, between two male lovers in a kind of theurgical menage-a-trois: the earthly tzaddikim below, and the male Godhead, mediated by *yesod*, the supernal tzaddik above. In Wolfson's view, the union is really a homoerotic one; though it takes place via the feminine power, it is really about stimulating the masculine one above her. See Wolfson, *Language, Eros, Being*, 593.

34. *Ein sof* is the limitless, boundless aspect of the Divine that preceded Creation. *Ayin* refers to the mystical understanding that all of existence is, fundamentally, nothingness.

16

Ḥeruta's Ruse

What We Mean When We Talk about Desire

Gail Labovitz

THE WEB SITE Negiah.org bills itself as "The First Abstinence Website for Jewish Teens."[1] It is sponsored by the National Conference of Synagogue Youth (NCSY), the youth movement of the Orthodox Union, and carries the slogan "NCSY says kNOw." Teens of both genders are invited to learn the risks of sexual activity outside marriage, to consider Jewish sources that speak to the question of restraint over one's urges, and to explore strategies for maintaining sexual abstinence.

How does the site suggest Jewish teens do this? Among the items listed on a page providing "Advice for More Successful Abstinence" is the following: "Limit time spent alone. It's normal to want to be alone with your bf or gf, but that's when the problems occur." Another page is entirely dedicated to this strategy: "Yichud: Don't Go It Alone." The page defines its key term, "The Gemara [Talmudic discussion] in Kiddushin (80b) discusses the prohibition for a man and a woman to be secluded alone together unless they are married or close relatives. This prohibition is called 'yichud' ('seclusion')," and concludes, "When it comes to abstinence, yichud is a very helpful halacha (Jewish law). Fighting temptation is much easier if you never put yourself in a situation private enough to become a problem!"

The most basic element of the law of *yichud* is found in the Mishnah (M), in *Kiddushin* 4:12: "A man may not be alone with two women, but one woman may be alone with two men." From the outset, then, it is clear that what motivates these laws—and simultaneously is reinforced by them—is the assumption that if a man and woman are secluded together, there is always the risk of inappropriate sexual activity. An example in another mishnaic law also illustrates this idea:

One who eats at the home of his father-in-law (*to be*) in Judea, without witnesses, cannot (*after the wedding*) make a claim that she was not a virgin, because he (*himself*) is alone with her. (M *Ketubot* 1:5)

In other words, the betrothed himself must be presumed to have engaged in sexual relations with his bride-to-be when they were left in private during his visit.[2] Equally apparent is that the rabbinic authors of these passages believe that desire—and whether one is likely to act on it—operates differently in men than in women, as is evident when a third person, and thus gender imbalance, is added to the mix. The behavior of a woman or a man in the presence of another man differs from their behavior in the presence of another woman.

Indeed, the same impression is seen on the negiah.org Web site. Overall the site appears to address boys and girls equally, encouraging both genders to refrain from sexual activity until married; yet often some sadly familiar, stereotypical gender references are made. For example, one page describes the risks of sexual activity as follows:

REGRET. This is especially true in the case of the young ladies. It's a Mars/Venus thing. Girls are more vulnerable. They see sex as a way of showing you care. Most boys don't. They see sex as a way of having sex.

A column attributed to a twenty-one-year-old woman writing under the pseudonym "Rita" advises girls:

1) In nearly every culture, there is a pattern: when a man looks for a wife, he prefers a virgin. This tendency has proven consistent even in Western cultures. . . . 2) If you have sex with someone who is not committed to you, the chances are he will never be committed to you, since men are quick to have sex and slow to marry.

In "The Guy's Side of the Story," the unnamed author, who identifies himself as a now married former member of NCSY, begins his essay in this way:

To all the guys who are reading this thinking, "Why the (heck) are they telling this stuff to my girlfriend? I want to get (lucky)! If I finish high school as a virgin, I will be the biggest loser come college."

I grew up non-Orthodox, and, despite a brief dalliance with Orthodoxy in college, I had never seriously considered the laws of *yichud* and their origins until after receiving my doctorate, when I spent a year working on the Feminist Sexual Ethics Project (FSEP) of Brandeis University.[3] Among my assignments was to write a short essay on the early rabbinic sources of the laws of *yichud*—to understand and explain the ideas regarding sexual desire embedded in these laws. As already noted, these laws are first recorded in the Mishnah, which was redacted at around the turn of the second century C.E., and are then elaborated in the commentary of the Palestinian Talmud (PT) and the Babylonian Talmud (BT).

While studying the texts at hand, I pondered whether the rabbinic concept of *yichud* could contribute to a conversation about sexual mutuality. Could I provide the kind of reading promoted by the rabbinics scholar Daniel Boyarin, who calls for a "generous critique":

> . . . it is not my intention to construct arguments that would cover over or explain away those aspects of rabbinic Judaism that I find ethically problematic . . . but rather, I would say, to construct from it a "usable past," discovering and marking out those areas within the culture that can serve us today and finding ways to contextualize and historicize recalcitrant and unpalatable aspects of the culture such that we can move beyond them.[4]

In examining these texts I encountered the extended and complex discussion in BT *Kiddushin* 80b–81b, which includes many intriguing stories. My aim in this chapter is to show that, within the stories of the Babylonian Talmudic discussion, there is a moment that is open to a generous critique. This moment, if reclaimed, has the potential to challenge the very nature of the questions that motivated the rabbis as they developed the laws of *yichud*.

As mentioned above, male and female sexuality are simply presumed not to be the same. Several other passages in this chapter of the Mishnah suggest that if a man has a legitimate sexual outlet—that is, a nearby wife—he may be less likely to engage in forbidden behavior, so perhaps it is male sexual desire that is at issue. On the other hand, the Tosefta (T), a collection of roughly contemporaneous materials, glosses the original Mishnah passage with a qualification suggesting that women are particularly lacking in sexual restraint and shame:

A woman may be alone with two men, even if they are both Samaritans, even if they are both slaves, even if one is a Samaritan and one is a slave, except (*if one is*) a minor, because she is not ashamed to engage in sexual relations in his presence. (T *Ketubot* 5:9)

So, too, the Babylonian Talmud begins its commentary to M *Kiddushin* 4:12 by addressing this question. It cites a source, which it identifies as also originating around the time of the Mishnah, that suggests a slightly different presumption about women and female sexuality: "What is the reason? It was taught by the school of Eliahu: Women are light-headed" (BT *Kiddushin* 80b). But the text does not go on to define what is meant by "light-headed."[5]

Instead, the rest of the Talmudic discussion turns in a very different direction. In fact, most of the discussion that ensues focuses on exploring masculine sexuality and the fear of succumbing to sinful sexual temptation.[6] Thus the rule of the Mishnah is modified by an early Talmudic scholar:

> "But one woman [may be alone with two men]": Rav Yehuda said, Rav said, "They did not teach [this rule] except regarding proper men, but regarding unrestrained men, even with ten, no. (BT *Kiddushin* 80b)

Much of the material that follows attempts to answer, more and less explicitly, a basic question raised in this statement: How does one define a proper man or a morally unrestrained man?[7] The stories in the Babylonian Talmud play a significant role in addressing this concern. In these episodes men—specifically, rabbis—find that they are potentially or actually aroused to sexual desire, and even to act on that desire, in the presence of a woman. Our central question thus takes on an added dimension: Does being a rabbi engaged in Torah study ensure that one will be a proper man? Even Rav, the rabbi who posited the distinction between proper and unrestrained men, may not place himself in the former category:

> Rav and Rav Yehuda were walking on the road; a particular woman was walking ahead of them.
>
> Rav said to Rav Yehuda, "Lift your feet before Gehenna [walk faster; pass the woman]."
>
> He [Rav Yehuda] said to him [Rav], "But it was Master himself who said of proper men that it is acceptable [for two men to be in the presence of one woman]!"

He [Rav] said to him [Rav Yehuda], "Who said that 'proper men' [refers] to ones such as me and you?"[8]

Perhaps even a rabbi and Torah scholar (and one committed to observing the laws of *yichud*) feels, and feels compelled to act upon, sexual desire in the presence of a woman.

Several stories that follow share this theme. Three stories in particular dramatize situations where a rabbi is unexpectedly confronted by a woman's presence and faces his ability to control, or not control, the sexual desire he (inevitably?) experiences as a result. That the three stories—the latter two in nearly identical language—all dramatize the same tension (and similar resolutions) emphasizes the concern the rabbinic authors and editors felt about sexual temptation:

(1) There were some female captives brought to Nehardea. They took them to the house of Rav Amram Ḥasida [the pious one]. [They took the ladder out from under them.][9] As one passed by, a light fell in the opening. Rav. Amram took the ladder—[which ten men could not set up—and set it up alone,][10] placed it, and started to ascend. When he reached the halfway point of the ladder, he stopped himself and raised his voice, "A fire at Rav Amram's!" The rabbis came. They said to him, "You have shamed us!" He said to them, "Better that you are shamed at the home of Rav Amram in this world and not be shamed by him in the World-to-Come." He adjured it [some texts add: the Evil Inclination/his Inclination][11] to leave him; it left him as a pillar of fire. He said to it, "See, you are fire and I am flesh, but I am better than you."[12]

(2) R. Meir used to scoff at those who committed sin. One day, Satan appeared to him as a woman, on the other side of the river. There was no ferry. He grasped the rope and was crossing over; when he reached the halfway point of the rope, he [Satan] released him. He [Satan] said, "If it were not that they decreed in the heavens 'Beware of R. Meir and his learning,' I would have valued your life at two meahs [a small coin]."

(3) R. Akiva used to scoff at those who committed sin. One day, Satan appeared to him as a woman, at the top of a palm tree. He grasped the palm tree and was ascending; when he reached the halfway point of the palm tree, he [Satan] released him. He [Satan] said, "If it were not that they decreed in the heavens 'Beware of R. Akiva and his learning,' I would have valued your life at two meahs."

The rabbi, at best, is able to stop himself halfway to his desired goal, as in the case of Rav Amram. Or, perhaps, the scholar's learning provides heavenly intercession on his behalf, once again at the halfway point to his goal, as in the parallel stories of Rabbi Meir and Rabbi Akiva.

Particularly striking, then, is the final story in the cycle,[13] that of Rav Ḥiyya bar Ashi and "Ḥeruta." In this story the recurring plot device of a rabbi and apparently pious man who is overcome by his sexual desires is allowed to play out to its conclusion:

> Rav Ḥiyya bar Ashi had a habit: every time he fell on his face, he would say, "May the Merciful One save me from the Evil Inclination." One day his wife heard him. She said, "Since it has been several years that he has separated himself from me [sexually], what is the reason that he said this?" One day he was studying in his garden. She dressed herself up [and] passed repeatedly before him. He said to her, "Who are you?" She said, "I am Ḥeruta and have just returned today." He propositioned her. She said, "Bring me that pomegranate that is on the top branch." He leapt up, and then brought it to her.
>
> When he came to his house, his wife was lighting the oven. He went to it and sat inside it. She said, "What is this?" He said, "What happened was thus and thus." She said to him, "It was I." [He paid no attention to her, until she brought him signs.][14] He said to her, "I nonetheless intended something forbidden." [All the days of his life that same righteous man fasted until he died of that very death.][15]

Like the protagonists of preceding stories, Rav Ḥiyya bar Ashi does not, initially, deliberately seek out a forbidden encounter in the garden or actively ignore the laws of *yichud*. But when temptation presents itself, this rabbi also succumbs to it. Torah learning, in which he is engaged at the very moment of "Ḥeruta's" appearance, is no protection against his sexual urges. Yet, where other rabbis stopped or were stopped halfway into their sinful journey, Rav Ḥiyya leaps to the top of the pomegranate tree; the storyteller only barely veils the implication that the rabbi then proceeds with similar alacrity to sexual intercourse with the desirable "stranger" in his garden.

For this and other reasons I highlight in a moment, this story is significantly different from what preceded it. Moreover, the story is full of strange elements, reversals, echoes of other stories in other sources. It is precisely these factors that open up this story to a new reading, one that reflects back on the rest of the passage in important ways. First, a rather obvious detail is missing from the story's opening, namely, that Rav Ḥiyya has not been sexually intimate with his wife for several years. Despite the importance to the story of the sexual abstinence in this marriage, and despite the importance of this circumstance for setting the rest of the story's events in motion, the narrator supplies no explicit information as to why the rabbi has separated himself from his wife in this way.[16] This abstinence is further problematic in that elsewhere in rabbinic sources a man's sexual activity with his wife is overwhelmingly presented as legitimate and laudatory, even obligatory.[17] More specifically, Rav Ḥiyya's withdrawal from marital relations seems to contradict other rules found in chapter 4 of M *Kiddushin*; as noted above, these materials imply that the very presence of a legitimate sexual outlet for a man is protection for him against inappropriate sexual temptation or behavior or both.[18]

Another strange point in the story comes at the moment when the rabbi addresses the "stranger" in his garden.[19] In this case we have rare extra detail that is not strictly necessary for the plot to proceed. The critical point, it would seem, is that the rabbi is quickly aroused by the apparently unfamiliar woman, and he does not resist acting on that desire. The storyteller adds, however, an intriguing bit of dialogue (although not the proposition itself!): Rav Ḥiyya asks the woman who she is, she gives her "name," and she even adds that she has "just returned today." As Shlomo Naeh has observed, "the apparent superfluity of this dialogue is precisely the reason to view it as important for understanding the story in which it is set. This fact . . . allows us to infer that it plays a key role in establishing the interpretation of the entire story."[20] Several comments, then, can be made about this exchange.

In the stories that preceded this final episode, women are hardly characters at all; what they are or are not doing in the stories is mostly irrelevant to the actions and reactions of the male protagonists. The woman on the road ahead of Rav and Rav Yehuda is not said to be doing anything but walking, and she does not ever interact with them. The former captive in the upper story of Rav Amram's house merely passes by the opening to the lower floor,[21] and the narrative does not address how she might have reacted had Rav Amram completed his ascent of the ladder. In the stories about Satan and R. Meir and R. Akiva, there is no "real" woman at all. On the other hand, Rav Ḥiyya's wife is an active participant in this last tale. She speaks her mind from the first time she appears, even before she takes on her disguise. Once disguised, not only does she continue to speak but she is named, as only very few other women are in the Talmud. Indeed, in the exchange in question she names herself; she is self-defining.

As Wendy Doniger writes, in a study of stories of sexual masquerade in Hindu literature but also with reference to biblical and Western literary examples:

> Women are riddles throughout this corpus, but they are also riddlers. The riddle is itself a double, often turning on the double meaning of a word or a phrase: the trick is to find out what the second meaning is, to identify the surrogate—which is also the point of so many of the stories of sexual masquerade.[22]

It is reasonable to assume, then, that the name Rav Hiyya's wife gives for herself and to her husband, the name that the storyteller goes out of his way to give to his audience, should influence the course and meaning of the events in the story. As Jeffrey L. Rubenstein notes regarding Talmudic narratives, "Names of characters regularly feature in a type of wordplay such that the symbolic meaning of the name substantively relates to the narrative content."[23] Indeed, the name "Heruta" evokes immediate associations with *herut*, freedom. This root could also suggest a freed slave; the sexual histories and morals of such women are often treated with suspicion in rabbinic literature.[24] Both Marcus Jastrow and Michael Sokoloff note an alternate reading of "Hedv'ta," which Jastrow translates as "reveller" or "wedding party" (perhaps meaning in this context a member of a wedding party), and Sokoloff as "bride." In Jastrow's reading the name may again be intended to signal the woman's sexual availability. In Sokoloff's, there is a hint toward the relationship that Rabbi Hiyya and this woman do/should share: she has been his bride; she is perhaps seeking to renew their marriage sexually.[25] Yet another meaning of *heruta* is a dried palm branch or twig. Linking the name and the statement that "I have just returned today," Yona Fraenkel offers another interpretation: her statement intimates that that which was withered and dry (whether the marriage, his sexual ability, his desire) can return/has returned to freshness and flourishing.[26] Finally, Naeh refers to the use of the word *heruta* in Syriac Christian discourse of sexual ethics, where it carries paradoxical meanings of sexual restraint and self-control, what we might call chastity on the one hand, but also freedom and sexual license, on the other.[27] Each of these possibilities highlights various aspects of the sexual and emotional underpinnings of the story.

The response of Rav Hiyya's wife to her situation also significantly echoes and parallels the story of Judah and Tamar in Genesis 38, a story whose plot also hinges on disguise and an act of female sexual agency.[28] As already noted, one might argue that Rav Ḥiyya has a conjugal duty to his wife; as in the biblical story, then, a man is withholding from a woman a marital/sexual relationship to which she is entitled. Like Tamar, Rav Ḥiyya's wife disguises herself, and in her disguise makes use of her sexual desirability. So, too, does she claim a token from the man who seeks her sexual company as proof of his intentions, and (in some readings of the story) later presents tokens to the man that make clear the identities of the partners to a sexual act.

Finally, Rubenstein draws attention to the use of irony in Talmudic storytelling: "Reversals, which are related to situational irony, also feature prominently in BT stories. . . . Irony and reversals . . . have a didactic function too in effectively communicating lessons to the audience."[29] Prior to this point in the Talmudic discussion, we could well argue that the reversals in the stories indeed serve a didactic purpose, that is, to caution against pride or overconfidence where sin (particularly sexual sin) is concerned. The rabbi whose very name deems him "pious" will feel his illicit desires burn in him as a pillar of fire; the rabbi who scoffs at sinners will prove himself to be susceptible to temptation in his path. Is the reversal in this story, as in the other stories, in the figure of the apparently pious man brought low, the man who thought he had conquered his sexual urges taught that they remain potent? Or might the reversal be enacted by the woman, who breaks free of her sisters' depictions as the object of male desire, and takes upon herself the freedom to be the one who desires, the one who pursues, a sexual agent? And what of the irony that what Rav Ḥiyya perceives to be a sexual sin is not exactly a sin, that the woman involved is not who Rav Ḥiyya thought her to be but is the woman permitted to him all along, the woman to whom he may even be said to have a sexual obligation, his own (unnamed) wife?

In fact, "Ḥeruta's" story lends itself to rather intriguing parallels with a story in BT *Nidah* 20b, as read and interpreted by Rachel Adler.[30] In that passage the character Yalta contests Rabbah bar bar Ḥana's ruling that a blood sample she has brought to him is impure (that is, menstruous, meaning that she cannot have sexual relations with her husband); she consults Rav Yitzhak for another opinion. Although, by rabbinic principle, one rabbi should not contradict the ruling of another, Yalta convinces Rav Yitzhak to overturn his colleague's judgment with a claim that Rabbah bar bar Ḥana was, on this occasion, unable to rule properly because of pain in his eye. As Adler notes of this story, "There are two ways of reading the narrative, one of which is considerably less destabilizing than the other."[31] The first possibility is that Rabbah bar bar Ḥana was indeed unable to provide an accurate ruling because of circumstances; Yalta has a legitimate grievance, one that is unique to this situation and that can be contained within the rules and procedures of the rabbinic system. A "darker, more ironic" alternative, however, is to read Yalta's actions as "calculated attempts to manipulate the system." Yalta may thus be understood as "the trickster in the tale, the folkloric prankster who incarnates and unmasks what is arbitrary, chaotic, or unjust in our universe," a "legal guerilla."[32]

"Ḥeruta's" actions, I argue, are also open to a reading of this latter sort. In taking on a disguise and assuming her role as Ḥeruta, Rav Ḥiyya's wife readily offers herself for interpretation as a trickster figure. Indeed, she follows on the heels of another well-known trickster already introduced in previous stories: Satan, who challenges men's—rabbis'—assumptions about themselves and their virtue.[33]

We could reasonably claim, then, that Ḥeruta's disguise is an opportunity for the androcentric perspective of the entire discussion up to this point to be unmasked. Where men have tried to demonstrate their need to be separated from social interactions with women, for their own good, Ḥeruta demands that a man see her, interact with her, and attend to her sexual needs. Similarly Doniger has written that one common motivation in stories of disguise and sexual deception is that "the self does not wish to be regarded as only partial, and wishes to play more roles than those the partner would allow . . . and so slips into the role of another personality: 'I am both this person and that person.'"[34] Rav Ḥiyya has not allowed his wife to play the role of sexual partner; more broadly, male rabbis have not allowed women to actively participate in their own sexual lives or in the making of rules and standards meant to guide interactions between the genders. Through her disguise, Ḥeruta may be understood to challenge the validity—or at least the completeness—of the central concern of the discussion that preceded her appearance, that is, rabbis' fears about their own susceptibility to sexual temptation and forbidden acts. Ḥeruta's story creates an opening for readers to shift their perspective in a way that throws everything the Talmud has said prior to this moment into an ironic light. When read as a "legal guerilla," Ḥeruta resists the idea that men could ever consider or legislate controls on their own sexuality without considering the sexuality—the sexual needs and desires—of the women who are their sexual partners.[35]

It is not particularly original to suggest that every reader cannot help but bring, more or less consciously, his or her personal circumstances and concerns to the act of reading and interpreting a text. Together with Rubenstein, I recognize that "my reading—an interpretation—is conditioned by my culture, historical context, social situation, and other 'forestructures,' not the least being the canons of the university."[36] Where Rubenstein looks for some objective standards to judge a reading, in this instance I again endorse Boyarin's call for a "generous critique." Reading text with attention to varied interpretive possibilities leads Boyarin to assert that "it is incumbent on us, as scholars and as cultural critics, to discover other faces in the same texts—faces that can be more useful for us in re-constructing our own versions of culture and gender practices."[37] In her multiple identities, and the slippage between them, Rav Ḥiyya's wife/Ḥeruta allows us to glimpse just such a face. Because the possibility for reading Ḥeruta as legal guerilla is present in the text, there is no reason why I should not—and every reason why I should—claim this reading from among other possibilities[38] and hold it up as a model toward creating, as the Feminist Sexual Ethics project had hoped to do, "sexual ethics focusing on meaningful consent and mutuality." In this spirit I embrace Ḥeruta as a foremother who demands of us that no proper consideration of sexuality and gender should proceed unless *all* who are affected are included as participants in the discussion. For this reader, at least, Ḥeruta's ruse has the potential to achieve far more than perhaps its perpetrator, or even its recorder, ever imagined it could.

NOTES

1. http://www.ou.org/abstinence (accessed 10/13/08). "Negiah" means touching and refers to the observance of a prohibition on physical contact between a male and a female who are not married to each other.

2. See also M *Gittin* 7:4, 7:7, and 8:4, and *Avodah Zara* 2:1; Tosefta (T) *Ketubot* 1:4 and 3:2, *Gittin* 5:4 and 5:8, and *Avodah Zara* 3:1–2. This assumption, of course, proceeds from and constructs other significant assumptions about gender, desire, and the like; see Miriam Peskowitz, *Spinning Fantasies: Rabbis, Gender, and History* (Berkeley: University of California Press, 1997), 49–76.

3. See www.brandeis.edu/projects/fse (accessed 10/13/08). I thank members of the FSEP team, notably Bernadette Brooten, project director; Kecia Ali, senior research analyst; and Molly Lanzarotta, who read my initial translations and writings on this material. Gratitude is also due Kristin Lindbeck, Ishay Rosen-Zvi, Miriyam Glazer, and Aryeh Cohen, who each provided constructive criticism to my earlier explorations on this topic. See also the FSE Web site, given at the start

of this note, for my brief introduction to the topic of *yichud* laws and the rabbinic texts in which they are set out.

4. Daniel Boyarin, *Carnal Israel: Reading Sex in Talmudic Culture* (Berkeley: University of California Press, 1993), 19–20.

5. This exact phrasing ("women are light-headed") appears in only one other instance in the Babylonian Talmud, and in a context that is decidedly not sexual; BT *Shabbat* 33b describes the presumed likelihood that a woman will not be able to withstand torture. The phrase may thus suggest a general weakness of will that includes, but is not limited to, susceptibility to sexual inducements.

6. This attention to male experiences of sexual desire is not the only possible approach to the laws of *yichud*; other sources suggest that their purpose is to protect women from male sexual predation. See, for example, BT *Sanhedrin* 21a–b, and *Avodah Zara* 36b; also see Hauptman, *Rereading the Rabbis*, 49, 54.

7. A similar limitation also appears in the Palestinian Talmud (PT) as well (*Kiddushin* 4:11, 66c): "R. Abin said: Regarding what are these words said? Regarding proper men, but regarding [morally] unrestrained men, she may not be alone even with one hundred men." However, there is no further attempt there to define the categories.

8. Various readings for this last phrase exist in manuscripts, early printings, and citations by commentators. Nonetheless, the force of the question and the answer remain functionally the same for our purposes here.

9. This sentence appears neither in the Vatican and Munich manuscripts nor in the Spanish recension. Replacing the ladder, however, appears in all versions (see next 10), meaning the ladder must have been removed previously. Further, in an episode appearing before this one, a rabbi who is visiting a colleague explicitly requests that the ladder between floors of the house be removed from underneath him, so that he will not be tempted by—or at least able to act on—sexual desire for his host's wife.

10. The phrase "which . . . alone" does not appear in the Vatican or Munich manuscripts or in the Spanish recension, all of which read, instead, "he placed it."

11. See Vatican 111 ("the Evil Inclination") and the Spanish recension ("his Inclination").

12. In other words, Rav Amram experiences his desires as alien to himself, an anarchic fire that must be expelled if it cannot be extinguished. That it takes the form of a pillar of fire is intriguing, as this is a heavily laden, charged, and sometimes phallic symbol in rabbinic literature. Other uses of this image (in addition to biblical citations) in the Babylonian Talmud appear in *M.K.* 25a, *Ketubot* 17a, 62b, and 77b; and *Nazir* 50b. The example in *Ketubot* 62b is particularly notable for the use of this imagery in a sexualized context; see Aryeh Cohen, *Rereading Talmud: Gender, Law, and the Poetics of Sugyot* (Atlanta, Ga.: Scholars Press, 1998), 108.

13. A story intervenes between the previous three and this one that relates to trickery by Satan in disguise rather than sexual temptation.

14. This sentence does not appear in the Vatican or Munich manuscripts or in the Spanish recension.

15. This sentence does not appear in either the Vatican or Munich manuscripts.

16. The medieval commentator Rashi suggests that the rabbi's restraint is the result of old age, and thus the loss of desire (and perhaps ability). See Eliezer Diamond's brief discussion of possible roots for Rashi's comment: Eliezer Diamond, *Holy Men and Hunger Artists: Fasting and Asceticism in Rabbinic Culture* (Oxford: Oxford University Press, 2004), 38. If this is the case, however, the challenge may be raised that the rabbi's prayer is effectively superfluous, for how do improper urges threaten him?

Shlomo Naeh has read this story in light of ascetic practices of celibacy among Syriac Christians, and given the rabbinic bias toward marital sexuality (see just below), as a critique of Rabbi Ḥiyya's behavior; see Shlomo Naeh, "Freedom and Celibacy: A Talmudic Variation on Tales of Temptation and Fall in Genesis and Its Syrian Background," in *The Book of Genesis in Jewish and Oriental Christian Interpretation*, ed. Judith Frishman and Lucas Van Rompay, 73–89 (Louvain, Belgium: Editions Peeters, 1997). See also Yona Fraenkel, "Prominent Trends in the Transmission History of the Text of Aggadic Narratives," *Proceedings of the Seventh World Congress of Jewish Studies: Studies in the Talmud, Halacha, and Midrash* (1981): 59–61 (Hebrew).

17. See M *Ketubot* 5:6; and BT *Ketubot* 61a–62a.

18. A strong articulation of this point can be found in Ishay Rosen-Zvi, "The Evil Inclination, Sexuality, and the Yichud Prohibitions: A Chapter in Talmudic Anthropology," *Te'oriah u'Bikoret* 14 (1999): 80 (Hebrew).

19. In fact, there is room to ask whether Rav Ḥiyya's wife initially intends to disguise herself and deceive him. The word used to describe what she does before presenting herself to him is *kashta*, from the root *k,sh,t*. In many contexts this root means to adorn oneself (as with jewelry, cosmetics, hair-styling, or nice clothing), and represents something a married woman is encouraged and expected to do so as to remain attractive and desirable to her husband (although a woman might also adorn herself for a lover; see, for example, M *Sotah* 1:7; and T *Sotah* 3:3). Examples are far too numerous to list here, but see Marcus Jastrow, *A Dictionary of the Targumim, the Talmud Babli and Yerushalmi, and the Midrashic Literature* (New York: Judaica Press, 1996 [1886]), 1429–1430; and, similarly, Michael Sokoloff, *A Dictionary of Jewish Babylonian Aramaic of the Talmudic and Geonic Periods* (Ramat Gan: Bar Ilan University Press; Baltimore, Md.: Johns Hopkins University Press, 2002), 1048.

On the other hand, the word translated here as "passed [. . . before him]" is *ḥalfa*, from the root *ḥ,l,f,* which also carries meanings of "to change, exchange," "to substitute, exchange . . . to switch"; see Jastrow, *A Dictionary*, 471–472; and Sokoloff, *A Dictionary*, 465. This root is also the source of the word *ḥiluf/a*, meaning contrary/opposite/instead of; see Jastrow, *A Dictionary*, 456; and Sokoloff, *A Dictionary*, 455. In context, then, this word choice is quite resonant.

20. Naeh, "Freedom and Celibacy," 75–76.

21. Nor is it clear what Rav Amram saw: the woman, her shadow, or perhaps some sort of light cast from her body. For examples of particularly beautiful/desirable bodies radiating light, see BT *Ketubot* 65a (Ḥoma, wife/widow of Abaye), and *Berakhot* 5b and *Bava Metziah* 84a (Rabbi Yoḥanan). Both *Ketubot* and *Berakhot* use the phrase that appears here, *nafal nehora*, "light fell."

22. Wendy Doniger, "Enigmas of Sexual Masquerade in Hindu Myths and Tales," in *Untying the Knot: On Riddles and Other Enigmatic Modes*, ed. Galit Hasan-Rokem and David Shulman, 217–218 (Oxford: Oxford University Press, 1996).

23. Jeffrey L. Rubenstein, *Talmudic Stories: Narrative Art, Composition, and Culture* (Baltimore, Md.: John Hopkins University Press, 1999); idem, *Talmudic Stories*, 246; see also 247.

24. See Fraenkel "Prominent Trends," 60 n. 73. On the sexual availability/vulnerability of enslaved women as constructed in rabbinic literature and culture, see Catherine Hezeer, Jewish Slavery in Antiquity (Oxford: Oxford University Press, 2005), 179–201; and Gail Labovitz, "The Purchase of His Money: Slavery and the Ethics of Jewish Marriage," in *Beyond Slavery: Overcoming Its Religious and Sexual Legacy*, ed. Bernadette Brooten, forthcoming.

25. Jastrow, *A Dictionary*, 426 (and see, too, 460 and 500 for additional possibilities); Sokoloff, *A Dictionary*, 432. This version of the name would be directly related to the noun "*ḥedva/ḥedv'ta*," meaning joy/rejoicing. See also Tal Ilan, *Silencing the Queen: The Literary Histories of Shelamzion and Other Jewish Women* (Tübingen, Germany: Mohr Siebeck, 2006), 88.

26. Fraenkel, "Prominent Trends," 60. See Jastrow, *A Dictionary*, 500; and Sokoloff, *A Dictionary*, 482.

27. Naeh, "Freedom and Celibacy," 76–83; see also his discussion of the rest of her statement, 84–85, noting meanings of turning and changing in the word *hadari*.

Rashi does not address the meaning of the name itself but states that it was "the name of a well-known prostitute in the town." Although nothing in the story itself explicitly suggests this reading (perhaps Rashi imported it from the story of Judah and Tamar—see below), this understanding of Rav Ḥiyya's wife's disguise has been adopted, at least in passing, almost unanimously by modern scholars who have written about the story; the notable exception is Ilan, *Silencing the Queen*, 88–90.

28. The plucking of the pomegranate from the top of the tree also has hints

of Adam and Eve eating the fruit of the Tree of Knowledge in Genesis 3. See Naeh, "Freedom and Celibacy."

29. Rubenstein, *Talmudic Stories*, 247–248.

30. Rachel Adler, "Feminist Folktales of Justice: Robert Cover as a Resource for the Renewal of Halakhah," *Conservative Judaism* 45, no. 3 (1993): 40–55.

31. Ibid., 53.

32. Ibid. Adler's reading is explicitly indebted to Robert Cover, "The Folktales of Justice: Tales of Jurisdiction," in *Narrative, Violence, and the Law: The Essays of Robert Cover*, ed. Martha Minow, Michael Ryan, and Austin Sarat, 173–201 (Ann Arbor: University of Michigan Press, 1992). For another interpretation of this story (to which I am indebted for having inspired part of my title for this essay), see Charlotte Elisheva Fonrobert, "Yalta's Ruse: Resistance against Rabbinic Menstrual Authority in Talmudic Literature," in *Women and Water: Menstruation in Jewish Life and Law*, ed. Rahel R. Wasserfall, 60–81 (Hanover, N.H.: University Press of New England, 1999).

33. As noted above, Satan also appears in the intervening story that I have not cited here. Indeed, some intriguing linguistic and thematic links exist between that story and this one; see Shulamit Valler, *Women in Jewish Society in the Talmudic Period* (Israel: Hakibbutz Hameuchad, 2000), 49.

34. Doniger, "Enigmas of Sexual Masquerade," 218.

35. Indeed, it may be noted that it is the redactor of the passage who chooses to include this story and places it at this point in the discussion. Although rabbinic literature rarely, if ever, includes authentic representations of female voices (one may also question its representation of male voices), Boyarin suggests that another approach to feminist reading "promises to be more fruitful for the Talmud, namely the search for male opposition, *within the Talmud itself*, however rudimentary, to the dominant, androcentric discourse" (*Carnal Israel*, 228; emphasis in original).

On the other hand, it may well be this disruptive potential that Ḥeruta has at this moment to overturn the androcentric perspective of the previous stories and discussion that provokes the equivocal ending this story has been given (especially in the Venice and Vilna printings of the Talmud). Rav Ḥiyya and the redactor of the passage remain ambivalent about the events of the story. Like the biblical patriarch Judah, Rav Ḥiyya acknowledges wrongdoing when the full details of the sexual encounter come to light. Yet, he only acknowledges that his misdeed was to have sex with a woman he had legitimate reason to think was forbidden to him; he does not accept responsibility for sexually depriving his wife or even indicate any recognition of this as a fault. In the Babylonian Talmud, as we generally encounter it (that is, in its standard printing), moreover, Rav Ḥiyya so punishes himself out of guilt for what he has done, and is deemed "righteous" as he does so, that his wife will come to suffer the ultimate deprivation of his presence, namely, widowhood (but see note 16 above). In addition, the story is followed by several traditions meant to illustrate the idea that one ought to be held liable even for a permitted act if one performed it under the misapprehension that it was forbidden and with the willful intent to perform the supposedly forbidden act.

36. Rubenstein, *Talmudic Stories*, 32–33.

37. Boyarin, *Carnal Israel*, 21.

38. Although it should be acknowledged that other plausible interpretations do exist: see my article "Of Proper and Unrestrained Men: Textual Ambiguity and the Reading of Law, Narrative, and Desire in the Babylonian Talmud," *Hebrew Union College Annual*, forthcoming.

17

Love the One You're With

Laura Levitt

Only now, I find more and more women-identified women brave enough to risk sharing the erotic's electrical charge without having to look away, and without distorting the enormously powerful and creative nature of that exchange.

— Audre Lorde, "Uses of the Erotic"

David said before God, "My father Jesse did not intend to sire me, but intended only his own pleasure. You know that this is so because after the parents satisfied themselves, *he turned his face away and she turned her face away* and You joined the drops." (my emphasis)

— Vayiqra Rabbah 14.5, ed. Margoles, 2:308; quoted in David Novak, *Jewish Social Ethics*

WHEN I FIRST considered contributing to this volume I was haunted by the relationship between the two texts of which the epigraphs to this chapter are taken, and to the work of two unlikely writers: the Jewish feminist theologian Judith Plaskow and the Jewish social ethicist David Novak. The passage from Vayiqra Rabbah comes from Novak's book, *Jewish Social Ethics*. Ten years ago I referred to this particular rabbinic narrative and Novak's reading of it in my account of Judith Plaskow's groundbreaking feminist theology of sexuality.[1] Plaskow's work and Novak's book still remain a peculiar pair, precisely because Plaskow relies so heavily on Audre Lorde's classic essay, "Uses of the Erotic: The Erotic as Power."[2] As I explained then, Lorde's essay is the central contemporary feminist text informing Plaskow's Jewish feminist vision of sexuality. What struck me then, and continues to inform my thinking about a Jewish feminist approach to sexuality is the notion of not "turning away." This strangely constant notion connects the passage from Vayiqra Rabbah's text to Lorde's. In their own ways, each shares a sense of the power of presence, and each insists on this presence as a kind of ideal. They demand that we not turn away from the one we are with, that we more positively love that person. With this vision in mind I found myself turning to the words of singer, songwriter Steven Stills for the title of this chapter, "Love the One You're With."[3]

To understand what a radical vision of the erotic might mean to (Jewish) feminists today, I reframe my original critique of Judith Plaskow's feminist theology of sexuality and her move from radical mutuality to long-term partnership, which includes gay and lesbian relationships. I ask what it might mean for us now, after the explosion of gay and lesbian marriages, to rethink the erotic as just that: radical mutuality, not tied to either monogamous marriage or long-term partnership. In other words, what might it mean to love the one we are with? As I show when I reframe and revisit my original critique of Plaskow's work, a more capacious and erotic future may be offered by radical mutuality, the road not taken.[4]

For Audre Lorde, not turning away is a brave act. It is about being present and open to the person with whom one shares "the erotic's electrical charge," and I do not think this need only be an account of what transpires between "women-identified women" as Lorde's language suggests. What seems most important is to be open to such an exchange with others, regardless of gender.

The Vayiqra Rabbah passage is much narrower in its account of right sexual relations. It is more concerned about negative consequences than presenting its erotic ideal, all within the confines of hetero-marriage. The text tells the tale of an erotic encounter between a husband and wife, and it is told in the voice of the biblical King David speaking to God. Here we learn that when husband and wife "turn away" from each other, the child that should have been or could have been conceived as a holy gift from God, if not God's presence itself, is wasted. Here the individually satisfied partners are left with nothing lasting; as David says to God, "You join the drops;" wasted seed indeed.[5]

Novak presents the Vayiqra Rabbah passage as part of a larger argument about the transcendent power of the erotic:

> It is mistaken, it seems to me, to consider the essence of sexual love to be pleasure, although it is certainly a *sin qua non* of it, for in all other bodily pleasures, such as eating, drinking, bathing, we seek a heightened sense of awareness of our bodies. Our pleasure is essentially a

taking-in, that is, our desire is to make our world around us an extension of our own bodies. In heterosexual love, on the other hand, we seek ecstasy, which comes from two Greek words, *ex histemi* meaning "to stand out." In other words, our sexuality intends transcendence. Eros seeks spirit. It seems that in true eros we seek to *go beyond our bodies through them*. For a moment we experience a going beyond the body, which is ordinarily the limit of the soul. Nevertheless, sexual love in itself lasts only for a moment before the body, the ever-present finite, mortal vessel, claims the soul once again.

Unlike Audre Lorde's embodied eros, Novak's eros flees the body. He believes that the goal of eros is ultimately to transcend the body, and that the embodied act of sexual engagement should be about seeking spirit. Strangely, despite this account of sexuality, Novak uses the Vayiqra Rabbah passage as a proof text. He concludes the discussion I have just cited by asserting, "This is pointed out in the following aggadah." He then cites the Vayiqra Rabbah text, which interests me. Despite the case Novak wants to make about sexual engagement as seeking spirit, not bodily pleasure, the cited text makes a different argument; it demands a physical presence between husband and wife, a face to face encounter, where neither partner turns away. Thus, despite Novak's particularly phallic and disembodied reading of a narrowly defined hetero-married sex, he, like Plaskow, offers readers something beyond the normative vision explicitly called for in his text. That he cites this passage from Vayiqra Rabbah suggests possibilities strangely closer to what Audre Lorde proposes. What goes wrong in the Vayiqra Rabbah text is that husband and wife turn away from each other. What is right in Lorde's text are those rare moments in which any of us are fully present in our erotic relations with others. And, as I will show, Lorde's insistence on not turning away as an ideal in and of itself, functions in Plaskow's more normative text in much the same way that the Vayiqra Rabbah text functions in Novak's book. In both instances, the cited texts say more than the authors seem to want to say, complicating, even contradicting, the authors' theologizing and moralizing.

Much has changed since I first wrote about these issues a decade ago. Public discourse has shifted dramatically from debates in the early 1990s about gays in the military to the question of gay marriage. As I began working on this chapter, the state of New Jersey joined a few other American states in legalizing gay and lesbian domestic partnerships, not quite marriage but a huge step in that direction. The New Jersey law enables gay and lesbian couples to share virtually all the rights and privileges of married heterosexual couples in New Jersey. And yet, despite the fact that gay marriage is now legal in Massachusetts, during this same ten-year period the vast majority of other states have passed constitutional amendments defining marriage as solely a relationship between one man and one woman. This, too, may be a sign of how much things have changed. Many of the defenders of hetero-marriage perceive it as under serious attack, so threatened that they now need to use the law to secure its normative status. This perceived threat is not only exacerbated by changes in the law but also by profound changes in social practice. Since 1997 huge numbers of gay and lesbian couples have, in fact, married. Gay and lesbian couples of various backgrounds have held commitment and marriage ceremonies, rituals often performed by clergy without state sanction, in order to affirm their long-term monogamous commitment to each other. They have made these vows before friends and family. Many of these ceremonies have been performed by liberal rabbis. Reconstructionist, Reform, and some Conservative rabbis now regularly perform these rites and bless these unions.

In this sense, Plaskow's vision was prophetic. In the early 1990s she predicted what has now come to pass in many liberal Jewish communities and in American culture more broadly, a liberal appreciation for gay marriage. Although this affirmation has emerged with great resistance, it has happened.

I do not want to diminish this accomplishment. In many ways this is a truly revolutionary social and cultural achievement, but I contend that something was lost in this transformation. In this chapter I return to my reading of Plaskow's theology of sexuality in order to look more closely at the possibilities lost in this cultural affirmation of gay marriage. I return to Audre Lorde and the notion of not turning away. I argue that it was precisely this radical affirmation of the erotic and its challenge to both monogamy and even liberal marriage that got lost in the pursuit of gay marriage.

Toward a New Theology of Sexuality

The most powerful feature of Judith Plaskow's Jewish feminist theology is her discussion of sexuality. Here, more than anywhere else in her work, she sets out her vision of right relationships, using liberal marriage to describe not only right human relationships but also the covenant between God and Israel. In her theology of sexuality, Plaskow considers diverse loving relationships and explicitly argues against marriage as an exclusively heterosexual contract. By calling for respect, responsibility, and honesty, she opens up the possibility of affirming different kinds of sexual relationships.

It is important here to clearly point out that Plaskow directly advocates the "erotic" as a theological value. Relying on the work of the black feminist poet and activist Audre Lorde,[6] Plaskow argues that sexuality is a source of liberation. Citing Lorde, she writes "And when we fail to understand sexual feelings as an expression of the power of the erotic, we reduce them to mere sensations that we then fear and seek to suppress."[7] In this respect, Plaskow's work explicitly addresses sexuality's moral and spiritual power. Given this, Plaskow reads Martin Buber's *I and Thou* and the biblical *Song of Songs* as charged with the power of the erotic, a power that she describes as an ambivalent presence within rabbinic Judaism.[8]

Like the rest of her theology, Plaskow's writing about sexuality begins with an explicit critique of the Rabbis. In considering the Rabbis' ambivalence toward sexuality, she identifies three key problems. First, she argues that the Rabbis address sexuality under the guise of an "energy/control" model, according to which "sexuality is an independent and sometimes alien energy that must be held in check through personal discipline and religious constraints. While the sexual impulse is given by God as a normal and healthy part of human life, sanctified within its proper framework, sexuality also requires careful, sometimes rigorous control in order that it not violate the boundaries assigned it."[9] The second problem she identifies is that the Rabbis define sexuality too narrowly; they define heterosexual marriage as the only proper venue for Jewish sexual expression. And, third, Jewish women are the explicit concern of most rabbinic accounts of sexuality. As she explains: "To speak of control is necessarily to speak of women—of the need to cover them, avoid them, contain them in proper (patriarchal) families where their threat is minimized if it cannot be overcome."[10]

In each of these cases, Plaskow argues that the Rabbis acknowledge and give power to sexual expression, but they use this power to control Jewish women, not liberate them. She rejects this legacy and offers a liberal alternative allowing unmarried others to be included in a new conception of "right relationships." She then turns to Martin Buber's I-Thou relationship to describe a kind of mutuality, a relationship that need not be marital. As she explains, "Relationships between human beings need not hover at the 'threshold of mutuality' but can express themselves in language, so that acknowledgment of the other as a person can be both given and received."[11]

This vision of mutuality also appears in Plaskow's liberal reading of the Song of Songs. "Unabashed by their desire, the man and woman of these poems delight in their own embodiment and the beauty surrounding them, each seeking the other out to inaugurate their meetings, each rejoicing in the love without dominion that is also the love of God."[12] As her use of Audre Lorde's notion of the erotic suggests, the erotic, for Plaskow, is both holy and powerful. The question is, what kinds of relationships does Plaskow envision as possible outside "the sacred garden" and "in the midst of daily demands," in the present?

Plaskow argues that her mutual vision of the erotic sharply contrasts with "the structures of marriage as Judaism defines them."[13] Although these arrangements still define Jewish women as subordinate to Jewish men, she focuses on their failure to recognize "the possibility of loving same-sex relationships."[14] Plaskow points out: "A first concrete task, then, of the feminist reconstruction of Jewish attitudes towards sexuality is a radical transformation of the institutional, legal framework within which sexual relations are supposed to take place" (145). Besides advocating lesbian and gay relationships, she also calls for a reaffirmation of consent as a criterion for her liberal feminist position. As Plaskow explains,

> In the modern West, it is generally assumed that such a decision [mutual consent] constitutes a central meaning of marriage, but this assumption is contradicted by a religious (and secular) legal system that outlaws homosexual marriage and institutionalizes inequality in its basic definition of marriage and divorce.

In this way, Plaskow opens up the legal definition of marriage to include gay and lesbian relationships without altering the structure of liberalism's legal framework. For her, marriage continues to be about consent, which she uses as an answer to patriarchy as well. Marriage, she contends, will not be about the acquisition of women by their husbands or the sanctification of potential disorder through the firm establishment of women in the patriarchal family, but about the decision of two adults to make their lives together, lives that include the sharing of sexuality.

This is where Plaskow's argument begins to break down, because she cannot fully distinguish between the modern Western legal tradition and her feminist alternative. She cannot account for the fact that the patriarchal family is not just a rabbinic problem; therefore, even her efforts to affirm lesbian and gay relationships are based on a liberal premise of inclusion. Lesbian and gay relationships are affirmed in their likeness to liberal marriage, not in their queerness.

Plaskow's Erotic Ideal

According to Plaskow, sexuality and spirituality are linked:

> I believe that radical mutuality is most fully possible in the context of an ongoing, committed relationship in which sexual expression is one dimension of a shared life. Long-term partnership may be the richest setting for negotiating and living out the meaning of mutuality, responsibility, and honesty amid the distractions, problems, and pleasures of every day.

Plaskow qualifies her definition of "radical mutuality" and chooses "long-term partnerships" as the only means, or at least the strongly preferred one, to its end.

Given the contingencies of everyday life as she experiences them in the United States, ongoing committed relationships like marriage make sense, although such relationships may be neither desirable nor possible for others. Thus, "to respond to the realities of different life decisions and at the same time affirm the importance of sexual well-being as an aspect of our total well-being," Plaskow offers criteria for making sexual choices.

> We need to apply certain fundamental values to a range of sexual styles and choices. While honesty, responsibility, and respect are goods that pertain to any relationship, the concrete meaning of these values will vary considerably depending on the duration and significance of the connection involved.

She argues that respect, responsibility, and honesty must be understood contextually and can vary considerably. In so doing, she offers contingent criteria that are potentially inclusive of various kinds of sexual possibilities. I affirm these moves, but I become troubled when Plaskow begins to apply these criteria.

In her application of these criteria to specific relationships, Plaskow's position shifts from its initial contingency, which is the aspect of her efforts I find most compelling in terms of reimagining the erotics within Jewish communities. Once Plaskow presents examples, what she first expressed as an individual opinion quickly becomes a normative assessment.

> At its fullest, respect may mean regard for another as a total person; at a minimum, it may mean absence of pressure or coercion, and a

commitment, in Lorde's words, not to "look away as we come together." If we need to look away, then we should walk away.

In this way, Plaskow sets up a hierarchy. For her, "fullness" is the ideal
and, reformulating Lorde's statement, she makes "not turning away" into a
minimal requirement. However, in my view, Lorde's position is much more
in keeping with Plaskow's initial contingency. Although there is a hierarchy
in Lorde's text, it is not presented as normative. According to Lorde, each
person needs to figure out what she or he values most, and then act accord-
ingly. As Lorde explains,

> Yes, there is a hierarchy. There is a difference between painting a back
> fence and writing a poem, but only one of quantity. And there is, for
> me, no difference between writing a good poem and moving into sun-
> light against the body of a woman I love.[15]

Lorde is clear about what she values, without demanding that others
make the same assessment. My concern is that Plaskow's construction of a
maximum and minimum standard erases this kind of contingency. By pre-
suming that long-term monogamous relationships are a norm, Plaskow ultimately demands that others adhere to this single standard.

Again, what makes more sense to me is her initial approach, with the
contingent application of her criteria of respect, responsibility, and honesty
within particular contexts. These criteria could offer a more affirming strategy and open up the possibility of different kinds of sexual expression.

In her final assessment of the erotic, Plaskow directly pleads for gay
and lesbian relationships, but this time without appealing to her criteria of
respect, responsibility, and honesty. Instead, she turns to God and theology,
and she spiritualizes sexuality.

> If we see sexuality as part of what enables us to reach out beyond our-
> selves, and thus as a fundamental ingredient in our spirituality, then
> the issue of homosexuality must be . . . a question of the affirmation
> of the value to the individual and society of each of us being able to
> find that place within ourselves where sexuality and spirituality come
> together.[16]

Ironically, in this account Plaskow's justification for gay and lesbian sexuality returns to a Jewish tradition, building on a legacy of Jewish mysticism to

give weight and authority to her theological claims. Following this tradition, she writes that "sexuality can be a medium for the reunification of God." Her innovation is simply that this reunification need not take place in exclusively heterosexual relationships: "The reality is that for some Jews, it has been realized only in relationships with both men and women, while for others it is realized only in relationships between members of the same sex." Here again, Plaskow's strategy is not to transform the tradition but to bring gay and lesbian Jews into something that already exists so that their relationships become yet another means to holiness.

This theological argument further distinguishes Plaskow's efforts from Audre Lorde's work on the erotic. For Plaskow, the bonds of the erotic lead to God:

> In recognizing the continuity between our own sexual energy and the greater currents that nourish and renew it [community], we affirm our sexuality as a source of energy and power that, schooled in the values of respect and mutuality, can lead us to the related, and therefore sexual, God.

This position contrasts with her more contingent criteria of respect, responsibility, and honesty. Instead of affirming a vision of diverse and even contradictory erotic relationships, here Plaskow returns to a more unified liberal vision of community. Instead of affirming differences, here again a singular Jewish community demands that all Jews adhere to a single sexual norm. Although she includes gay and lesbian relationships in her normative ideal, she does so only to the extent that they resemble the liberal contract of marriage. By reading against the grain of her argument for establishing this norm, I want to imagine other erotic possibilities. I want to respect and not judge the differences between different kinds of erotic relations. I believe that I share this position with Lorde, who also does not want to tell others, ultimately, what kinds of erotic relationships they should have.

I believe that Plaskow's normative claims and theological turn, despite her reliance on Lorde, do not fit neatly with Lorde's depiction of the power of the erotic as a liberating practice. By using Lorde's notion of "not turning away when we come together" as a minimal requirement for sexual relationships, Plaskow misses the power of Lorde's plea. Lorde's demand is by no means minimal. "Not turning away" is a symbol of the fullness of relating to another. For Lorde, the image of "not turning away" is an expression of radical mutuality. As Lorde explains,

Only now, I find more and more women-identified women brave enough to risk sharing the erotic's electrical charge without having to look away, and without distorting the enormously powerful and creative nature of that exchange.[17]

Lorde views "looking away" as a form of distortion that can have many manifestations. As I read it, "turning away" includes Plaskow's efforts to justify sexuality as "Godly" or "holy."[18] As Lorde writes, "These occasions are almost always characterized by a simultaneous looking away, a pretense of calling them something else, whether a *religion* [my emphasis], a fit, mob violence, or even playing doctor."[19] These distortions, including religion, are, according to Lorde, quite dangerous. They limit one's ability to be fully present with another.

Although Lorde speaks of the erotic as spiritual, she does not want to confuse it with something outside herself. She writes,

> that deep and irreplaceable knowledge of my capacity for joy comes to demand from all of my life that it be lived within the knowledge that such satisfaction is possible, and does not have to be called *marriage*, nor *god*, nor *an afterlife*.

Not having to attribute this experience of the erotic to something external is one of the challenges of "not turning away." Thus Lorde offers a way of thinking differently about an erotic self in relation to others. Lorde is concerned about living life fully:

> When we begin to live from within outward, in touch with the power of the erotic within ourselves, and allowing that power to inform and illuminate our actions upon the world around us, then we begin to be responsible to ourselves in the deepest sense. For as we begin to recognize our deepest feelings, we begin to give up, of necessity, being satisfied with the suffering and self-negation, and with the numbness which so often seems like their only alternative in our society. Our acts against oppression become integral with self, motivated and empowered from within.

For me, Lorde's construction of the erotic also offers a new perspective on relationships and selves in their complexity, over and against the sexual contract and other forms of individual and social oppression. Among these,

Lorde includes resignation, despair, self-effacement, depression, and self-denial. In this way she acknowledges how she has internalized and sustained various histories of oppression within herself, even as she works against them. In these ways her text speaks to me and is a reminder of how the erotic is powerful and liberating without having to contain its powers within an overarching framework. This contingency is what is inviting about Lorde's work. In other words, the contingent nature of Lorde's notion of the erotic opens it up to different possibilities. In this case, the possibilities it opens are Plaskow's two different interpretations of the theology of sexuality.[20] The specificity of Lorde's account, as opposed to its all-inclusiveness, makes it highly appealing to me. I do not have to share Lorde's position to learn from her; I can apply her approach to my own situation, and this may even lead to contradictory results.

Lorde's notion of the erotic is at the heart of Plaskow's theology of sexuality, giving shape and texture to some of Plaskow's most powerful accounts of community, relation, and belonging. In these moments, Lorde offers an alternative to Plaskow's normative vision of liberal inclusion. I have focused on Plaskow's reading of Lorde because I see it as a promising site of contradiction within Plaskow's text. Through reading Lorde, Plaskow begins to push at the seams of her own liberal feminist stance. What I have tried to demonstrate is that these are, indeed, liberating moments. Within Plaskow's understanding of Lorde, she offers a more contingent feminist notion of erotic community that challenges her liberal theological vision. It is this partial vision that I carry with me out of Plaskow's text as an alternative to her liberal feminist position.

A Return to the Present

Ten years ago I concluded my critique of Plaskow's work by arguing that, throughout her feminist theology, she critiques the dynamics of domination within rabbinic Judaism and adamantly resists that legacy by turning to liberalism as a feminist alternative. My disappointment was that, despite her careful critique, Plaskow used theology to legitimate and prescribe a version of the sexual contract of marriage, which is already seriously challenged by feminist political theorists for the ways it does not liberate women.[21] With this critique in mind, I argued that Plaskow never challenged the ways that marriage, and especially liberal marriage, is itself an asymmetrical power relationship and, as such, not a useful model of mutuality and respect. Fortunately, as

I explained then, this is not all that is going on in Plaskow's text. By turning to Audre Lorde's notion of the erotic, Plaskow points to a different vision of feminist community, a vision I want to reaffirm now as an alternative to both liberalism and the promise of gay marriage in the present.

Lorde's position echoes the vision that the political theorist Marla Brettschneider presents in *The Family Flamboyant*, where Brettschneider boldly shows the ideological and institutional work that monogamy and liberal marriage do to support alienated forms of relation in the present.[22] She further complicates the notion of marriage as the answer to the kinds of inequities Plaskow described. Brettschneider argues that part of the problem is structural. These private relations are supposed to do all the work of nonalienating engagement; they are supposed to compensate for the larger alienation and disconnect that mark contemporary American culture. As Brettschneider explains, monogamy and marriage "are *supposed* to provide counter spaces to the alienated forms of relation in politics and economics. Yet, . . . they each carry through—in their own modalities—the very same dynamics of alienation as found and noticed more commonly within the public sphere of politics and work."[23] For me this is "turning away" writ large. It is a vision of the erotic I do not want to continue to affirm.

By returning to my reading against the grain of Plaskow's text and thinking again about the relationship between the Vayiqra Rabbah passage and Lorde's essay, I want to build a bridge from Lorde through Plaskow to Brettschneider. Maintaining Plaskow's criteria of respect, responsibility, and honesty, I want to more fully appreciate those rare and powerful moments when we can and do love the ones we are with. Building on the work of Martin Buber, Brettschneider explicitly challenges the institutions of marriage and monogamy. As she explains,

> In the expectations and promises of monogamous marriage the present is lost, and relation becomes an object with a pretense to the future as real. For Buber this is a stultifying of the present. It is not the aliveness promised by the ideological vision, but instead "cessation, suspension, a breaking off and cutting clear and hardening, absence of relation and of being present."[24]

We are no longer able to connect to ones we are with. To do that means embracing a vision of the erotic that does not already presume a single normative erotic ideal even for (Jewish) feminists.

NOTES

A portion of this essay comes from Laura Levitt, *Jews and Feminism: The Ambivalent Search for Home* (New York: Routledge, 1997), chap. 6. It is reproduced and reframed here with permission from Routledge.

1. See Laura Levitt, *Jews and Feminism: The Ambivalent Search for Home* (New York: Routledge, 1997), chap. 6.

2. Audre Lorde, "Uses of the Erotic: The Erotic as Power," in idem, *Sister Outsider* (Trumansburg, N.Y.: Crossing Press, 1984), 53–59.

3. Stephen Stills, the first single release from his self-titled first solo album, 1970. The song was subsequently recorded and performed by Aretha Franklin, the Isley Brothers, The Jackson Five, and Luther Vandross, among others.

4. Here my move back to a past reading to imagine a different future is very much built on the kind of critical practice first presented by Walter Benjamin and powerfully rearticulated in a more explicitly Jewish context by Jonathan Boyarin. See Walter Benjamin, "Theses on the Philosophy of History," in idem, *Illuminations* (New York: Schocken Books, 1968), 253–264; and Jonathan Boyarin, *Storm from Paradise: The Politics of Jewish Memory* (Minneapolis: University of Minnesota Press, 1992).

5. David Novak, *Jewish Social Ethics* (New York: Oxford University Press, 1992). A final powerful connection in this regard is Buber's notion of "God turning his [*sic*] face away" from Israel. See my analysis of this concept as it appears in Eugene Borowitz, "Renewing the Covenant," in Levitt, *Jews and Feminism*, chap. 5.

6. Lorde, "Uses of the Erotic."

7. Plaskow, *Standing Again at Sinai*, 196.

8. On this ambivalence, see Plaskow, *Standing*, 185–191.

9. Judith Plaskow, "Towards a New Theology of Sexuality," in *Twice Blessed: On Being Lesbian, Gay, and Jewish*, ed. Christie Balka and Andy Rose (Boston: Beacon, 1989), 141.

10. Plaskow, "Towards a New Theology of Sexuality," 142. See also *Ezekiel* 16:62–63.

11. Plaskow, *Standing Again at Sinai*, 157.

12. Plaskow, "Towards a New Theology of Sexuality," 144.

13. In this account, Plaskow, like many other liberal theologians who build on the work of Buber imagining a relational covenant, does not directly refer to the rabbinic marriage contract, or *ketubbah*, in her account of what becomes a marital covenant. This is also the case in Eugene Borowitz's work. For more on this issue in Borowitz, see Levitt, *Jews and Feminism*, chap. 5.

14. Plaskow, "Towards a New Theology of Sexuality," 144.

15. Lorde, "Uses of the Erotic," 58.

16. Plaskow, "Towards a New Theology of Sexuality," 150.

17. Lorde, "Uses of the Erotic," 59.

18. In my original reading of Plaskow's work, this is where I draw the connection to Novak's text. For that reading, see Levitt, *Jews and Feminism*, 196 n. 30.

19. Lorde, "Uses of the Erotic," 59.

20. Lorde herself writes about these connections in "Age, Race, Class, and Sex: Women Redefining Difference," in *Out There: Marginalization and Contemporary Cultures*, ed. Russell Ferguson, Martha Gever, Trinh T. Minh-ha, and Cornel West (Cambridge, Mass.: MIT Press, 1990), 281–288.

She writes:

> Black women and white women are not the same. For example, it is easy for Black women to be used by the power structure against Black men, not because they are men, but because they are Black. Therefore, for Black women, it is necessary at all times to separate the needs of the oppressor from our own legitimate conflicts within our communities. This same problem does not exist for white women. Black women and men have shared racist oppression and still share it, although in different ways. Out of that shared oppression we have developed joint defenses and joint vulnerabilities to each other that are not duplicated in the white community, with the exception of the relationship between Jewish women and Jewish men. (284)

In a panel on cultural appropriation sponsored by the Women's Section of the American Academy of Religion (AAR), Kansas City, November, 1991, Plaskow critically assessed her "appropriation" of Lorde's text. For this discussion, see "Special Section: Appropriation and Reciprocity," *Journal of Feminist Studies in Religion*, 8:2 (fall 1992): 91–122, esp. 109–110.

21. Carole Pateman, *The Sexual Contract* (Stanford: Stanford University Press, 1988).

22. Marla Brettschneider, *The Family Flamboyant: Race Politics, Queer Families, Jewish Lives* (Albany: State University of New York Press, 2006). I am grateful to Rebecca Alpert for calling this book to my attention. See Rebecca Alpert, "The Family Flamboyant: Race Politics, Queer Families, Jewish Lives by Marla Brettschneider," *Bridges*, 12:1 (spring 2007): 128–131.

23. Brettscheider, *The Family Flamboyant*, 109.

24. Ibid., 133. The passage from Martin Buber cited here is from Martin Buber, *I and Thou* (New York: Collier Books, 1958), 13. On the use of Buber by both Borowitz and Plaskow, see Levitt, *Jews and Feminism*, chaps. 4, 5. In my reading of Borowitz in chapter 4, I challenge his conflation of the I-Thou relationship with marriage.

18

Eden for Grown-Ups

Toward a New Ethic of Earth, of Sex, and of Creation

Arthur O. Waskow

TWO MYTHIC TALES—the Garden of Eden and the Song of Songs—are the Hebrew Bible's richest, deepest explorations of the place of people in the world and the relationships of human beings to the earth. The first is a tale of the painful awakening of the human race from an unconscious infancy into a tense adolescence and the drudgery of adulthood, and the second can be seen as a vision of that adulthood renewed, refreshed, made fully playful and conscious at the same time. The Song of Songs is Eden for grown-ups.

From one standpoint, the story of Eden seems to embody and command the dominion of men over women, as well as rigid roles in life for women and men. This is indeed how most of Judaism, Christianity, and Islam have viewed the story. The dominant figure, the "real creation," seems to be a man, and woman is merely an afterthought. The woman is weak: she hearkens not to God but to the cunning serpent; she challenges God impetuously, and brings sin and trouble into the world; and she visits upon all future women their subservience to men and their pain in childbirth. From this angle of vision, all of it—the whole story—seems to be both warrant and command to keep women in their place.

Suppose, however, that humankind began not as "male" or "man" but as embryonic or infantile "androgyne." It is written in the Torah (Gen. 1:26–27) that "God said, 'let us make man in our image, after our likeness' . . . and God created man in His image, in the image of God He created it; male and female he created them." The Bible not only asserts that human beings, male and female, were created in God's Image, but in the same breath God speaks of the Divine Self not as "My Image" but as "Our Image," as if to say, "I, too, am Male and Female."

Genesis 1 and 5 sometimes describe Adam as "he" and sometimes as "they," shifting back and forth from singular to plural, as if the Bible were trying to say simultaneously that there is a single humanness in both men and women, and that in this single humanness there is also a doubleness —maleness and femaleness—both of which are real, and both of which have a part in making the one human form.

At this point in the Creation story all the elements of "male" and "female," and all the other aspects of humanity, are still cloudy and undifferentiated.

The notion that Adam was originally androgynous—somehow both "male" and "female"—has long been recognized. Nineteen hundred years ago, ancient Jewish commentators acknowledged this and suggested a second level of perception. In the classic Midrash Rabbah, R. Jeremiah ben Eleazar referred to the passage "In Our Image, male and female" as indicating that Adam was androgynous; R. Samuel ben Nahman suggested that Adam had two "backs" and two "faces," one male, the other female. Another rabbi disagreed, drawing not on Genesis 1 but on the Bible's second Creation story, in Genesis 2, to say that Adam had only one "face," which was masculine, and that Eve was created from his rib. But Samuel and Rabbi Levi replied that she came not from a rib but from Adam's side (the Hebrew *tzela* can mean either "rib" or "side").[1] Whoever wrote the words of Genesis and rabbinic commentary could tell, from looking at the world, that men and women each had both masculine and feminine aspects. Once this way of thinking enters the world, separating men and women into utterly distinct roles and spheres of life becomes difficult.

What does it mean to use the descriptives "male" and "female"or "masculine" and "feminine" to define behaviors and characteristics that could appear in both sexes? These terms have become linked with two other polarities: mastery and mystery, activism and nurturance.

The Bible's second Creation story, which focuses on the Garden of Eden, distinguishes between the roles of men and women. As the Adam of Genesis 2 evolves, from this "s/he" is removed the "she." Whether she is differentiated as a rib or a side from the human body, the masculine aspect of the human being goes forward, still known as *adam*—the human. The woman becomes a specific figure lifted out of the undifferentiated ground, and the female or feminine aspect becomes more focused, more active. The emergence of this female aspect necessarily, dialectically, defines what remains as male or masculine.

Why does the woman emerge from what then remains defined as man?

Why does the man not emerge from—is not birthed by—the woman, as we might expect? Perhaps it suggests that, in the Garden of Delight, a man could give birth; in Eden, the roles we know to apply in ordinary history are not locked in. Even after this birth, this separation, clearly the two remain bone of each other's bone, flesh of each other's flesh.

But a radical change happens in the Garden, an event that triggers what we know as ordinary history. First the Woman and then the Man eat in some troublesome, perhaps growthful and also disobedient way. In this moment and even more thereafter, the roles of man and woman become sharply differentiated.

As their choice of independent action defines their growing past the innocent, infantile idyll of the early Garden, they are warned that outside the Garden, in their more grown-up life, domination and conflict will take command. Men will have to struggle to win food from the earth; the earth will rebel against this control; men will rule over women.

Yet the whole tenor of biblical hope is that the Garden can somehow be rediscovered, re-created, reawakened within us and around us; more on this momentarily.

But it will not be the Garden as it was; human beings will not be as childish, unaware.

In the original Eden, God was Mother/Father, giving orders; in Eden for mature grown-ups, human beings will have internalized parental values or will have come to their own values and will be able to guide their own lives.

In the original Eden, human beings were childishly unconcerned with sexuality, or with the sexual differences between them; they were "naked and not ashamed." In the new Garden, men and women will be fully equal, and to be fully human is to encompass both traditionally "masculine" and "feminine" aspects of being human. In that new Garden, human beings may again be unashamedly naked—but not because they are innocent of sexuality.

In the original Eden, food came easily from every tree, even from the forbidden tree. The earth gave its abundance fruitfully and joyfully. In the new Garden of Delight, exhausting toil will no longer be the human lot, for each will live under his or her own vine and fig tree to eat there unafraid. This is the vision we keep before us in the world of striving and strife that characterizes contemporary adulthood.

Modernity has convinced many of us that God now intends women and men to be equal in shaping society and governing families. We see

God's message to Eve—"He shall rule over you"—in the same light as God's message to Adam—"You shall toil with the sweat pouring down your face"—not as a command to be obeyed but as a prediction or description of a reality that is pain and sorrow. That reality is meant to be overcome through historical transformation. Just as today we work to make work less toilsome, so today we rule out hierarchies of ruling that automatically privilege half of humanity above the other half.

Many of us believe that God's statement to the first Adam—"Be fruitful and multiply and fill up the earth and subdue it"—has already been fulfilled and overfulfilled, to the point of danger to the entire human race and the planet. Thus its corollary, "Procreate as many children as possible," is no longer God's will.

Does the Bible give us a vision of this higher, fully mature Garden? Yes, in the Song of Songs, one of the greatest love poems in all human literature. It is erotic, playful, passionate, funny, tipsy with love for the spring, the flowers, the smells, the legs and breasts and forehead of each lover's sweet beloved. Each is naked and unashamed, celebrating the body of the other.

If there is a dramatic plot to the Song, it is about lovers who seek each other, who passionately celebrate each other's bodies, but who vanish from each other just when they are about to join. The story is also about watchmen and brothers who seek to impose order—brothers of the leading woman who seek to make her follow the rules, watchmen who beat her up when she wanders at night.

Yet she is not deterred, and the stuctures of orderliness prove evanescent. Order rules our ordinary lives, and there are only flashes of spontaneity; but in the Song spontaneity is everywhere, and there are only flashes of rules and order.

The Song offers us an Eden—but not the infantile unconscious Eden of Genesis 2; it is an Eden for fully matured grown-ups. We have a Garden —and we have a man and woman living in it.

But God's Name never appears in the Song—as if the Parental God of Eden is indeed gone—as would surely be the case if the Parent's children had fully grown up. And gone, too, are the adolescent stirrings of a fearful sexuality that shadow Eve and Adam: in the Song, sexuality is vigorous and playful, unforced and unforcing. "Do not rouse the lovers till they're ready," says the Song again and again.

With all their Eros, however, the lovers never quite consummate their love, never quite achieve orgasm. They vanish into the hills just when one might expect a consummation. This is never said to be a result of asceticism or a cause for mourning. The joy of Eros does not need a climax, according to the Song: the joy is in the process, just as God is in the Process.

The Song is a hymn to fluidity and flow, rather than to rigidity and structure. The form of the Song is itself a hymn to flow, which is why it is so hard to be sure whether there is a story in it. It is intended to be evanescent: now you see it, now you don't. Like the lovers. Like love. Like God. Here humans have at last been able to eat from the Tree of Life. The Tree of Distinctions—of Knowing Good and Evil—has taken its proper place within the Garden. "*Adam*" is not simply embedded as part of *adamah*, as in the beginnings of humanity—human embedded in the humus, the earthling in the earth. Nor is there a bitter hatred between them. There is a free and playful relation.

And of the two lovers, the woman leads the story. She speaks more than the male lover does; she seeks, and she is the more active partner. She leads androgynously—assertively but fluidly.

And the man of the Song is also androgynous—vigorous and virile but also nurturing, fluid, mysterious. In the Song Adam and Eve are again androgynous but not quite like the original Adam, for each is still a separate man and woman, each bearing within an aspect of the other.

Interpreting the Song as a culmination of the mytho-history beginning with Eden would teach women and men a way of looking at the past that is a compound of less triumph and anger and more sadness and joy. It would remind us to accept that there was some value, as well as some loss, in the process of change; that our history has been a spiral of change, and periodically we gave up something that would have been valuable to keep; that we gave it up because we rightly saw something more valuable to be learned that seemed to contradict it; and that at the next level of the spiral we can reappropriate, relearn what we gave up, this time more richly and more knowledgeably.

In about 120 CE, as the Rabbis of the Sanhedrin voted to include the Song in the canon of sacred texts, they transformed the Song from an erotic poem, sung in wine halls and beloved by the people, into a spiritualized allegory, fit mainly for mystics, in which the lovers are understood as Israel and God. The Church drew on this approach to see the Song as an allegory of love between Christ and the Church.

There would be a spiritual symmetry, as well as an irony, if the Song became for our own generations an important lesson for sexual ethics and practice in a new ethos, in which pleasure and joy were simultaneously earthy and spiritual; an ethos in which we saw the absence of God's Name in the Song as an invitation to sense God as present throughout the Song, not in one of its particular characters but in every breath of the Song's music, in all its form and content.

On that transformative day, when the Sanhedrin faced the question of whether the Song was to be understood as Holy Writ, some of the Rabbis wanted to keep it out of the Bible altogether. Rabbi Akiba fought to include it, and he won. He said that all the Writings (*Ketuvim*) were holy, but the Song of Songs was the Holy of Holies; that it was holiest precisely because it did not mention God's Name; and that the day on which the Song was created was of equal worth to the day on which all the rest was created. Did he mean "all the rest" of the Writings that the Sanhedrin was debating? Or did he mean "all the rest" of the world, so that the Song is practically a new Creation, the look and sound of a whole new world for earth and earthling? We do not know. He did not assert that the Song replaced all other reality, or all the other Writings—but stood equal to them.

What would it mean to integrate this very different world as half of our consciousness and action? The Song calls forth a submerged and subversive alternative to the male domination of sexual relations, and even to the assumptions of marriage and procreation. The sexual ethic of the Song of Songs is focused not on children, marriage, or commitment but on sensual pleasure and loving companionship.

Although the Song at every explicit level is clearly heterosexual, it points toward a world where men need not rule over women and procreation is not the only purpose of sex. In that world, it is not frightening for two men to be loving sexual partners; no one need worry which one will rule over the other, "as with a woman." In that world no one has to fear that, with no man to rule over them, two women in sexual partnership are frightening. In that world, no one needs to worry about same-sex partnerships not producing more children, for producing children is not the only point of sex. And in that world, the ethic of playful sexuality that has informed much of gay sexuality can come out of the gay ghetto, just as the family ethic can come out of the heterosexual ghetto. Instead, all adult consensual relationships can partake of both worlds that stand equal to each other, instead of splitting them apart.

In that world "Adam" and "Eve" are now grown up, and because the Song never mentions God, the Parent has evidently been absorbed into the children's own identities. Moreover, they are no longer focused on their own parenthood, on their own children, or on the process of wringing from the earth just barely enough food to keep themselves and their family alive. For their relationship with the earth is as fluid, playful, loving, and pleasurable as their relationship with each other.

What if we were to take the Song as a lesson for our epoch? What if we were to view the human race as a whole as if it had entered the period of maturity that a happily married couple enter when they no longer need or want to have more children? When they no longer need or want to toil on the earth, to "fill it" or "subdue it," because these tasks are already accomplished? When they no longer need or want to do everything according to the clock or calendar but can live more fluidly, more attuned to their internal rhythms?

In the Song of Songs, these grown-up humans continue to connect sexually for the sake of pleasure and love—and so could the human race or the Jewish people. Without denigrating the forms of sexuality that center on children and family, we might find the forms of sexuality that focus on pleasure more legitimate at this moment of human history than ever before, standing equal with the family ethic, not subservient to it or obliterating it.

NOTE

1. See Genesis Rabbah 8:1; and Leviticus Rabbah 14:1.

Glossary

adam. Person, human being. The reference to "Adam" in the Book of Genesis most likely comes from the word *adamah,* or earth/ground, from which the first human was formed.

Adonai. A "polite" way to refer to the most sacred name of God.

aggadah. A genre of literature that includes stories, legends, folklore, and interpretations of the Bible.

aguna. A woman who is "chained" to her marriage because her husband refuses to give her a Jewish divorce. See *get.*

androgynos. A person described in the Mishnah and Talmud as having both male and female sex traits. Today an androgynos would likely be described as "intersex."

Ashkenazi. Jews of (or relating to Jews of) Northern, Central, or Eastern European descent.

assur. Forbidden.

Avot d'Rabbi Natan. A collection of midrashim (aggadot), probably dating to the eighth to tenth century.

ayin. A reference to the mystical understanding that all of existence is, fundamentally, nothingness.

ba'al/ba'alut. **Ba'al** may be translated as "master," as with the head of a business or household; "owner," as with the owner of property; and "husband." It is also the name of an ancient Near Eastern deity; discussions of idolatry in the Bible are often connected to injunctions against *Ba'al* or accusations of worshiping *Ba'al.* **Ba'alut** is generally translated as "ownership" or "mastery."

Baraita. A teaching (or a collection of teachings) of the oral legal tradition that was not codified in the Mishnah but is often cited in Talmudic discussions.

Bavli. Babylonian; generally refers to the Babylonian Talmud.

be'ilah. A woman who has had sexual intercourse, who "has been intercoursed."

Beit Din. A rabbinic court, generally comprised of three rabbis.

betulah. A virgin. Colloquially, an unmarried woman.

biyah/biah. Sex; originally one of the ways that a woman could be betrothed for marriage.

chulent. A type of stew cooked by Ashkenazi Jews, often eaten on the Sabbath.

Chumash. A book containing the five books of the Torah: Genesis, Exodus, Leviticus, Numbers, and Deuteronomy.

d'var Torah. Literally, "word of Torah." A sermon or homiletic teaching.

davvening. Prayer. Yiddish, either from the Latin "divinus," meaning "the Divine," or from the Lithuanian word meaning "gift."

denar. An ancient unit of currency.

erva. **May** be translated, variously, as "nakedness," "sexually forbidden," or "intimate"; also a referent for genitals.

Ein Sof. Literally, "without end." The kabbalistic term for the boundlessness of the Divine or the abstract state of existence prior to God's creation of the world.

Exodus Rabbah. A homeletic (midrashic) collection of stories relating, to some degree, to the Book of Exodus, redacted around the eleventh or twelfth century.

family purity laws. Practices in connection with the prohibition against cohabitation with a menstruant.

frum. Religious; a Yiddish-ization of the German word for "pious."

geder. Fence.

Gaon of Vilna. Rabbi Eliyahu ben Shlomo Zalman, an influential eighteenth-century rabbinic authority.

Gemara. Rabbinic analyses of the Mishnah and other, sometimes digressive discussions that, together with the Mishnah itself, comprise the Talmud. (Gemara and Talmud are often used interchangeably.) The Gemara probably dates from 350–550 CE.

get. A writ of divorce; in Judaism, only the husband has the power to grant a divorce. (See *aguna.*)

gevurah. The name of one of the kabbalistic *sefirot*; can be translated as "strength," "judgment," "power," or "severity."

gilui arayot. The category of sexual relations forbidden in the Torah, including incest, adultery, and relations with a menstruant.

gittin. Of, or relating to, a *get*; also the tractate of Talmud that deals with Jewish divorce.

halakha (n.), *halakhic* (adj.). Literally, "the way." Jewish law, referring to the laws set out in the Torah or developed through the oral and legal tradition.

harkakah/harkachot. Literally, "distancing." The custom of imposing stringencies connected to the prohibition against cohabitating with a menstruant; for example, a husband and menstruating wife would not touch, share food, and so forth.

Hasidut. A strain of Judaism founded in the eighteenth century as a way to approach God with both contemplative meditation and fervent joy. Hasidism is comprised of many sects, and most of them are modeled on the teachings of a particular rebbe, or spiritual leader.

Hasmoneans. The ruling dynasty of ancient Israel from 140–37 BCE. During this time ancient Israel was an autonomous Jewish state.

hekdesh. Consecrated. An object consecrated to the ancient Jerusalem Temple is forbidden to be used for non-sacred purposes.

hevruta. Study partner. Traditionally Jewish study is done in pairs.

Hillel (the Elder). An important sage who lived in the last century before the common era, founder of an important intellectual dynasty (The House of Hillel), and quoted in many important Jewish texts. He is often cited in debate with Shammai.

Hillel Center. Hillel is an international organization focused primarily on fostering Jewish life on college campuses.

huppah. The Jewish wedding canopy, often synonymous with the marriage ritual itself.

k'rovei Yisrael. Literally, "relatives of Israel" or "ones close to the Jews." Refers to non-Jews married to Jews, as suggested by the authors of *A Place in the Tent: Intermarriage and Conservative Judaism.*

Kabbalah. Literally, "receiving." One arm of the Jewish mystical tradition.

kadosh. Holy.

Joseph Karo. The sixteenth-century author of the *Shulchan Aruch,* an authoritative code of Jewish law, and several other important Jewish writings.

karet. Excommunication.

kavanah. Intention.

kedeshim. See *qedesh.*

ketubah. The Jewish wedding contract.

Ketuvim. Literally, "writings." The section of the Bible that includes Psalms, Proverbs, Job, Daniel, Ezra-Nehemia, Chronicles, and the five scrolls, of which the Song of Songs is one.

kiddushin. The first part of the Jewish wedding ceremony, originally constructed as a separate betrothal ritual. Technically *kiddushin* is a ritual effecting the groom's acquisition of the bride and/or her sexuality.

kinyan. Acquisiton.

kippah/kippot (sing./pl.). A yarmulke; a Jewish head covering.

Kohen. A descendent of the Jewish priestly line of Aaron.

Koi. An animal mentioned in rabbinic texts that defies easy categorization; in some ways it is like a wild animal, in other ways like a domesticated animal, and in still other ways it resembles neither.

konei/kona. One who acquires. See *kinyan.*

kosher. Literally, "fit." Permitted for use or consumption according to Jewish law.

Lamentations Rabbah. A homeletic (midrashic) collection of stories relating, to some degree, to the Book of Lamentations, redacted in the fifth and/or seventh century.

Levirate marriage. In biblical times, if a married man died but had not left heirs, his wife was obliged to marry her deceased husband's brother, and the first child of this union was considered to be her late first husband's progeny.

Levite/Levitical. Descendants of the biblical tribe of Levi; Levites had special roles regarding the Tabernacle (and, later, the Temple) and its functions.

ma'aseh. A story.

Maimonides. An important twelfth-century Jewish sage, philosopher, physician, and legal decisor.

malchut. Literally, "kingship." The name of one of the kabbalistic *sefirot.*

maneh. An ancient unit of weight and, as such, a currency.

mamzer/mamzerim (sing./pl.). The offspring of certain forbidden unions. *Mamzerim* are forbidden to marry Jewish-born non-*mamzerim.*

mechitzah. A partition, usually used to describe a partition separating women and men in prayer, used primarily in Orthodox synagogues.

midrash. See **aggadah.**

mikveh. Ritual bath; a pool of water used for purification.

Mishnah. An interpretation and explication of biblical law handed down through oral tradition, first compiled in written form around 200 CE. The Mishnah is one of the two major divisions of the Talmud.

Mishneh Torah. An important code of Jewish law, authored by Maimonides in the late twelfth century.

mitzvah/mitzvot (sing./pl.). Literally, "commandment." One of the 613 directives issued by the Torah; also used more casually as "good deed."

Moloch. Either the name of a god or idol worshiped in the ancient Near East or a sort of sacrifice practiced during the biblical era. The Torah commands not to let one's seed pass through Moloch, and not to sacrifice one's children to Moloch.

moredet. Literally, "rebellious one." A woman who refuses to engage in marital relations with her husband.

Nahlaot. A neighborhood in Jerusalem.

negiah. Touch. It is a custom in some Orthodox communities not to engage in any physical contact whatsoever (including, say, a hand on a shoulder) with members of the opposite sex, unless one is related or married to the person in question.

nidah. Menstruation. The Torah stipulates that sex with a menstruant is forbidden, and many legal opinions and customs have been developed in regard to this.

onah. Literally, "time period." The maximum amount of time that can pass between a husband's conjugal visits to his wife, which sometimes depends on his occupation; also a euphemism for the conjugal obligation in a general sense or for conjugal visits.

Oz VeHadar Levusha. "Strength and splendor/beauty are her clothing." A phrase from the "Woman of Valor" passage in the Book of Proverbs (chapter 31), and the title of a recent book on modesty.

Palestinian Talmud. See Yerushalmi.

payes/payot. Sidelocks.

Pesikta Rabbati. A ninth-century collection of midrashic (homeletic) material.

Pharisees (n. pl.)/**Pharisaic** (adj.). Members of a political/social/intellectual movement in the Second Temple period. The Pharisees were the precursors to what later became known as Rabbinic Judaism.

pikuach nefesh. Literally, "watching over a life." The principle that the mandate to save a life trumps almost all other commandments in Jewish law.

pilagesh. Concubine.

Purim. A holiday in the spring celebrating the thwarting of a plot to destroy the Jews of ancient Persia; the holiday is marked by festive rejoicing and often dressing in costumes.

qedesh (male), *qedeshah* (female), *qedeshim* (pl.). "Cultic" or "temple" prostitutes associated with non-Israelite rituals, as described in the Hebrew Bible.

Qumran. The site associated with the Dead Sea Scrolls and the sect that composed them.

Ramban Nachmanides. An important thirteenth-century Spanish rabbi, physician, Kabbalist, and biblical commentator.

red heifer. The Torah explains in Numbers 19 that the process of becoming once again ritually pure after contact with a corpse requires the ashes of an unblemished red heifer.

Rosh Hashanah. Literally, "the head of the year." The Jewish New Year and the beginning of the Days of Awe that lead to Yom Kippur.

Shabbat. The Sabbath, the seventh day of the week, a day of rest. Saturday.

safek. Doubt, doubtful.

Samaritan. An ethno-religious group found in the ancient and medieval Near East. A very small population of Samaritans still lives in the Middle East today.

Seder Eliyahu Rabba. A midrashic (homeletic) collection, and half of a larger collection redacted around the tenth century CE.

Sephardim. The Jews, and the descendents of the Jews, who settled in Spain and Portugal until the expulsion of Jews from Spain in 1492 and from Portugal in 1496.

sefirah (n., sing.), *sefirot* (n., plural), *sefirotic* (adj.) The Divine attributes or emanations described in Kabbalah. These include the seven "lower," more earthly attributes and three "higher" transcendent attributes.

Shammai. An important sage who lived around the time of the common era, known as the founder of an important intellectual dynasty (The House of Shammai) and quoted in many important Jewish texts. He is often cited in debate with Hillel.

Shechinah. Jewish mystical literature describes the Shechinah as the feminine, immanent aspect of God.

Shema. Literally, "hear." The prayer, "Hear, O Israel, God, our Deity, God is One" and a number of fixed verses that follow. A central aspect of Jewish liturgy.

shiksah. A Yiddish term, usually derogatory, referring to a non-Jewish woman.

Shlomo Carlebach. A twentieth-century rabbi and songwriter associated with a renewed interest in the spiritual dimensions of Judaism.

shofar. A ram's horn that is blown, creating a very distinctive sound, most notably (but not exclusively) on Rosh Hashanah.

shuk. Market.

Shulchan Aruch. An important code of Jewish law, composed by Rabbi Yosef Caro in the sixteenth century. Other legal decisors have written extensive commentaries to it.

Sifre Zuta. A midrashic (homeletic) commentary on the book of Numbers.

Sifra. A halakhic (legal) midrash (homeletic commentary) to the book of Leviticus.

slivovits. A distilled alcoholic drink made from plums.

Sotah. A married woman suspected by her husband of adultery. The Torah and later Rabbinic literature describe an elaborate ritual by which her guilt or innocence may be determined.

Stam. The anonymous editorial voice of the Talmud.

sugya. Talmudic discussion.

taharah (n.), *t'horah* (adj.). Ritual purity, or to be in a state of ritual purity.

Talmud. A compilation of legal discussions and interpretations, arguments, theological explanations, and homeletic material that includes and often directly pertains to the Mishnah. The Babylonian Talmud (also called the "Bavli," generally the collection referred to when discussing the Talmud) was compiled over the first five centuries of the Common Era. The Palestinian Talmud (also called the "Yerushalmi") was probably redacted in the fourth or fifth century CE.

Tanakh. Hebrew Bible. An acronym of *Torah* (the Five Books of Moses), *Neviim* (the books of the prophets), and *Ketuvim* (other writings).

tefillin. Phylacteries; black leather straps and boxes containing biblical verses that are affixed to the arm and the forehead during weekday morning prayer.

Temple. The Holy Temple in Jerusalem was the site of highest worship in ancient Judaism. It stood from 957 BCE until its destruction by the Babylonians in 586 BCE, and then was rebuilt and stood from 515 BCE until its destruction by the Romans in 70 CE. From the Temple, offerings to God, including animal sacrifices, were carried out.

tiferet. Literally, "adornment." The name of one of the kabbalistic *sefirot.*

tumtum. A person, described in the Mishnah and Talmud, whose genitals are obscured, making gender classification difficult to discern.

toevah. Generally translated as "abomination." This word is used in the Bible to describe (and condemn) a number of acts, including incest, idolatry, eating unclean animals, and, most famously, the act of "a man lying with another man as with a woman," as mentioned in Leviticus 18:22 and 20:13.

Tosefta. A collection of materials roughly contemporaneous with the Mishnah.

Tosafot/Tosafist. Tosafot are medieval commentaries on the Talmud, and the Tosafists were those who wrote them.

treyf. Nonkosher.

tshuvah. Literally, "returning" or "answer." Can refer either to the process of repentance for sin and return to a relationship with God or to a Jewish legal responsum, the answer to a question about Jewish law.

tumah (n.), *t'meah* (adj.). Ritual impurity, or to be in a state of ritual impurity.

tzaddik. Righteous person.

tzelem Elohim ("image of God") The Torah in Genesis states that God created humankind "in the image of God."

tzimtzum. Contraction, self-withdrawl.

tzitzit. Ritual fringes attached to the edges of a four-cornered garment, which serve as a reminder of the Torah's commandments.

tzniut/tznius. Modesty.

v'ahavta. Literally, "and you shall love." A passage from Deuteronomy that is recited as part of the Shema prayer.

Vayiqra Rabbah. A homiletic (midrashic) collection of stories relating, to some degree, to the Book of Leviticus, redacted around the mid-seventh century.

white days. According to the Torah, a person who has an irregular discharge must wait a week after the cessation of flow to be sure that the discharge has ceased completely before undergoing ritual washing. According to Talmudic and later interpretations of Jewish law, this additional week should also apply after normal menstruation, before ritual washing in the *mikveh* and resuming sexual relations.

Yerushalmi. Jerusalemite; as a text, refers to the Palestinian Talmud, composed in and in part relating to the land of Israel. See also **Talmud.**

yeshiva. A center for Jewish learning.

yetzer ha ra. The evil inclination.

yetzirah. Literally, "creation" or "formation." In contrast to *briyah*, which is a sort of creation that is understood to be something only God can do, *yetzirah* is a kind of creation that both God and human beings can enact.

yichud. Literally, "seclusion." Generally speaking, when two members of the opposite sex (or certain combinations of members of the opposite sex) are secluded together, Jewish law presumes them to have engaged in sexual relations. Laws of *yichud* often define whose seclusion falls under this assumption.

Yom Kippur. The Day of Atonement, during which Jews fast and attempt to ask forgiveness for their sins and shortcomings.

yonah. Dove.

zav (male), *zavah* (female). A woman or a man who has abnormal bodily emissions, usually genital.

zemirot. Sabbath songs.

zenut. Prostitution or, more generally, licentiousness.

Zohar. Literally, "radiance." An important group of books of Kabbalah, probably written in thirteenth-century Spain.

zonah. A prostitute or, more generally, a woman deemed to be licentious.

Contributors

REBECCA T. ALPERT is a rabbi and Associate Professor of Religion and Women's Studies at Temple University. She is the co-author, with Jacob J. Staub, of *Exploring Judaism: A Reconstructionist Approach* (Reconstructionist Press, 1985), the author of *Like Bread on the Seder Plate: Jewish Lesbians and the Transformation of Tradition* (Columbia University Press, 1998) and *Whose Torah? A Concise Guide to Progressive Judaism* (New Press, 2008), and the editor of *Voices of the Religious Left: A Contemporary Sourcebook* (Temple University Press, 2000); she also has published numerous articles. She teaches in the areas of religion and contemporary social issues: sexuality, the politics of race and gender, and medical ethics, and is currently at work on a book on Jews in black baseball.

WENDY LOVE ANDERSON has written about history, transgression, and Western religious traditions in venues ranging from *Church History* (vol. 75, no. 4 [December 2006]) to *Fear and Trembling in Sunnydale: Buffy the Vampire Slayer and Philosophy* (Open Court, 2003). Her current project deals with the roles of Jewish characters in Christian hagiography, but she hopes someday to publish a book-length history of Jewish intermarriage. She holds a Ph.D. from the University of Chicago Divinity School, and teaches at Webster University in St. Louis, Missouri.

JUDITH R. BASKIN is Knight Professor of Humanities at the University of Oregon. Her books include *Pharaoh's Counsellors: Job, Jethro, and Balaam in Rabbinic and Patristic Tradition* (1983), *Midrashic Women: Formations of the Feminine in Rabbinic Literature* (2002), and the edited collections *Jewish Women in Historical Perspective* (2nd ed., 1998) and *Women of the Word: Jewish Women and Jewish Writing* (1994). She is also the author of numerous scholarly articles. Dr. Baskin served as president of the Association for Jewish Studies from 2004 to 2006.

ARYEH COHEN is Associate Professor of Rabbinic Literature at the American Jewish University. He is the author of *Rereading Talmud: Gender, Law, and the Poetics of* Sugyot and the co-author, with Shaul Magid, of the collection *Beginning/Again: Toward a Hermeneutics of Jewish Texts*. He is currently working on a feminist commentary to Tractate *Shabbat* of the Babylonian Talmud and a book on rabbinic conceptions of the just city. Cohen is a pioneer of the movement to add social justice issues to the curriculum of rabbinical schools, and he co-teaches the first course in the country on worker justice issues for rabbinical students and business leaders.

ELLIOT N. DORFF, Rabbi (Jewish Theological Seminary, 1970), Ph.D. (Columbia, 1971), is Rector and Distinguished Professor of Philosophy at the American Jewish University (formerly the University of Judaism) and Visiting Professor at the School of Law of the University of California at Los Angeles. In 1999–2000 he served on the U.S. Surgeon General's Task Force to create a responsible sex ethic that diminished the spread of sexually transmitted diseases and sexual violence. The chair of the Conservative movement's Committee on Jewish Law and Standards, he wrote the Rabbinic Letter on Human Intimacy that became the voice of the Conservative movement on sexual matters as well as the rabbinic ruling on family violence. The author of more than two hundred articles and fifteen books on Jewish thought, law, and ethics, his book, *Love Your Neighbor and Yourself: A Jewish Approach to Modern Personal Ethics* (Jewish Publication Society, 2003), contains both those documents.

ESTHER FUCHS is Professor of Near Eastern Studies and Judaic Studies at the University of Arizona in Tucson. She is the editor and author of numerous publications on feminist biblical theory and interpretation, Modern Hebrew literature, and Israeli feminist scholarship. Her recent publications include *Sexual Politics in the Biblical Narrative: Reading the Hebrew Bible as a Woman* (Sheffield Academic Press, 2000) and *Israeli Women's Studies* (Rutgers University Press, 2005). She is currently at work on a collection of essays titled *Reading against the Grain: Feminist Scholarship on Jewish Sources* (Jewish Publication Society, forthcoming).

BONNA DEVORA HABERMAN is a lecturer and researcher at Hebrew University in Jerusalem where she teaches Jewish Gender Studies. She returned to Israel in 2004 with her spouse and five children, having taught at Harvard University and at Brandeis University, where she founded and directed the Mistabra Institute for Jewish Textual Activism. Her recent manuscript commissioned by the Jewish Agency, *Israel Spirit Matters*, is a text-based vision for Zionism in crisis. She is completing *Beyond the Wall: From Text to Action*, a Jewish feminist liberation theology. She is the initiator of an Israeli movement for women's public participation and leadership in Judaism, Women of the Wall.

ELLIOT ROSE KUKLA has been an activist, writer, and educator for more than a decade. He has taught widely about sexual and gender diversity in Judaism in the U.S., Canada, and Israel. His writing appears in numerous magazines and anthologies. Elliot is currently a Chaplaincy Resident at the University of California at San Francisco Medical Center, specializing in Mental Health Chaplaincy. Before moving to San Francisco, Elliot served as the first rabbi of the Danforth Jewish Circle, in Toronto, Canada. Elliot was ordained by Hebrew Union College—Jewish Institute of Religion in 2006.

GAIL LABOVITZ is Assistant Professor of Rabbinic Literature at the American Jewish University and chair of the Department of Rabbinics for the Ziegler School of Rabbinic Studies. She has also served as a senior research analyst in Judaism for the Feminist Sexual Ethics Project at Brandeis University and as the coordinator for the Jewish Feminist Research Group, a project of the Women's Studies program at the Jewish Theological Seminary of America. She is currently at work on a book about constructions of marriage and gender relations in classical rabbinic literature. She is also an ordained Conservative rabbi.

MELANIE MALKA LANDAU is Associate Director of the Australian Centre for Jewish Civilisation at Monash University, Melbourne, Australia, where she is also a lecturer and community educator. She teaches in the fields of Jewish Law, and Rabbinics and Gender Studies, and she is the coordinator of a new program in Communal Service and Leadership. She is currently completing her Ph.D. on a feminist analysis of *kinyan* (acquisition) in rabbinic marriage. She is the co-editor, with Michael Fagenblat and Nathan Wolski, of a recently published collection titled *New Under the Sun: Jewish Australians on Religion, Politics, and Culture*, and she edits the new series, Monash Publications in Jewish Studies. She facilitates personal and group processes as well as larger-scale events around life-cycle rituals and peace-building initiatives. From 2001 to 2003 she was a Jerusalem

Fellow at the Mandel School for Social and Educational Leadership. She is learning, growing, and loving with two children, Ktoret Ashira and Ariel Raya, and a partner, Michael Fagenblat.

SARRA LEV is Assistant Professor of Rabbinic Literature at the Reconstructionist Rabbinical College in Philadelphia. Before coming to rabbinical school she walked across the United States on the Great Peace March and lived in the Women's Encampment for a Future of Peace and Justice. Since then she has been active in the cause for a just peace between Palestinians and Israeli Jews. She believes that a rabbi's role, above all, is to engage in social justice as a function of living a life connected to the divine, and she teaches rabbinic texts with great love and deep critique toward that end.

LAURA LEVITT is the author of *American Jewish Loss after the Holocaust* (New York University Press, 2007) and *Jews and Feminism: the Ambivalent Search for Home* (Routledge, 1997). She is the co-editor, with Miriam Peskowitz, of *Judaism since Gender* (Routledge, 1997); and also co-editor, with Shelley Hornstein and Laurence Silberstein, of *Impossible Images: Contemporary Art after the Holocaust* (New York University Press, 2003). She edited "Changing Focus: Family Photography and American Jewish Identity," *The Scholar & Feminist Online*, 1.3 (winter 2003); available at www.barnard.edu/sfonline. She coordinates the Greater Philadelphia Women's Studies Consortium. She is also director of the Jewish Studies Program at Temple University, where she teaches in the Department of Religion and the Women's Studies program.

SARA N. S. MEIROWITZ studies and teaches at the Conservative Yeshiva and works as a freelance editor and a medic in Jerusalem. An alumna of Yale University, she worked as an acquiring editor at the MIT Press for seven years before going to Israel in 2006 on a Dorot Fellowship. Her other publications include pieces in the edited collection *The Women's Seder Sourcebook* (Jewish Lights, 2003), and in the journals *Lilith* and *Feminist Collections*.

JAY MICHAELSON (www.metatronics.net) is a visiting professor at Boston University Law School and a Ph.D Candidate in Jewish Thought at Hebrew University, as well as the director of Nehirim: GLBT Jewish Culture and Spirituality (www.nehirim.org), the chief editor of *Zeek: A Jewish*

Journal of Thought and Culture (www.zeek.net), and a columnist for the *Forward*. An active member of New York's "Pride in the Pulpit" project and a contributing editor of the *White Crane Journal* of gay spirituality, Jay writes and teaches frequently on issues of sexuality and religion; his work has appeared on National Public Radio, and in *Tikkun, Slate, Blithe House Quarterly*, the *Jerusalem Post*, and anthologies including *Mentsh: On Being Jewish and Queer* (Alyson, 2004) *and Righteous Indignation: A Jewish Call for Justice* (Jewish Lights, 2007). He was a recent finalist for the Koret Young Writer on Jewish Themes award, and his most recent books are *God in Your Body: Kabbalah, Mindfulness, and Embodied Spiritual Practice* (Jewish Lights, 2006) and *Another Word for Sky: Poems* (Lethe Press, 2007).

HAVIVA NER-DAVID is a writer, teacher, spiritual counselor, and activist. She received her rabbinic ordination from an Orthodox rabbi in Jerusalem and her doctorate from Bar Ilan University. She is the founding director of Reut: The Center for Modern Jewish Marriage, where she runs premarital seminars for couples and private counseling sessions. Her first book, *Life on the Fringes: A Feminist Journey Towards Traditional Rabbinic Ordination*, was published in 2000 by JFL Books, and she is in the process of finishing her latest book, *Finding Chanah's Voice: A Feminist Rabbi's Challenge to Religious Patriarchy*. Rabbi Dr. Ner-David is on the board of Women of the Wall, in which she has been active for years, and Rabbis for Human Rights. She lives in Jerusalem with her husband and six children.

DANYA RUTTENBERG is the author of *Surprised by God: How I Learned to Stop Worrying and Love Religion* (Beacon Press, 2008), and the editor of the anthology *Yentl's Revenge: The Next Wave of Jewish Feminism* (Seal Press, 2001). She is currently in the process of co-editing three volumes on Jewish ethics, together with Rabbi Elliot Dorff, for the Jewish Publication Society's Jewish Voices/Jewish Choices series. She has published in a wide variety of books and periodicals, including *Encyclopedia Judaica, Best Jewish Writing 2002*, the *San Francisco Chronicle, Salon, Bitchfest, Righteous Indignation, The New Jewish Feminism*, and *The Women's Movement Today: An Encyclopedia of Third-Wave Feminism*. She also serves as contributing editor to both *Lilith* and *Women in Judaism*. Ruttenberg received her B.A. in Religious Studies from Brown University, was ordained by the Ziegler School of the American Jewish University, and teaches and lectures nationwide. She lives in the Boston area. More information can be found at http://danyaruttenberg.net.

NAOMI SEIDMAN was born in Brooklyn and studied at Brooklyn College and the University of California. She is presently the Koret Professor of Jewish Culture and is director of the Richard S. Dinner Center for Jewish Studies at the Graduate Theological Union in Berkeley. She published *A Marriage Made in Heaven: The Sexual Politics of Hebrew and Yiddish* (University of California Press, 1997) and *Faithful Renderings: Jewish-Christian Difference and the Politics of Translation* (University of Chicago Press, 2006). Her present project is related to a larger study, titled "The Sexual Transformation of Ashkenaz." She is also at work on a novel.

ARTHUR O. WASKOW, since 1969, has been one of the creators and leaders of Jewish renewal and of several important interfaith projects addressing issues of peace, justice, and the healing of the earth. He founded The Shalom Center (www.shalomctr.org) in 1983 and has been its director since then, shaping it into a prophetic voice in Jewish, multireligious, and American life. His *Freedom Seder* (Holt, Rinehart, Winston, 1969) seeded a generation of Passover haggadot that addressed the issues of our time. His books *Seasons of Our Joy* (Beacon Press, 1991), *Godwrestling* (Schocken, 1978) and *Godwrestling—Round 2* (Jewish Lights, 1996), *Down-to-Earth Judaism* (William Morrow, 1995), and, with his wife, Rabbi Phyllis Berman, *A Time for Every Purpose Under Heaven* (Farrar, Straus & Giroux, 2003) have helped renew and reshape Jewish thought and practice in every sphere of life. With Benedictine Sister Joan Chittister and Sufi teacher Saadi Shakur Chisti, Rabbi Waskow co-authored *The Tent of Abraham: Stories of Hope and Peace for Jews, Christians, and Muslims.* He taught for seven years at the Reconstructionist Rabbinical College and has been a Visiting Professor of Religion at Swarthmore and Vassar colleges and Drew and Temple universities. In 1995 the United Nations named him one of forty Wisdom-Keepers from around the world in connection with the Habitat II conference. In 2007 *Newsweek* named him one of the fifty most influential American rabbis.

Index of Sources

Subject Index

CPSIA information can be obtained
at www.ICGtesting.com
Printed in the USA
JSHW050032130820
7260JS00002B/49